NO GLOBAL

No Global

The People of Ireland Versus the Multinationals

Robert Allen

Pluto Press
London · Dublin · Sterling, Virginia

First published 2004 by Pluto Press
345 Archway Road, London N6 5AA
22883 Quicksilver Drive, Sterling, VA 20166-2012, USA

Distributed in the Republic of Ireland and Northern Ireland by
Columba Mercier Distribution, 55A Spruce Avenue,
Stillorgan Industrial Park, Blackrock, Co. Dublin, Ireland.
Tel: + 353 1 294 2556. Fax: + 353 1 294 2564

www.plutobooks.com

British Library Cataloguing in Publication Data
A catalogue record for this book is available from the British Library

ISBN   0 7453 2211 5 hardback
ISBN   0 7453 2210 7 paperback

Library of Congress Cataloging-in-Publication Data

Allen, Robert, 1956-
  No global : the people of Ireland versus the multinationals / Robert
Allen.
      p. cm.
Includes bibliographical references and index.
  ISBN 0-7453-2211-5--ISBN 0-7453-2210-7 (pbk.)
  1. Chemical industry-Environmental aspects-Ireland. 2.
Pollution-Ireland. 3. International business enterprises-Ireland. 4.
Environmental protection-Ireland-Citizen participation. I. Title.
  TD195.C45 A436 2004
  363.7'09417-dc22
                                                    2003019936

10 9 8 7 6 5 4 3 2 1

Designed and produced for Pluto Press by
Curran Publishing Services, Norwich
Printed and bound in the European Union by
Antony Rowe Ltd, Chippenham and Eastbourne, England

Contents

Preface

This book is based on *Guests of the Nation: People of Ireland Versus the Multinationals* by Robert Allen and Tara Jones, published by Earthscan, London, in 1990, which is now available online at www.bluegreenearth.com. Readers interested in the history of opposition to mining in Ireland and the story of the opposition to Gulf in Bantry should consult the 1990 edition, for these chapters are not included in this edition. The remaining original chapters have been rewritten and include new material. This edition also includes three chapters not in the 1990 edition and a new chapter based in part on the original epilogue. Acknowledgements and credits for the original research can be found in the 1990 edition. For this edition, my admiration goes out to Derry Chambers, Eanna Dowling, Adrian Peace, Anne Ruimy; and my thanks go to Jim Page (for his permission to reproduce lyrics from *Hiroshima Nagasaki Russian Roulette* – www.jimpage.net), Mary Bourke and Martin Storey at the CSO, to Carmel Cronin and Linda Fitzpatrick of CHASE, to Rory Finegan, to Mary, John and Selina Hanrahan, to Audrey Hogan of the Ringaskiddy and District Residents Association, to Kieran Keohane, to Ger Mullally, to Liam Somers, to Hilary Tovey, to John Waters, to Simon White, everyone at APRN throughout the 1990s; and to Clare O'Grady Walsh, Aynia Brennan, Sian Brennan, David Watchorn (all Greenpeace), David Healy; and finally to Roger at Pluto because he wanted to see it back in print.

Thanks also go to Tomas for drafting the original analysis for *Guests of the Nation, Against Money and Power*, which I have shamelessly plundered for the second half of this edition's chapter of the same name, and part of the original draft of the Raybestos story.

This book is dedicated to every person in an Irish community who fought and continues to fight against the hazards of corporate industry, to Ali, Allan, Anne, Carl, Erik, Kate, Peter, Philip, Tim,

Steve, and as always to my daughters Ciara and Jenny and my grandchildren Conor and Matthew.

Notes

IR£1 = €1.25

Sources

Material for this book is based on research by the author or by researchers on behalf of the author, including interviews, observations, statistics and recordings of meetings. Anything not credited in the sources chapter is from a primary source. Secondary source material is acknowledged and cited in the sources chapter or in the bibliography. Some material is sourced from press releases, from quotes and statistics first published in national and regional newspapers, a list of which is also included in the sources chapter, and from material that is not in the public domain - such as correspondence, leaflets, booklets and reports. The main examples are the reports on oral hearings, the source is the stenographer's report if one has been employed, specifically the oral hearings of Merrell Dow and Sandoz, which are not in the public domain.

Introduction:
A Toxic War

In 1972 the first battle against the Irish state's policy of attracting foreign direct investment occurred in Cork when An Taisce, the conservationist group, challenged Pfizer, the US chemical corporate, to prevent it polluting Cork harbour. Four years later a second, arguably more significant, battle saw Schering Plough abandon a IR£27 million (€33.75 million) investment for a pharmaceutical factory at Killaloan, in County Tipperary, following threatened High Court action by a group of residents, who had objected to the planning application. These disputes would define the opposition to the hazards of globalisation; as Hilary Tovey put it, one was an 'official' urban-based movement that relied on expert knowledge to resolve environmental problems, as An Taisce had done; the other was a 'populist' rural movement that used whatever means possible to achieve its aims.

This book covers the history of these movements with a greater emphasis on the 'populist' community campaigns (because it is hardly accurate to credit these campaigns as being part of a movement). Sean O'Faolain, writing about pagan celtic society, described the celtic Irish mind as 'atavistically indestructible, [with] an ineradicable love of individual liberty'. If one word describes the history of the community opposition to the globalisation of Ireland it is 'atavistic'. And by 1978 it was clear that some communities preferred Irish ways and Irish laws, such as they were defined in local environments.

Thus in County Clare a community stopped Beecham from setting up a pharmaceutical factory by using the planning and legal process (an event that led to the state changing the planning laws – a tactic it would continue to use throughout the 1980s and 1990s). The success was repeated a year later when the community in Nohoval, in County Cork, stopped the council from establishing a toxic dump, in what would be the first battle to throw together the conflicting interests of agriculture and industry, and the realisation that the state was beginning to radically alter the country's dependence on agriculture for its livelihood. As the Nohoval farmers celebrated their legal victory in 1980, a combination of anarchists, residents and workers saw off Raybestos Manhattan, which packed its bags and returned to America. The toxic war was on and it was about to get rough.

South Tipperary farmer John Hanrahan became a hero in the war when he took his local chemical corporate Merck Sharp and Dohme to the courts in Dublin, the judges ruling that toxic emissions from an incinerator on the Merck site had led to the deaths of hundreds of animals belonging to the Hanrahans.

That was in July 1988; a month later the pattern of the 1970s was repeated as the communities in east Cork and west Waterford rallied to prevent Merrell Dow building a pharmaceutical factory in Killeagh, in County Cork. Now the battles were coming thick and fast. The communities in Cork harbour challenged the council to do something about the emissions coming from Penn Chemicals and Angus Fine Chemicals (later Hickson's Pharmachem). When the communities learned that yet another chemical factory was headed for the harbour, they formed alliances with each other and objected to the planning application of Nordisk Gentofte, the Danish insulin manufacturer. Those alliances were needed, for the empire was about to strike back. The Swiss were coming, flanked by an armed and irascible state in the form of their IDA battalion.

It would be the last major battle, fought against a background of skirmishes that saw communities all over the country defend themselves against the terrors of the chemical industry and the complicity of the state. In Derry, for example, the communities would prevent DuPont from building an incinerator. Sandoz (now Novartis) won but the state lost. The Swiss corporate was the last to build a chemical factory in Cork.

Who won the war, so? Sandoz finished the construction of its factory in Ringaskiddy in 1994. But during the period since, the farmers in Askeaton, in County Limerick, have fought the state and industry over industrial emissions they believe have resulted in the deaths of hundreds of their animals, and ill-health among their neighbours. To the state it is a mystery, to the communities it is corruption, lies and secrecy.

This is the story of a war that is now becoming sophisticated.

1 The Politics of Pollution

> Though you search
> for the Holy Grail
> You're not going to find it
> in the Chemical World
>   Peter Hammill

It started in 1958 when Thomas Kenneth Whitaker, Secretary of the Department of Finance, and Sean Lemass, Taoiseach, introduced the Programme for Economic Expansion that, among other economic initiatives, sought to attract foreign investment to Ireland. Whitaker and Lemass believed the state could entice, with grants and tax concessions, the highly professional corporates and get them to train Irish people in corporate management. By 1970, with the restructuring of the Industrial Development Agency (IDA), local authorities in league with the state body saw only the success of bringing the corporates to Ireland, and ceaselessly pursued every corporate thinking of locating a subsidiary in Europe. While many under-developed or less-industrialised countries questioned whether they should provide a home or haven for the most hazardous sector of this industry, the IDA and the local authorities were blinded by the jobs these corporates would bring, with little or no regard for health and safety and none for the environment. Ireland became a 'pollution haven' before anyone gave it a thought. Those who did were immediately marginalised.

The growth of toxic industry (particularly US originated) in Ireland was seen as a local phenomenon, but globally it was not unique. In 1970 US chemical industry investment in Ireland was $22.25 million. Within three years it had climbed to $173 million and by 1981 it had increased to $1,121 million (approximately 6 per cent of the chemical industry's worldwide investment total) – by 2002 the IDA was quoting total investment at $12 billion. Over the same period in Mexico a similar increase occurred: in 1973 it was $503 million, in 1981 it was $1,144 million. In Brazil investment increased from $343 million in 1973 to $1,384 million in 1982. In Australia between 1973 and 1983 US chemical industry investment rose from $498 million to $1,277 million. In Ireland and Mexico, after 1981 investment fell off for several years before picking up again at the end of the decade. By 2002 the electronics and software industries had replaced the chemical and pharmaceutical industries as the jewels in Ireland's corporate crown – responsible for 32 per cent of exports against 25 per cent from the chemical industry.

That 13-year period from 1970 to 1983 saw Ireland host five of the giants of the US chemical industry – Penn Chemicals (subsidiary of SmithKline Beckman, later SmithKline Beecham), Pfizer, Merck, Schering Plough and Syntex (now Roche) – which accounted for nearly 70 per cent of pharmaceutical industry output. The reasons that these companies came to Ireland were straightforward. Aside from the lack of safety and environmental regulations, which appealed to US corporates who wanted to escape the escalation of occupational and environmental regulation in their homeland, of particular interest to the industry was the large amount of that increasingly rare resource, unpolluted groundwater, that was available – approximately 15,000 m^3/person/year, about five times that of many other European countries.

This threat from polluting industry was never taken seriously when the corporates believed all they had to do was fly in, do a deal with the local elites, sign a few papers and build a drugs factory. The heavy presence of chemical corporates in Ireland meant that domestic and European Community legislation designed to protect the environment, public health and workers' safety wasn't worth a damn. The legislation existed but the laws were not adequately or stringently enforced, largely because the state and the local authorities who hosted hazardous industry believed a quiet word in the ear of the offending corporate was better than a journey to the (local) court house. Although it could be argued that Ireland's membership of the European Community should have protected it from the alien policies of chemical corporates, specifically the policies these corporates practice in the less-industrialised world, the problem was not the legislation, but the way it was being interpreted.

European Union environmental directives were not worth the paper they were written on because they had not been incorporated into Irish law (with appropriate enforcement legislation), as the confusion over the implementation of the directive on environmental impact assessment showed. After it was scheduled to come into force in 1988, Europe chastised the Irish government for failing to implement it properly and it was a further two and a half years before it was incorporated into Irish law. In 1992 Liam Cashman of the EU Office of the Environment told an Irish activist that he was concerned about the interpretation of EU legislation by local authorities in Ireland.

If the Irish people were ignorant of what the corporates were doing to their land and to their health, all that changed around 1978, two years after Merck Sharp and Dohme had established its factory in Ballydine, County Tipperary, when neighbouring farmers began to complain about pollution they insisted was coming from the chemical factory. No one in authority, it appeared, could help them, until one farming family, the Hanrahans, decided *ya basta* (enough) and took on Merck, the local authority, the state and its apparatus, sending a clear message to other communities. Very few people in Ireland knew about toxic pollution until the Hanrahans made it an issue throughout the 1980s when they fought Merck in the courts, determined to prove that pollution from the factory had poisoned their animals and damaged their health.

Despite the high profile the Hanrahan story had in Irish society, the state was using all its power to pretend that opposition did not exist, at first unsure where the opposition was coming from. Padraic White, former Head of the Industrial Development Authority (now called the Industrial Development Agency), speaking on 10 February 1989, made this very clear. According to White, corporates thinking of locating in County Cork would look elsewhere in Ireland or overseas if the hostility from local communities persisted. The speech was a well timed piece of propaganda to assuage the feelings of the corporate executive officers in the corporates whose developments were being opposed, White would explain later, by small undemocratic groups made up of people who had radical social and environmental tendencies.

There was some irony in this speech because the debate about the impact of globalisation on Irish society had been filed during the 1970s and 1980s under subversives, cranks, greens, communists, anarchists, dreamers and troublesome farmers. Yet here was White castigating local communities while claiming at the same time that radical tendencies were the real reason for the opposition. It was true that the developments his agency were promoting in Ireland were being opposed by anarchists, communists, environmentalists and republicans, but like many at the time, he was wrong to believe what other politicians and the media were saying about this opposition, that it was at one extreme the work of elite groups or at another the work of people who were responding to the victory of the Hanrahan family against US chemical corporate Merck Sharp and Dohme in the Supreme Court in 1988.

In reality, it was part of a resurgence in community opposition to development plans that people considered toxic or hazardous or plain wrong. It was the beginning of an opposition to the impact of globalisation on Irish society before anyone knew what globalisation was. It was a feeling that people had, that these developments were wrong for the country. 'The vibrancy that keeps us people alive is one of our major strengths. Are we going to allow the government to enforce developments that destroy our way of life?' Michael 'Mitey' McNally, of the Allihies Resource Development Group – one of the founder members of the Irish Rural Link – said at the time. Anthropologist Adrian Peace put it another way some years later in a study of an Irish coastal fishing and farming community. Irish communities are no longer 'inseparable from the international economic system, which establishes the parameters of power within which localised strategies have to be worked out'. Which is exactly what happened in Tipperary, and was becoming apparent in other communities, particularly in east Cork when Merrell Dow attempted to establish a pharmaceutical factory in Killeagh in the late 1980s.

This opposition to globalisation was not confined simply to the chemical and pharmaceutical industries; it included opposition to extractive industries such as mining and quarrying, to intensive mariculture such as fin-fish farming, to the dumping of toxic waste and the building of toxic incinerators, and to a variety of developments from broadcasting masts to meat factories, to tanneries, to the use of Irish sea and air ports by foreign military, in fact to anything that people believed was harmful or hazardous to their lives and their way of life. It also included myriad single issue campaigns such as protests against hard drugs, health cuts, post office closures, railway closures, border road closures, the rod licence and about education, child care, unemployment, tax, public transport, inadequate infrastructures, farming inequality, gender rights, water quality, cultural activity, barter, rural resettlement, pot holes, local/pirate radio and organic farming.

The late 1980s and early 1990s were a watershed for economic and industrial development in Ireland, because the protests were becoming generational, loud and effective, and by the end of the century the opposition to globalisation grew in the form of civil disobedience and direct action against telecommunication masts, road building (and road widening), genetically engineered crops, pollution of waterways and the continued use of air and sea ports by the US military. But never far away was always the threat from the toxic world, particularly the emissions and wastes from corporate industry, hanging like the sword of Damocles over communities who feared toxic emissions and waste. Some communities were determined that would not be their fate and so Merrell Dow's decision to flee back to the United States was regarded as an expedient business consequence. The sensible people in Cork knew better.

Merrell Dow's failure to locate in a high food-producing region was also a watershed for social resistance to the US-dominated toxic industry in Ireland. This community battle, more than any other in the Irish toxic war that was now a reality, was a turning point – for the industry, for the state and for communities. Yet the people of Killeagh and the surrounding area, who opposed Merrell Dow in the, late 1980s, were no different from any community anywhere in the world where potentially hazardous industry has attempted to find a home. In an Irish context the Killeagh opposition was not unique. Communities in Clare and Tipperary had seen off the chemical industry during the 1970s, and in Cork in 1980 Raybestos Manhattan packed its bags and went back to the United States after local opposition to the handling and dumping of its asbestos waste became too intense.

All of these communities were united by one concern: toxic pollution and waste and their health and environmental implications. John Beecher, one of the principal original objectors to Merrell Dow, was visibly shocked when he learned what the extent of that pollution could be.

> I couldn't believe that everything, just everything – the land, the air, rivers, sea, the cows – all of it could get destroyed by those dreadful American Merrell Dow bigshots. And just to think that on top of it all, the Irish government was in there as well, pushing and pulling and squeezing them into place at Killeagh.

That the Merrell Dow saga is regarded as a turning point in the politics of globalisation in Ireland and in standards of environmental control had as much to do with a change in IDA and state policy regarding its programme of industrialisation as with the 18-month campaign itself which impacted indelibly on Irish life, coinciding as it did with the Hanrahan family's victory in the Supreme Court over Merck.

State policy had been to encourage polluting industry. The ruling in the Hanrahan case had done nothing to appease communities concerned about an industry that appeared to make up the rules as it went along, in conjunction with the relevant local authority. So when Longford-born Dr Conor Gearty of King's College, London, writing in the August 1988 issue of the *Irish Law Times*, praised the judges in the Supreme Court 'for a decision that is as just as it is courageous' eyebrows were raised until it became obvious that he was critical of the ruling. Gearty did not find much hope in the ruling for similar actions against toxic industry in the future. The common law on which the judgement was based, said Gearty, is inherently biased against individuals, because it requires the plaintiff, who is likely to be the least able to obtain the necessary information about the operations of the defendant's activities, to provide proof of causation. In making the Hanrahan ruling the Supreme Court had, said Gearty, a chance to restructure the law in a way that would have favoured individuals against corporate polluters but failed to do so. The law remained structured in favour of potentially polluting industry. The fact that the Supreme Court ruled in the Hanrahans' favour was, according to Gearty, a signal from the highest court in the land that it was prepared, in the right situation, to interpret the law in a way favourable to the plaintiffs in order to achieve a result that accorded with justice and fairness.

Justice and fairness are not words associated with globalisation, whether we are talking about chemical corporates or the courts of the land. The courts interpret law that has been designed to protect the ruling elites and when Gearty wrote that it is 'the task of government, central and local to protect its people' he displayed a naiveté of the ways of capitalism that is not uncommon among his profession. There were several lessons, as he put it, to be learned from the Hanrahan case, that it is wrong to 'dump danger on the deprived' and that 'the planning system failed to anticipate the problems and, far from resolving them, did not even spot them when they occurred'. It would not be the last time, because the corporates were beginning to realise they needed to get their spin doctors working.

Ireland has a strong chemical industry lobby. Some observers would say it became paranoid during the time of the Merrell Dow opposition and there is some justification for this. Having decided that Ireland was a suitable 'pollution haven' the chemical and pharmaceutical corporates, in collusion with the state and unwitting local authorities, got used to getting their own way. As one critic of the industry put it:

> In the game the multinationals were playing in Ireland, when the multinationals picked the tune it was the local communities that did the dancing. Basic to this are the relations of dependency implicit in the development model followed by the IDA. Thus when pollution or other operating problems arose, or when corporates needed further concessions from local authorities, the corporations played their trump card, the threat to pull out.

Pfizer, the embodiment of the fledgling chemical industry in Ireland, was the first to play this card in 1972 after An Taisce in Cork challenged the corporate over its pollution policy. Pfizer lost this battle but lessons were learned, particularly by those who advocated an Ireland flush with the biggest players in the chemical industry. A year later, Sinn Féin issued a policy document in which it attacked the IDA's industrial development strategy which, the Sinners insisted, was geared to attracting dirty industry:

> Not only do we try to get the dirty outcasts of European [sic] industry to come to Ireland, we pay them large grants to come. We have totally inadequate pollution control standards and we are prepared to allow the construction of such technological time-bombs in the most beautiful and scenic parts of our country. Sinn Féin says that the prostitution of the environment and the amenities of Ireland in this manner must be resisted. We cannot allow the capitalists of Europe and North America to unload the filth, which is no longer tolerated in their own countries and in many instances, on our door-step in return for jobs which it would be the duty of any proper Irish government to provide in the first place.

Fine rhetoric this was and prophetic it would be too but the document was ignored. Not for the captains of industry to consider anything other than short-term capital gains. The Hanrahans' horror and the agony at Askeaton were waiting to happen.

The chemical industry was able to harness this power because of attitudes inherent in state and government policy during the 1960s and 1970s. H. J. Leonard, an American academic who studied the impact of the chemical industry in Ireland and analysed the 'pollution haven' hypothesis, was told that IDA officials were 'not much concerned with assessing the environmental implications of most industrial projects for which overseas firms were seeking grant assistance'. In the late 1960s/early 1970s the IDA 'generally assumed that some of the industries migrating to Ireland would be ones that faced an inhospitable climate at home owing to concern about pollution'. But it went deeper than that:

> To ensure the co-operation of the local governments actually responsible for approving specific industrial proposals, IDA officials held a series of closed-door meeting to advise local officials that, for the sake of the economy and jobs, some of the dirtier industrial facilities from the advanced industrial nations might have to be sited on terms that offered less stringent pollution controls than in Europe or the United States.

Two decades later the tune changed. 'We do not want jobs at any cost', the IDA announced as the campaign intensified against Sandoz, the Swiss chemical giant that went on to build a IR£170 million factory in Ringaskiddy, County Cork. 'We will strongly support action by regulatory authorities to ensure clean industry', the IDA added, changing its rhetoric from the early 1970s. And the reason for its change of mind? 'Within industry there is a good balance across many sectors – food, pharmaceuticals, electronics, etc. – which do not offend the environment', the IDA press officer Colm Donlon told an industry seminar in February 1990, as the anti-toxic campaigners geared up for Sandoz's planning hearing. 'We must keep it that way if any growth is to be achieved', he added.

Growth was an important word in the IDA's vocabulary and was being heard frequently in the early 1990s as the Irish economy moved into a period of unprecedented growth. The Organization for Economic Cooperation and Development (OECD), acknowledging that the state's industrial and domestic fiscal policies were beginning to work, summarised Ireland's industrial development in 1985 as:

better than countries and regions against which it is competing in the race to attract foreign direct investment. Ireland has a higher proportion of output in fast-growing electronics, chemicals and food-processing, and a lower proportion of output in traditional industries, including mechanical engineering, textiles and clothing.

These sectors have been declining ever since. The result is a dual economy with, on one side, a modern industrial sector consisting largely of electronics and chemicals and on the other, declining traditional industries such as crops, meat, food, drink, tobacco, wood, textiles, clothing, footwear and concrete products. The modern industrial sector uses Ireland primarily as an 'export platform' and here again electronics and pharmaceuticals are the twin pillars of this success. This type of dependent development, which includes a massive public debt and an economy dominated by foreign capital, has led to massive repatriation of profits from corporates operating in Ireland.

While the IDA argued, particularly since Merrell Dow tried to come to Ireland in 1988, that it was no longer attempting to attract polluting or dirty industry – it claimed it was spending its promotional budget on indigenous food industry – there are many reasons why the chemical industry located in Ireland, and they have more to do with internal and external economics than health and environmental implications. Ireland was chosen as a manufacturing base because of high productivity, labour flexibility, relatively low labour costs, low or non-existent taxation, political stability, government-funded incentives, a highly educated and English language workforce, unpolluted groundwater and, most significantly, high rate of return on capital investment.

According to the IDA, Ireland was the most profitable industrial location not only in Europe but in the world during the 1970s and 1980s. Between 1977 and 1982 the average rate of profit on US capital investment in Ireland was 30.7 per cent, higher than Japan and Italy by 13 points and double that of Germany. Although it dropped to 23 per cent for the period 1982–7 – four times the EC average – by 1996 it was climbing back up, at 24 per cent for the period 1991–6, at which it stood in 2003. Between 1980 and 1985 IR£4,035 million in profits were repatriated by corporates operating in Ireland.

John McMahon, Chief Economist with the IDA, estimated that 85 per cent of profits leaving Ireland during the period when the rate of profit was highest were from the electronic and chemical industries. During the Hanrahan–Merck Sharp and Dohme legal battle the US corporate admitted that its weekly profits from Bally-dine came to $1 million. According to Kieran Keohane, 'as much as one seventh of all the profit made by subsidiaries of US pharmaceutical corporations in the EC in 1984 and 1985 was made by subsidiaries of US corporations operating in Ireland'. J. Stewart noted:

> Surveys by the US Department of Commerce of US firms operating in Ireland show profit margins greater than those in other countries, particularly for firms in the Chemicals and Allied Products sector. This sector accounts for between 62 per cent and 76 per cent of net earnings of US firms operating in Ireland for the period 1973 to 1980.

In other words capital investment could be recouped within one to two years. Given that most of the chemical corporates located subsidiaries in Ireland between 1970 and 1990 they have all been making huge profits for a long time. The value of the chemical industry to Ireland's gross national product is evident from the number of chemical corporates operating subsidiaries. There were approximately 280 pharmaceutical and healthcare companies in Ireland in the early 1990s employing 14,000; by 2002 this had dropped to 200 but those employed 28,000. Of these 73 are foreign, and according to John Lloyd of the IDA's pharmaceutical, chemical and healthcare division, 18 are from the top 20 corporations. '[They] include 28 bulk active ingredient producers, 13 producing generic pharmaceuticals and 32 producing proprietary finished pharmaceuticals.' Total exports from the industry were approximately $4.5 billion in 1990; by 2002 they had increased to $18 billion.

Despite the glorious campaigns and the energetic protests, Ireland is now a toxic country, with little to distinguish it from many post-colonial industrial nations in environmental, economic and political considerations. Those who opposed toxic capital and toxic industry from the 1960s until the mid-1990s were up against money and power. Yet it took over 20 years of constant protest for the chemical industry in Ireland to finally spend some of its money on environmental control. In 1989, in response to the criticisms about environmental control that had dominated the debates about Merrell Dow and latterly Sandoz, the major chemical companies stated they would add approximately IR£75 million to their environmental control budgets. This figure is placed in perspective when it is revealed that between 1970 and 1988 the industry invested only IR£95 million.

As the Environmental Protection Agency (EPA) was being put in place – a process that took five years – the chemical industry began to make curious sounds about environmental standards. Fine Gael's attempts to introduce environmental protection agency legislation were defeated in November 1989. On 2 February 1990 Mary Harney said the government intended to introduce its own EPA bill during the current session. When the bill was published, community and environmental groups were critical of its contents. 'You'd go out of business anyway', Frank McCoy, Personnel Manager of Angus Fine Chemicals (now Hickson's Pharmachem) in Cork, said two years before the place blew up, sending the harbour communities into a justifiable panic. It is arguably the only point that the industry and the environmentalists agree on. 'I don't see why we shouldn't have the highest standards, in Ireland', said Geraldine O'Brien of the Cork Environmental Alliance. 'Why do we have to have German standards or US standards?'

For many years the chemical industry in Ireland has been oblique about environmental control and standards. For a manager like Frank McCoy to admit openly in 1991 – while the industry was under fire from communities – that higher pollution standards were required was seen as a significant progression by the state and the regulatory authorities but not by environmentalists and anti-toxic campaigners who remained convinced that the state would continue to protect the interests of the chemical corporates. And that is exactly what they alleged happened in 1997 when Aughinish Alumina complained the extra expense imposed on it by the EPA.

The fledgling Irish EPA inherited a system of pollution control that did not protect the environment and the health of the human and animal populations, Greenpeace claimed during its 'Stop Legal Pollution Tour' in the summer of 1993 when the group highlighted 'toxic' pollution in Cork, Limerick, Meath, Tipperary and Wicklow. A nationwide investigation into pollution licensing and monitoring led Greenpeace to the conclusion that there was 'an absence of understanding and knowledge of humane environmentalism and an ambivalence towards the concept of environmental protection' in both central and regional government. Greenpeace wanted the EPA to begin a programme to phase out and eventually ban the most dangerous toxic chemicals and espouse the principle of clean technology. Environmental audits, it insisted, should be made mandatory for industry and the public should be given full access to environmental information. But it was Greenpeace's argument that the government should arrest its industrial strategy and adopt a policy which supports 'pollution free' industry that was slightly revolutionary for the global environmental group. And, it appeared, much too visionary for a state far too dependent on corporate investment. Greenpeace said:

> Ireland is less polluted than its European neighbours. With the political vision, the future of Ireland can be a place where the development of pollution-free technology can co-exist with an indigenous food and crafts industry, an eco-tourist industry and a thriving service industry to make Ireland a post-industrial model for the rest of Europe.

Given the Irish state's dependence on capitalist development, critics of the EPA questioned whether it could provide a new environmental dawn. A few months before it was established on 26 July 1993, its first Director-General Liam McCumiskey, who had been prominent in Irish environmental research and administration for many years before he joined the EPA, said he was philosophical about the expectations being imposed on the fledgling EPA. 'You can't press a button and put all kinds of staff into place overnight. They have to be trained', he said, indicating that it would be up to five years before the EPA took over all the functions in the legislation. The EPA, which took two years to go through the Dáil and a further year of preparation, was set up to complement all existing environmental legislation. The EPA's specific functions required it to licence, regulate and control all activities 'with potential for major impact' on the environment, monitor polluting industry and make the data available to the public, support and advise public authorities on environmental matters, promote and coordinate environmental research, liaise with the European Environmental Agency and advise on new domestic, EC and international environmental legislation.

'Most of our pollution is of an organic nature', he said, noting that pollution from the chemical industry in Ireland is 'minuscule'.

Ireland has four times more water resources on a per capita basis than most of the countries in Europe. McCumiskey stressed that the quality of Irish waters must be maintained and improved where necessary. 'This does not mean that there are to be no further discharges. The agency will be considering both new and existing sources of pollution in the context of water quality and the need for sustainable development.' He was adamant there would be 'minimal environmental impact' from discharges if the best available technology not entailing excessive costs (otherwise known as BATNEEC) was used. He insisted that for licensable activities the EPA would be seeking to prevent pollution using BATNEEC, but where this was not practicable by minimising emissions. 'There is a growing realisation that the adoption of cleaner technologies can be beneficial not alone to the environment but also to industry. Nevertheless, it would be unrealistic to expect that all pollution can be avoided, even in the medium term', he said. 'There is little point trying to get a company to achieve a zero discharge if the costs are going to be huge when a 90 per cent removal will have minimal impact on the environment.' Licence applications, he said, would be handled individually.

> What we'll be looking at very carefully is what impact the emissions or discharges from that company has on the environment. If its impact is so small that we can't measure it – if that's the case then I think we couldn't be insisting on an unreasonable level of investment to reduce down a load.

Everyone, he said, would become involved in environmental protection:

> While the regulatory system will still play an important role into the next century, other instruments will have to be used like the economic and fiscal instruments. If we want economic and social development a clean environment is an absolute prerequisite. If we haven't got a clean environment even for our high tech industries, they won't locate here.

McCumiskey said he believed the availability of environmental information would 'make people more informed' which he hoped will allow them to 'come to a rational and sensible conclusion' on pollution issues. Better enforcement, compliance and monitoring, he said, would eventually allow the EPA to establish exactly what is being discharged and emitted into the environment. In the long term, he said, the EPA should be able to publish a toxic release inventory.

These comments would have had greater credibility if the Irish state was seen to take ecological and environmental issues seriously, but the feeling that the EPA was a new emperor in the same old clothes was rampant among communities who feared toxic industry in all its forms. The global concern about the ecology of the planet was not debated in the Ireland of the early 1990s. While the rest of Europe was getting heavily into alternative energies, organic farming, sophisticated recycling schemes and waste minimisation – and especially away from the products of chlorine chemistry – Irish society, with no support from the government, was making futile gestures. 'Recycling aluminium cans in the company cafeteria and ceremonial tree plantings are about as effective as bailing out the *Titanic* with teaspoons', was green entrepreneur Paul Hawken's view of these 'woefully inadequate' gestures. Hawken continued:

> How can business itself survive a continued pattern of worldwide degradation in living systems? What is the logic of extracting diminishing resources in order to create capital to finance more consumption and demand on those same diminishing resources? How do we imagine our future when our commercial systems conflict with everything nature teaches us?

Instead, in Ireland, the industry became even more defensive. When Greenpeace set out around the Irish coastline in August 1993 armed with the first of its Stop Legal Pollution documents, industry didn't like what the green NGO had to say. In *The Irish Times* on 19 August 1993 Professor James Heffron criticised Greenpeace and said the organisation 'would be far more constructively employed in taking positive action to eliminate the major risk factors for avoidable human cancer deaths and in helping government and industry systematically to reduce all emissions, industrial, municipal and domestic in a realistic planned programme'. In *Business and Finance*, published the same day, the Federation of Irish Chemical Industries' Neil Buckley said the chemical industry in Ireland was 'a success story without any significant environmental blemish over the past 25 years'. In the same report the Federation's Joe Harford said Greenpeace was using quasi science and that it was 'scaring the living daylights out of people'.

It was a tired old argument and one that shook Greenpeace because the organisation believed, as many environmentalists and anti-toxic campaigners did, that the toxic war was being won. The first realisation that it was not had come a year earlier in March 1992 when Clare O'Grady Walshe of Greenpeace Ireland and the leader of the Progressive Democrats Mary Harney, then Minister for Environmental Protection, clashed over a government award to Merck Sharp and Dohme, the Hanrahans' neighbour. But this particular story began even earlier. It started when Greenpeace decided it was time that the Hanrahan case had a higher profile – outside Ireland. During the summer of 1991 Greenpeace took John Hanrahan to Brussels to launch its international anti-incineration campaign. Greenpeace had also objected to the granting of an air emission licence to Merck Sharp and Dohme, and called on the government to hold a public enquiry into the events that brought the farmer and his family up against the corporate in Dublin's Four Courts. In August 1991 Walshe sent a six-page document on the Hanrahan case to every TD in the country and to the relevant government departments. No one responded until after Eolas presented the government-sponsored 'good environmental manage-ment award' to Merck. The replies to Walshe's circular were actually critical of Greenpeace's stance on Merck.

Undeterred, Walshe decided to organise an 'action' on the Liffey to protest about the presentation of the award to Merck by Mary Harney. Using two inflatables, Greenpeace displayed a banner which read: DOES POLLUTION PAY? ASK MERCK SHARP AND DOHME. Walshe said the award to Merck was 'a terrible insult to the Irish people' and 'by giving this award, Mary Harney is endorsing incineration'.

Harney responded: 'I have a duty to encourage better environ-mental practice in industry and to acknowledge progress of this kind where it occurs. Negative and continued confrontation is not the way forward.' She added that the government was committed 'to major improvement of the environmental regulation of industry through the establishment of the EPA'. The award, Harney stressed, would 'enhance the confidence of the public and industry alike in the fair application of high environmental standards and controls'.

What worried the anti-toxic campaigners was the question of whose standards and whose controls. (Merck stated in a press release on 23 March 1992 that it had spent IR£6 million on environmental protection at its Ballydine plant since 1987 and proposed to spent a further IR£7 million up to the end of 1993. 'Our aim', said Merck, 'is to set the standard for our industry by keeping abreast of the latest technology, replacing and upgrading our equipment, finding newer and better ways of producing our products and training our employees to the highest level of operating practices. Our commitment to continuous improvement in all aspects of environmental performance makes good business sense and hopefully will result in future expansion and the creation of additional jobs.'

Harney, like many before her, had missed the point. It was not just a question of standards and controls, it was something more fundamental, something that every community in the midst of a toxic factory or incinerator feared. John Hanrahan and his family had been poisoned and the government, industry and its apologists didn't think this was a problem. And if it was a problem it was better that we didn't hear about it. We certainly wouldn't hear the full story from John Hanrahan because he had come to trust no one, not even those anti-toxic campaigners who had helped him in his struggle against Merck.

Until the case was finally settled in July 1988, John Hanrahan, who had taken over the family farm from his mother Mary, was reluctant to be drawn into the social, health, political and economic arguments inherent in the case. He would give evasive answers to any journalist's probing questions and then suddenly lapse into intense monologues about a particular aspect of the case, which served to confuse rather than inform. It was as if John Hanrahan had lost the ability to think coherently or simply didn't remember whole chunks of his life. The fact that the entire case should have been a matter of public record because of its implications for human health from toxic pollution did not occur to sections of the media, and John Hanrahan believed he was powerless to do anything about the 'silence' from the corridors of power in Dublin.

Hanrahan instead choose to challenge Merck in the courts. When it was over he said he had the greatest faith in the Irish legal system. 'We have been treated with respect and honour. Anything we asked for from the court, we got, because we told the truth.' Mary Hanrahan reiterated what her son said. 'This is the valley of tears', she said, standing in the sitting room of her home, after the settlement in December 1990, acknowledging the location of the farm in the picturesque Suir Valley in South Tipperary. 'Our story was true, you see. We were very pleased that in the end we got, I suppose you could say, justice. But at what price? That is something none of us can say.'

There has been a price, and the Hanrahans and their neighbours are slowly paying it: irreparable damage to their health. Selina Hanrahan, John's wife, has endometriosis, which has been identified with dioxin contamination. The rise in cancers in the area around Ballydine has increased dramatically, to the extent that no longer do the people of the valley shrug their shoulders in bemusement. Now they know. They know what has caused their illnesses.

Those who have studied the Hanrahan case believe that Merck got off lightly, estimating the total cost to the company at around IR£5 million. No one in Merck would comment on how much it spent fighting the Hanrahan family, but for a company that records its profits in billions it was a small price to pay. We don't even know how much the Hanrahans received in compensation because Merck insisted that the terms of the settlement remain secret. Barristers in Dublin's Four Courts have claimed that the Hanrahans got less than IR£1 million. But the money doesn't really matter. The price to the Hanrahan family is incalculable. The greater price is the effect on public opinion, which is exactly what Merck wanted to achieve when it forced an undisclosed settlement.

The great toxic disasters of the modern era happened elsewhere, out of sight, out of mind and certainly out of Ireland. Yet Merck's poisoning of the Ballydine environment occurred in front of our eyes in Ireland, but it is as if nothing strange happened in this place Mary Hanrahan calls the 'valley of tears'. This astute remark had much to do with the local knowledge that those farming families who have suffered as a result of Merck's emissions have cried their tears in secret. The Hanrahans' decision to challenge Merck in the courts was courageous, but the circumstances that caused the suppression of the human suffering in the Ballydine area diluted the argument that there is a health risk from exposure to low levels of chemical compounds. It wasn't so elsewhere in the world.

Since July 1991, when an unprecedented gathering of scientists at Wingspread, Wisconsin in the United States discussed how the organohalogen compounds we know as pesticides, industrial chemicals and synthetic products affect sexual development in wildlife and humans, more and more scientists are realising that these compounds are responsible for the destruction of species all over the planet. More significantly is the reason: the failure and break-down of endocrine and immune systems. As the human endocrine system is virtually identical to that of other vertebrates such as fish, birds and mammals, scientists believe humans are next, unless, as the Wingspread scientists put it, something is done to abate and control the chemical compounds industry is pumping into the environment.

While many scientists are unequivocal in their belief that chemical and nuclear pollution is responsible for many of the modern illnesses in the western world, the absence, particularly in Ireland, of establishment-reviewed epidemiological studies and the inability to trace the flight and subsequent destination of any particular pollutant means that the debate remains unfocused, the case 'unproven'. Industry, as Martyn Day, an environmental lawyer, put it, 'has the advantage of knowing that the difficulty in ascribing any one pollutant to any one illness is enormous'.

Evidence of pollution – the problem which confronts the local doctor – has allowed the chemical industry to argue that its processes are not to blame for illnesses among industrialised and the wider communities. Chemicals are regarded as relatively harmless if clinical damage cannot be detected. According to those prepared to accept that there is a real problem, animal models, clinicopathological studies and epidemiological investigations are even regarded as not sensitive enough to detect the effects of low-level exposures to chemicals. Animal models are used to study the effects of high doses of chemicals but as Nicholas Ashford and Claudia Miller note in *Chemical Exposures: Low Levels and High Stakes*, 'rats, mice and other animals are unable to tell researchers if they have headaches, feel depressed or anxious or are nauseated'. They conclude, 'thus, the subtle effects of low-level chemical exposure may be missed completely'.

Epidemiological studies point to associations between events, but as multiple chemical sensitivity is the consequence of multiple triggers resulting in multiple health effects, according to Ashford and Miller, 'epidemiology may be an insensitive tool'. And clinicopathological studies, because they rely on the presence of a clinical sign, laboratory measurement or tissue pathology, are, note Ashford and Miller, 'not likely to be sensitive to the early effects of low-level exposures, that is prior to end-organ damage'. Inflammation of the airways is one of the first indicators of toxic pollution and multiple chemical sensitivity is the consequence of this exposure. Few doctors disagree that environmental pollution is the cause of respiratory illnesses. What they are unsure about is the cause, which, as we have seen from Ashford and Miller's comments, has more to do with the tools of the trade. Asthma is triggered by the pollutants common in our urban air, significantly oxides of nitrogen and sulphur, ozone and fine particles. That fine particles may be invisible killers is only beginning to gain greater credence than before, despite our knowledge of the London smog that killed 4,000 people in one week in 1952. The question, Dr Peter Montague of *Environment and Health Weekly* asks, 'is how much pollution causes how much damage and is there a threshold, an amount below which no effects are seen?'

This has been the debate throughout the past five decades because many authorities believe there is a safe threshold. But this has been questioned by scientists studying the effects of small particulates. Humans evolved to filter out large particulates by the hairs in the nose, mucous membranes in the throat and airways and other mechanisms. Small particulates, which are produced by modern combustion machines, pass through these natural protections straight into the lung. Because they originate in modern combustion processes most fine particles are coated with toxic metals and chemicals. In the deep lung air comes into contact with the bloodstream. Therefore, according to Montague, 'fine particles provide a uniquely efficient carrier, giving dangerous toxins direct entry into the blood stream'. Death rates from asthma have been increasing in the United States, Canada, England, France, Denmark and Germany throughout the past 50 years. In addition to asthma deaths the prevalence of asthma has been increasing steadily, and in major cities asthma is the leading cause of hospitalisation among children aged 5 to 15.

Asthma is a disease of the immune system. In an asthmatic the immune system overreacts to the presence of an external agent. The bronchial tubes (which connect the throat to the lungs) become inflamed, produce excessive mucous, and may constrict by muscular spasm. As a result the asthmatic feels like he or she is drowning for lack of air, which, for many, is actually what is happening. What is now beginning to concern some doctors is the possibility that the asthma increase is the result of damaged immune systems. In April 1994 *Science*, the magazine of the American Association for the Advancement of Science, agreed, claiming that immunologists were encountering a 'far more subtle' problem than AIDS: damage to the immune system from environmental pollutants. 'Everywhere these days doctors are seeing increasingly severe cases of immune-related diseases', Richard Stone wrote in an article titled 'Immunology: pollutants a growing threat'.

Far less subtle is the clinical damage from exposure to chemicals that scientists, workers and industrial communities have no doubt about. Cancer! The argument that occupational and environmental exposure to chemicals is causing a range of cancers not easily explained by age, diet or addiction has been uncompromised by those practitioners who study these phenomena. Scientists agree that one in three people in industrialised societies will get cancer during their lifetime and one in four will die from it. But the greatest risk is among those living near industrial plants, mines, chemical works and nuclear installations, and workers exposed to chemical and radioactive carcinogens. According to Samuel Epstein, Professor of Occupational and Environmental Medicine at the School of Public Health at the University of Illinois:

> some 75 per cent of all cancers develop in those over the age of 55. But there are notable exceptions, particularly some leukaemias, brain cancers and cancers of the tests, which strike mainly the young and have been increasing at alarming rates.

Epstein's work has led him to the conclusion that the rates for certain cancers are ten times higher among some industrial workers than within the general population. Based on exposure data, the US National Institute of Occupational Safety and Health (NIOSH) has estimated that approximately 11 million workers are exposed to occupational carcinogens. Two studies of workers exposed to tetrachlorodibenzo-para-dioxin (TCDD) – one of the most poisonous organohalogens, produced as a by-product of chemical manufacture and the combustion of chlorinated compounds – have also shown high increases of various cancers. Marilyn Fingerhut's study of 5,172 American chemical industry workers revealed a cancer rate 46 per cent above normal. A similar study of German workers revealed a rate 39 per cent above normal, but the German study also revealed that the cancer rates were 82 per cent for workers employed for 20 years or more. Although these studies have shown that high exposure to dioxin is a direct cause of cancer (and this has since been confirmed by studies of the population exposed to dioxin from the Seveso accident in Italy in 1976), Linda Birnbaum, Director of Environmental Toxicology at the USEPA and one of the scientists leading the agency's reassessment of dioxin, said she was also concerned about the chemical compound's impact on the human immune system, 'that much lower exposure to dioxin may result in adverse health effects that are very subtle and difficult to detect'.

The 21 scientists who had gathered at Wingspread to discuss sex hormones – the androgens that make males look and act like males and the oestrogens that make females look and act like females – in wildlife and humans were the first group of prominent scientists to show these correlations. As a result of their conference Dr Theo Colborn and her colleagues agreed that 'many compounds introduced into the environment by human activity are capable of disrupting the endocrine systems of animals, including fish, wildlife and humans' and they noted that 'the consequence of such disruption can be profound because of the crucial role hormones play in controlling development'. When these artificial chemicals enter the bodies of humans, animals and wildlife, largely through the food chain, they mimic hormones. What Colborn and her colleagues discovered is that the body mistakes these environmental hormones for natural hormones, but unlike natural hormones which carry a specific biological message and are then dispatched from the bloodstream, these environmental hormones remain in the body for long periods, causing continual biological destruction. Colborn and her colleagues also noted that most chemical endocrine disrupters mimic oestrogen, which many scientists now believe is the cause of the 50 per cent drop in the male sperm count since 1940, the twofold increase in breast cancer among women since 1960, the threefold increase in testicular cancer and twofold increase in prostate cancer since the 1940s, the phenomenal rise in endometriosis (virtually unknown outside the twentieth century) which now affects 5 million American women, and the increasing number of children born with abnormalities.

You would have been forgiven for not knowing anything about these studies if you lived amidst Ireland's toxic corporates. And when anyone tried to bring these up as serious issues they were met with a belligerent attitude that used emotional personal arguments, as witnessed in a letter to *The Irish Times* on 28 September 1994 in which Sean Ward, representing the Cork Pharmachem group, dismissed the work of Greenpeace's David Watchorn. Yet all Watchorn did was refer to the evidence that was out there in the public domain by peer-reviewed scientists.

What Watchorn did not know, at the time at least, was that the industry was becoming increasingly concerned about the activities of the green NGOs and their ability to attract publicity. A memo sent by Schering Plough on 14 April 1994 to P. Caffrey (Pfizer), B. Mohally (Janssen), P. O'Driscoll (FMC), B. Rutledge (Henkel), Dr. K. Goggin (Elanco) and M. Moran (IBEC) revealed that they wanted the state to do something about it.

> The all too familiar activities and tactics of Greenpeace and similar organisations can be expected to continue, indeed they will probably be intensified. We have a depressing familiarity with the effects of this which include the following:
> 1. increased costs for individual companies
> 2. discouragement of new investment and expansions
> 3. reduction in overall competitiveness.
> The government, through IBEC, should be requested to initiate appropriate action to counteract these effects.

It was clear to those working in Greenpeace and the Cork alliance that the industry was out to get them. When another leaked briefing document found its way into the alliance's office in Cork it surprised no one. The briefing suggested that dossiers should be compiled on known green activists and that residents' groups should be taken over by the industry. It also suggested that environmental figureheads should be compromised, but it was when a confidential file on Greenpeace members and their activities was presented to a reporter by a prominent member of the Pharmachem group that the greens realised what they were up against – lies and secrecy.

Despite EC legislation that was supposed to make it easier for communities to get information on pollution monitoring and enforcement, the information was not freely available in the Ireland of the 1990s, despite the formation of the EPA. The Cork alliance discovered this, only a year after the EPA had been set up, when one of its members went in search of what must at the end of the day have seemed like the Holy Grail, so tiring was the request for basic data on breaches of pollution licences from Cork County Council.

Whether or not there are laws to the contrary Ireland is still an elite, closed and secret society. (Attempts by the author to get the Irish state to make available any documentation between the corporate chemical industry and the state – transcripts of meetings and phone calls, letters, reports – have produced nothing; these don't exist apparently.) University science departments are funded largely by corporate industry; government-sponsored analysis is dictated by the demands of the industrial lobby; independent consultants work almost exclusively for government and industry, while regional and central government is slow to implement strategies that seek to improve the quality of natural and urban environments; and environmentalists use their skills to find permanent jobs or positions in academia, industry and government – even before they are compromised by industry.

Although the EPA promised a new dawn when it was established in July 1993, events in Askeaton in County Limerick have showed that the state has learned nothing from the Hanrahan case or even that it takes seriously the spectre of pollution and the consequent human and animal health problems and environmental damage. Progressive planning and environmental legislation has been drafted in favour of industry rather than people and their environments, and while the Hanrahan case is a source of comfort to those who believe in legal remedies, communities or individuals should not be compelled to fight costly legal battles to protect their health and environment. Throughout the 1990s that is the way it has been – single-issue legal battles that do not deal with the holistic problem.

The EPA has argued that in its ten-year history it has forced the chemical industry to clean up its act; it has achieved what it set out to achieve. The bad old days of the 1960s, 1970s and 1980s are over, Ireland is no longer a pollution haven, and Irish industry is now a properly regulated industry. The reality is different.

Back in the late 1950s the state policy – to invite foreign corporates to Ireland with promises of grants and concessions – was designed to provide jobs, albeit at a cost to the health of Irish communities and to the delicate ecology of the island. In return the corporates would employ and train Irish people, who would be able to create their own industries and keep their young at home. This idealistic image of big business was soon shattered as the corporations flooded into Ireland, took advantage of the concessions and then, when their markets faltered, cleared off to somewhere they could pay lower wages and extract greater profits. Despite the IDA's rosy image of Ireland and its people, some of these same people were not prepared to accept jobs at any price. Throughout the history of foreign capital investment in Ireland, there has been opposition to it. The people of Cork and Tipperary challenged the idea of globalisation at a time when no one anywhere in the world knew what such opposition really meant. Now that Irish agriculture is declining and rural values are being destroyed as the young flock to the cities and towns for work in factories that are always closing down we know why. So this is not a book about corporate Ireland or even about hazard, it is a collection of stories about people who did not want the alien influence of globalisation in their lives.

2   Ballydine: Tears in the Valley

From the moment that one man needed the help of another, and it was realised that it would be useful for one man to have enough supplies for two, equality disappeared; property was introduced, work became a necessity, and vast forests were transformed into smiling fields which had to be watered with the sweat of human beings, fields were slavery and misery were soon seen to germinate and grow with the crops.

Jean-Jacques Rousseau

The silver-haired woman is standing in the sitting room of her modest home, a large two-storey farmhouse built in the perfunctory tradition of those few Irish families who somehow managed to acquire and hold on to land when most of it was stolen by the English administration, acknowledging the location of her family domain in the picturesque Suir Valley in South Tipperary.

'This is the valley of tears', she says quietly. She is solemn, though it is possible to detect a trace of emotion in her voice. 'Our story was true, you see. We were very pleased that in the end we got, I suppose you could say, justice. But at what price? That is something none of us can say.'

Mary Hanrahan has the manner of a matriarch. This is not tradition. It is the consequence of a tragedy that has virtually destroyed her son and his family. For without Mary, her son John might never have endured the ordeal that could have easily wiped out many another man.

It is a cold December afternoon, dry and crisp without a hint of rain. The day is bright, patches of hazy blue can be seen in the winter sky. The Hanrahans should be elated. They have just received an out-of-court settlement against the US chemical corporation, Merck Sharp and Dohme, after a twelve-year legal battle to prove that emissions from the company's Ballydine factory – just beyond the hill and over the railway – were responsible for the death of 225 of the Hanrahans' farm animals.

[27]

It is 1990 and the war between the Hanrahans and Merck should be over, but it isn't. As far as the Hanrahans and many others are concerned, it will never be over until the chemical industry stops terrorising rural and urban communities with its toxic poisons. Significantly the Hanrahans were unable to prove that their own illnesses were the consequence of Merck's activities. This is a crucial element in this story, because the animals were not the only ones affected by Merck's toxic emissions. It's probably fair to say that no one in Ireland had ever heard of dioxin until the Hanrahans took on Merck. And even now it is not known what the extent of the dioxin contamination was around Ballydine. What is known is that people have illnesses associated with dioxin poisoning.

It all began in the spring of 1972, but the first most people heard about the Yankee chemical company and the jobs they were promising was on Wednesday 2 August later that summer when the County Tipperary Development Team called a meeting in Clonmel Council Chambers to permit Merck Sharp and Dohme to explain its plans to an invited audience of local organisations.

Over 40 people attended, including officers of the Tipperary and Waterford County Councils, town clerks from Clonmel and Carrick-on-Suir, representatives of the Irish Creamery Milk Suppliers Association, Clonmel and District Anglers, Chamber of Commerce, South-East Region Tourist Organisation, An Taisce, the Game Council, An Foras Forbartha (forerunner of the EPA), the Suir Valley Conservation Society, the IIRS (Institute for Industrial Research and Standards, later to become Eolas – the state's Science and Technology Agency) and the IDA.

'The role of the Planning Authority and the attitude of [Merck] to the pollution factors was the dominant factor of an exhausting meeting', the local weekly newspaper recorded at the time. Tom McManus, of the IIRS, reading from a report he had prepared ostensibly for the meeting, said that the institute believed Merck 'would operate a clean plant without detriment to any local activity'.

A few days later Merck submitted its planning application for a bulk chemical factory in a slight dip in the valley along the banks of the Suir river between Carrick-on-Suir and Clonmel in the north of the ancient Irish province known as Munster. As the second largest pharmaceutical corporate in the world at the time, obtaining this application from Merck Sharp and Dohme was a major coup for the IDA and the local authority. This was progress. It was what the state had decided was the antidote to the curse of emigration. Scientists with the IIRS, with no real understanding of what they had been asked to do by the state, carried out an environmental impact assessment of the factory. The plans were passed. McManus was the recognised expert in the IIRS at vetting new engineering or chemical factories, but it was the first time he had dealt with a factory of the nature of Merck's.

So it was a victory for the South Tipperary County Council, particularly County Manager Robert Hayes, who was also the chair of the County Tipperary Development Team. Hayes paid tribute to the development team 'who had worked night and day for six weeks' to bring Merck to Tipperary. Not forgetting the equally important role of the IDA, who had been negotiating closely with Merck for several years, he praised them too.

It was against a background of opposition to toxic industry that Merck Sharp and Dohme finally arrived in Ireland.

In 1976 Schering Plough decided to abandon a IR£27 million investment for a pharmaceutical factory at Killaloan, Clonmel, in County Tipperary following threatened High Court action by a group who had objected vociferously and ceaselessly to the planning application. The objectors' action, the Minister for Local Government, James Tully, announced in the Seanad on 6 April 1976, amounted to 'blackmail'. The South Tipperary councillor, Tom Ambrose, claimed that the whole country was amazed at the decision whereby a small minority was able to prevent a major industry coming into the area. Schering's impetuous decision angered South Tipperary County Council, who, with the assistance of the IDA, had hoped to secure a second chemical factory for the area, following Merck Sharp and Dohme. Had the Schering Plough application been accepted more chemical companies might have been persuaded to set up shop right along the picturesque Suir Valley. The dream of those who saw an industrial corridor stretching from Limerick and the Shannon to Waterford and the south-east coast had been shattered.

At first there had been over 140 major objectors to Schering's application, yet as the saga continued amidst the completion of Merck's factory at Ballydine, it appeared that the council would succeed. Gradually the council, by phoning the objectors 'up to five and six times', managed to whittle down the list and destroy the campaign against Schering. 'It was important to approach those remaining and get them to withdraw in the interests of South Tipperary', said a senior councillor. The Project Manager of the IDA's

Overseas Division, Richard Ryan, had said that the IDA was committed to getting Schering Plough to locate in the region. But it was too
late. The objections and the threatened legal action had indirectly
forced the multinational to abandon its Irish plans for the meantime
and move instead to Puerto Rico. It was a lesson the IDA, and to a
lesser degree South Tipperary Council, would not forget.

But the Americans from Merck were promising jobs – big jobs
that would keep sons and daughters from migrating, that would
keep them in their native homeland. Merck had promised 1,000
jobs, 400 to 600 to be employed when the factory opened in the
summer of 1976. In fact the workforce turned out to be no more
than 260 – a figure it has remained constant at ever since.

Merck had also arrived in Ireland against a background of inadequate planning and pollution laws, which gave insufficient legal
grounds for enforcement and compensation. It would be a year or so
before the Water Pollution Act, the Safety of Industry Act and the
establishment of An Bord Pleanála (the national planning appeals
board). The European Economic Community (forerunner of the EC),
which Ireland had joined in 1972, was still to define its objections,
policies and directives on the environment, particularly on air and
water pollution. In the meantime Merck, said one councillor, was 'a
great boost to Carrick-on-Suir, Clonmel and the whole area'.

Government restrictions and regulations for a factory such as
Merck's were confusing and ill-defined. Noel Murphy, the Managing Director of Gaeleo, a small Cork-based chemical company,
writing in an English chemical industry journal, was more succinct
and put Ireland, the chemical industry and the 1970s in perspective:
'companies have found Eire a good country to do business in'. And
there was praise for the 'sympathetic business-minded attitudes by
central government and local authorities'. The perils of toxic development, in that respect, were also new to both central government
and local authorities. It was not the function of the South Tipperary County Council to check Merck's credentials in the area of
pollution; that was the job of the IIRS and other technical advisors.
'You engage consultants because the council would not have that
expertise', was how Robert Hayes put it, therefore abrogating the
council immediately from any suggestion that it had failed to follow
the proper safety standards.

That attitude was to become a refrain of the following twelve
years. Merck would be seen to comply 'fully with the standards of
environmental control' set out in a state report on recommendations

for pollution control at the factory. 'It did not occur to the [county council] that Merck would not follow the conditions', one prominent official in the area said in 1988 after John Hanrahan had won his epic battle:

> What was the point of putting technical conditions into a planning permission and then doing nothing about it when it began to go wrong? The problem with the Hanrahan case was that nobody wanted to take responsibility. If it had been done properly this would not have happened.

What did happen in Ballydine brought a curious response from local officials and politicians, local farmers, local professional people, local deputies, the IIRS, the IDA and scientists from various institutions; in fact everyone who touched on the case right up to the hierarchy of government responded oddly:

> Some of the council officials did not give a damn about what was happening in Ballydine to the Hanrahans' farm, the animals and his family's health. A lot of people floated in and out of the council and didn't care what was happening on the ground. People did not read letters to each other. Officials are paid to solve problems but that did not happen in [Tipperary].

In the years between Merck's planning application in 1972 and the Hanrahans' victory in the Supreme Court in 1988 the personnel in the South Tipperary (South Riding) County Council changed constantly, with a few exceptions. The county engineer in 1972, who had accompanied County Manager, Robert Hayes, on a trip to Merck's factories in the United States prior to the May 1972 announcement that Merck were going to Tipperary, retired soon after. He is now deceased. Hayes himself left for the Dublin Port and Docks Board in November 1975 but subsequently returned for the opening of the factory in the summer of the following year.

Questions put to council members by journalists after the Supreme Court ruling about alleged negligence or duplicity were met with 'I wasn't here at the time. I can't really comment' and 'It's a long time ago, I don't think it would be fair for me to comment now, that is the job of the present council.'

In a statement issued on 11 July 1988, following allegations that the council had been negligent in relation to the Hanrahan family's problems, the acting County Manager, Ned O'Connor, refuted 'emphatically the suggestion made that there was any lack of impartiality or objectivity by the council in its investigations'. Taking the line advanced 16 years earlier, O'Connor named the 'independent expertise' and the 'best specialist advice in the country' who had carried out comprehensive scientific studies into the alleged pollution from the Merck factory. 'These investigations', (by An Foras Forbartha, An Foras Taluntais, the IIRS and Trinity College, Dublin) said O'Connor, 'failed to establish any direct link between the Merck Sharp and Dohme plant and the serious animal problems alleged.' On 5 July 1988 Justice Henchy, Chief Justice Finlay and Justice Hederman ruled differently in the Supreme Court.

For the medical profession in general the name Merck is associated with one of the world's foremost pharmaceutical companies, Merck and Co, Inc, of New Jersey, United States. Merck has the reputation of being one of the most responsible and ethical companies in the business. This reputation is generally dimmed when people are informed that Merck has admitted that it made questionable payments of over IR£3.5 million between 1968 and 1975 in 39 countries worldwide. Despite this, Merck's behaviour is generally perceived as a paragon of excellence in the US pharmaceutical industry. Merck Sharp and Dohme, Ireland is a Bermuda-registered subsidiary of Merck and Co, Inc.

Merck had been in operation in Ballydine, manufacturing bulk chemicals for 27 months when neighbouring farmers began to suspect that health problems, animal and human, were being caused by emissions from the factory. For 18 months the farmers complained to Merck and to the local authority until, in February 1980, South Tipperary Council commissioned Ian Jamieson of An Foras Forbartha to do a IR£2,000 study on air pollution around the area of the factory. Jamieson completed his report in October 1980.

He found no evidence of serious air pollution and he noted that acid vapour emissions were within EC limits. He did, however, make a recommendation:

> It is most important that the council should be aware of emissions of air pollutants from factory processes in order to confirm that these comply with the levels originally estimated. It may be that prior to this investigation the

council has had no information. In particular, it is necessary to ensure that the process gas scrubbing system continues to function properly and it is recommended that Merck Sharp and Dohme be requested to provide continuous records of emissions measured at the stack, together with the gas velocity at the stack, etc.

It wasn't until 6 November 1981 that Byron L. Rowe, General Manager of Merck, wrote to James O'Callaghan, the County Engineer, with the relevant information. This showed that between 'May and early June 1980' emissions from the factory violated the permitted levels. Rowe said this was because of 'severe mechanical problems' but 'repairs were made as quickly as possible'. Merck had broken its planning permission levels by four times the permitted amounts; South Tipperary County Council, nevertheless, took no action against the company.

The first problems with pollution in the area had occurred in 1978 and were perceived as minor. From 1980 animals began to die of a strange wasting disease, cattle miscarried, twin births and deformities increased and milk yields dropped. The problems were not confined to the Hanrahans; other farmers complained. Metal was seen to rust and corrode in the farmyards and houses closest to the factory. The tops of trees were pointed in the opposite direction from Merck. The farmers believed the Yanks were the problem and that was a problem in itself. Merck Sharp and Dohme was and still is the largest employer in the area, and the earlier experience of bitterness, divisiveness and intimidation associated with the farmers' opposition to Schering Plough, the other American chemical company that had wanted and failed to locate in South Tipperary, stopped many from speaking out. Yet the problems were real and investigations were called for.

On two occasions over the winter following the first Jamieson report, the county council met with local residents to discuss the problem and the implications for the area. At a meeting on 20 February 1981 it was suggested that a special committee be set up of technical experts in the pollution, agricultural, medical and veterinary areas to sort out the problem. (The first cattle deaths had just occurred at the Hanrahans' farm.) The County Manager, T. Rice, agreed with the idea of a committee. It was felt that such an independent body would solve or go close to solving the problem. It was never set up.

In November 1981 Jamieson informed the council that the findings of his second report, which he had begun the previous April, seemed to confirm what he had found in his first report. He suggested a further report be done using different methods. Trinity College was brought into the investigation.

In the meantime Jamieson's second report recommended that as a matter of urgency the animal health problems on Hanrahan's farm be fully investigated by veterinary and other appropriate authorities, and that the monitoring of emissions from the factory continue. He also stated that complaints be properly recorded and monitored by the council and subjected to serious investigation. 'Until an explanation for the health problems is found the possibility that some serious toxic substance, from whatever source, is responsible should not be ignored.'

When the report from Trinity's Botany Department appeared both the council and Merck were alarmed, but not just about its findings, which stated that there was 'clear evidence' that the surrounding countryside (lichens, grass, soil and silage) was being affected by emissions from the factory.

They were alarmed because it had been intended not to release the report publicly but to incorporate its findings with those of Jamieson. This plan was thwarted by Hanrahan's vet, Tom de Lacy, who procured a copy of the report which he produced at a meeting in Hanrahan's house on 27 September 1982. The county medical officer and Mark Lynch, who were both at the meeting, said they had been unable to get a copy. Later *The Irish Times* received a copy and it was then decided to release the report. The council wanted changes made in the report. Merck was simply concerned that it had been leaked to the media.

These investigations did nothing for the farmers. Each one appeared to exonerate Merck from any responsibility. The strategy of the state, local authorities and the Merck management had been to claim that the problems were confined to one farm (the Hanrahans'), that these problems were caused by John Hanrahan's mismanagement and that they had no connection with the Merck factory.

This strategy was undermined by the simple facts that problems existed on other farms near the factory, and that John Hanrahan had, until his cattle began to die, been a model farmer and was recognised as such in the locality. The Trinity study had provided circumstantial evidence to implicate the factory's emissions in the 'chronic levels of pollution' the investigators had found near its boundaries. Yet while that report suggested that the possible cause of the pollution was a toxic combination of chlorine and bromine (and it was hard to see where else such a contaminant could have come from in the local agricultural environment if not from Merck), it too was presented by the local authority as another exoneration of the company.

Earlier in May 1982 the pollution monitors were removed from Hanrahan's farm after the council claimed it had discovered 'acceptable levels of pollution'. The misrepresentation of the Trinity study angered local farmers who picketed meetings of the council; other farmers came forward to complain about the problems they had been suffering.

Farmer Paddy O'Meara, whose farm is on the opposite side of the road from the Merck factory, told an interesting story, one he has told many times to many people, journalists, county officials, and to officials and politicians from Dublin. Early one Sunday morning in May 1981 O'Meara, in a field with his cattle and sheep, watched as the cows began to sniff the air and the sheep ran to the opposite end of the field. The air was thick with a fog which began to burn in his chest. He went home, went to bed and when he awoke he couldn't breath. The doctor was called. 'Your system is rotten with poison', the doctor said to him. Where, asked the doctor, had he come in contact with poison? O'Meara mentioned the factory.

Paddy O'Meara was ill for several months. The cattle, in the field that day, he claimed faded away. He subsequently sold them to a dealer for half of their value. He also sold the sheep. His story was never investigated. He said in 1983:

> Trying to do anything about it is useless. I see Hanrahan
> across there trying to fight against them all and I say
> 'What's the use?' We got no hearing at any of the meetings.
> We just want a bit of clean air, that's all we want.

O'Meara provided a postscript. Between 1981 and 1983 he attempted to keep cattle in a field across from the factory but the cattle would have none of it. 'Whatever it was in the grass the cattle wouldn't stop in field.' He put barbed wire up to keep them in the field. One animal tore its chest open attempting to get out.

Though not as harsh as the Hanrahans' ordeal, O'Meara's accounts were not uncommon. Bertie Kennedy, another local farmer, died in August 1983. His wife claimed that all six doctors her husband visited asked him where he came in contact with chemicals. O'Meara's doctor refused to comment on his patient's case, as the doctors who heard Kennedy have done. There was no inquest into Kennedy's death.

Tommy Rockett, whose farm is opposite the Hanrahans, claimed that his cattle also refused to eat the grass. In 1981, particularly from April onwards, the cattle were seen coughing continuously. None of his animals died on the farm. 'They died in the meat factory, chemicals and all', was all he would say.

Another farmer said imaginatively that the emissions from the factory were 'like a fallout from an atom bomb'. Other farmers have had calving problems. One farmer lost a quarter of the calves born during the spring of 1981. Many farmers reported stampeding, cattle with streaming eyes, their children complaining of chest aliments, everyone feeling tired. Yet local GPs, vets and the county medical officer were either unable to say what the causes were, or claimed, as in the case of the county medical officer, that they were simply 'nuisance' complaints.

This pattern, investigations and allegations of pollution and ill-health around the factory, continued as John Hanrahan began a High Court action against Merck Sharp and Dohme. More reports were commissioned by the authorities and by several experts on behalf of John Hanrahan.

In 1983 the vet, de Lacy, and Hanrahan commissioned a private report on the events at the farm. They refused to release it to either the council or the Department of Agriculture, who later wrote to Hanrahan promising him confidentiality if he released the information he had on the cause of his cattle's death. But de Lacy and Hanrahan had already learned a lesson. 'The first place', alleged de Lacy, 'this information would go would be to the Merck Sharp and Dohme management.' He also stated that the council would have swept it under the table.

On 11 June 1984 ten Ballydine farmers placed a picket outside the council offices before a meeting of the South Tipperary County Council. Among the business that day was a summary report given by the county engineer, summarising two new reports on Merck's alleged pollution completed in May 1984 by the IIRS and An Foras Forbartha, which called for comprehensive testing for dioxin on farmlands close to the factory. Merck denied that dioxins were formed in its incinerator yet the company used it to burn chlorinated solvents – which produce dioxin when incinerated. Testing for phosgene, a toxic chemical originally used as an asphyxiant gas during the 1914–18 war whose major effect is on the lungs, was also called for.

After the council meeting one farmer, John Joe O'Connell, claimed that the number of unexplained cattle deaths near the Merck factory was much higher than the 200 plus admitted by local farmers. He said many of the farmers sent cattle to meat factories as soon as they began to show disease symptoms.

The council meeting did not resolve the issue; some observers said the obfuscation was apparent, particularly as few of the councillors knew or had seen the new reports. One reporter said it was 'extraordinary that South Tipperary County Council have waited so long to test for dioxin, or indeed for phosgene' as the first complaints had been registered six years earlier. One councillor had asked if dioxin was a dangerous substance. 'We're talking about things we know nothing about', he added.

Despite the concern from some councillors, according to TD Sean Tracey the allegations against Merck were 'casting a shadow over this magnificent industry'.

It has been said that Merck Sharp and Dohme have been too sophisticated for the councillors and politicians of South Tipperary. 'Merck had them all eating out of their hand', was how one local person put it. Merck, as part of its corporate policy, contributed an estimated IR£50,000 a year to health, education, environmental, civic and social projects all over the country, with a significant amount going into the local community during the years of its battle with the Hanrahans. This policy is crucial to Merck's overseas interests. According to the Securities and Exchange Commission in the United States, a body to whom Merck is obliged to supply information, the company has made annual donations of US$750,000 to countries where its factories are sited. In March 1976 it was reported that Merck's involvement in questionable payments allegedly 'involved illegal campaign contributions to US politicians and foreign pay-offs'. Merck's first contribution to an Irish cause, to the Rehabilitation Institute in Clonmel, coincided with the opening of the Ballydine factory. In the years since the factory opened it is estimated that Merck has made donations of well over US$1 million to Irish causes.

Not everyone was prepared to take the Merck shilling, though. During the height of the farmers' concerns in 1984 the Suir Valley

Residents and Protection Association was formed. Among its first actions was to object to a proposed IR£1.5 million laboratory extension at Merck on 20 June 1984. An Bord Pleanála overruled these objections and denied the farmers an oral hearing. The farmers claimed that the planning permission given to Merck amounted to 'planning behind closed doors'. Merck had not been required to give details of the chemicals and processes used in the new laboratory.

John Hanrahan moved a writ against Merck in February 1982. In March 1983 it was put down for trial. In February 1985 Hanrahan's High Court suit for damages against Merck, which was to run for 47 days into midsummer, began before Justice Ronan Keane, who heard how the Hanrahans' ordeal had begun six and a half years earlier on a cool August Sunday in 1978. Hanrahan, in the ritualistic manner of all farmers, was up with the dawn to tend to his animals. He immediately noticed that one of the farm dogs was weeping. There was a sweet sickly smell in the air. Wandering around his farm, which was cloaked in a thin fog, he saw other animals coughing and weeping.

By 1985 when he entered Dublin's Four Courts, Hanrahan was convinced that Merck was responsible for the mass grave in his farm which contained 225 dead animals – the result, he claimed, of emissions from its Ballydine factory. Merck, back in 1978, had told him that the emissions and the smells were harmless. In his evidence to the High Court John Hanrahan presented a death list – a chronology of the manner of deaths of 140 animals, between 1980 and 1984. This high mortality rate was questioned by both the Department of Agriculture (which kept Hanrahan's official herd file, which was made available to Merck's senior counsel but not to Hanrahan) and the company. The department calculated that only 65 animals had died during the same period and this was accepted by Justice Keane.

In its defence Merck argued that Hanrahan's problems were nothing to do with it, and that his ambitions as a farmer were the direct cause. Financial problems, overstocking and underfeeding had led to the deaths of his animals; to justify this mismanagement Hanrahan decided to blame the factory and seek litigation, Merck's defence argued. These accusations did not begin with the High Court. Shortly after Hanrahan began to complain to Merck about his problems on the farm, rumours of a diverse and persistent nature were prevalent: he was a bad farmer, his silage was contaminated, his cattle were diseased, he was a 'professional litigant' and 'gone in the head'. Some of these rumours even emanated from

Limerick and Dublin among people who were probably not sure where Ballydine was located. Yet the Hanrahans had a reputation as model farmers in South Tipperary. John Hanrahan and his mother Mary could claim descent from a 700-year farming dynasty in Ireland. During the High Court case, farming experts testified to the excellence of the Hanrahans' farm management.

Two and a half years earlier *RTE* had screened a film from America called *Bitter Harvest* about Rick Halbert, a Michigan farmer, who struggled to find the source of his cattle deaths. Halbert subsequently discovered that another member of the dioxin family, polybrominated biphenyls (PBBs) which had been inadvertently mixed with cattle feed, was the cause. The PBBs had entered the food chain. Lactating mothers found that their milk was unfit to drink. James Neufeld, a Canadian pathologist from the University of Winnipeg, visited the Hanrahans' farm and gave evidence in the High Court. The symptoms he had witnessed among the Hanrahans' animals and from results of post-mortems, he claimed, were consistent with chemical poisoning. There was, he added, an uncanny similarity with the Michigan case. Neufeld said he had taken samples of grain and silage at the Hanrahans' farm which showed traces of polychlorinated biphenyls (PCBs) – though no one has ever explained where these came from!

Trace levels of dioxin were found in milk samples taken from not only the Hanrahans' farm but neighbouring farms as well. Merck continued to insist that dioxins were not formed in its incinerator. At the time so little was known in Ireland about dioxin formation that it was able to confuse people with this propaganda. Yet all the Hanrahans, Mary, John, his wife Selina, their children, were now suffering from symptoms consistent with toxic – significantly dioxin – poisoning.

On 4 July 1985 the High Court case ended. Six weeks later Justice Keane found against the Hanrahan family. Within a month Avonmore Creameries had cut off its credit to John Hanrahan. Livestock and machinery were auctioned. In October the Hanrahan family was ordered to pay legal costs estimated at IR£1 million. The following year Tipperary County Council disconnected the water supply to the Hanrahans' farm. The family had refused to pay water rates until the council guaranteed them clean air.

But the High Court, as far as the Hanrahans were concerned, was only round one. In November and December 1987 an appeal was heard in the Supreme Court. Six months later Justice Henchy ruled in favour of the Hanrahan family.

Justice Henchy, in his conclusions, stated that Mary, John and Selina Hanrahan had:

> established that the defendants are liable to them in damages for the offensive smells emitted from the factory, that John Hanrahan is entitled to damages for the injurious effect on his health of the factory emissions, and that the defendants are also liable in damages for the cattle ailments to the extent that they were caused by factory emissions.

On several points Justice Henchy disagreed with the High Court decision. Justice Keane had denied that the odours 'were ever on such a scale or intensity as to justify the award of damages'. Justice Henchy said this 'conclusion was incorrect' and added that it was 'a misinterpretation of the relevant law'.

There were three 'possible sources' of atmospheric pollution caused by emissions from the factory, Justice Henchy ruled and referred to the incinerator.

> Because the function of the incinerator is to effect the destruction by combustion of dangerous waste chemicals and solvents and because the incinerator was for significant periods in the years in question running at below its design temperature and therefore at a heat which was not adequate to destroy dangerous and contaminated solvents, it is marked out by the plaintiffs as the primary source of atmospheric pollution on their farm.

Justice Henchy said there was evidence from a variety of witnesses 'of complaints such as a burning sensation in the throat and chest, reddening of the skin, irritation and teaming of the eyes and a smothering feeling in the nose, throat and chest'.

> While complaints of that kind seem to have been experienced by different people in the area, the plaintiffs seem to be the only people who claimed that the atmospheric pollution affected their health. Whether or not the Hanrahan farm vis-à-vis the factory was in a special meteorological position, there was unimpeached independent evidence that the complaints of physical ill effects in humans on the plaintiffs' farm were matched by observable distress in the animals on the farm.

Justice Henchy questioned whether Justice Keane's 'finding of no casual connection between those complaints and emissions from the factory can be sustained'. He went on to add: 'Even if all the complaints made by or on behalf of the plaintiffs are not accepted, there were uncontroverted items of complaints which suggested that the factory emissions were at the root of the trouble.'

Regarding the nature and extent of the factory emissions Justice Henchy stated that 'it appears to be an unquestionable fact that the defendant's factory is the main source of hydrogen chloride and hydrochloric acid mists in the Suir valley'.

> The possible effects of such emissions have to be considered in terms of factors such as air chemistry, meteorology, the height of the factory chimneys, the configuration of the Suir valley, local meteorological features (such as the inversion by which air is trapped in the valley when winds are light) and the effect of prevailing winds.
>
> Readings taken at the point of emission in the factory are therefore not necessarily a sound guide as to the consequences of the emissions in different parts of the valley. For example, some of the emissions take place at levels below that of the valley floor, and the top of the scrubber stack is on a level with the ground floor of the plaintiffs' house. The point has been taken that factory readings and the results shown by computer models do not take account of what actually happens in the Suir valley.
>
> The criticism has also been made that measurements of airborne concentrations on the plaintiffs' farm give no more than an average daily concentration, thus leaving out short violent emissions and not taking into account the deleterious effect, particularly on grazing animals, of prolonged low-level emissions of gases and mists of unknown degrees of toxicity.

Justice Henchy went on to refer specifically to Ian Jamieson's reports and concluded from his 'consideration of the scientific evidence as a whole' that:

> even if accepted in full it only shows what COULD or SHOULD have happened in the way of damage by toxic emissions. In the light of what DID happen in the way of

toxic damage, I consider that the defendants' evidence could not be held to rebut the plaintiffs' case. Theoretical or inductive evidence cannot be allowed to displace proven facts. It was proven as a matter of probability that John Hanrahan suffered ill-health as a result of toxic emissions from the factory.

It was a fact, and so found by the judge, that there was unusual damage to some plant life on the plaintiffs' farm in the relevant period, the only suggested source of this damage being the factory. And there was a volume of uncontroverted evidence given by eyewitnesses that animals were seen and heard to be ill and in distress at a time when the observer was experiencing foul chemical smells or weeping eyes or irritated skin, which could have been caused only by the factory.

It would be to allow scientific theorising to dethrone fact to dispose of this claim by saying, as was said in the judgement under appeal, that there was 'virtually no evidence in this case of injury to human beings or animals which has been scientifically linked to any chemicals emanating from the defendants' factory'.

Justice Henchy stated that there were many factors which proved that the factory emissions were the cause:

The causes
1. The plaintiffs' dairy herd was a thriving one up to the time when smells and other factory emissions were noticed.
2. The five veterinary surgeons who regularly saw and treated the animals in the relevant period were all of the firm opinion that what the animals were suffering from was caused by toxic emissions from the factory.
3. The factory incinerator, which was designed to burn, destroy and render harmless 7 tons a day of chemical solvents was run for long periods at temperatures which were too low to achieve the desired result, thus breaching one of the conditions of the planning permission for the factory and making damage to humans and animals highly likely.
4. The ailments suffered by the cattle – evidenced by stream-

ing eyes, coughing, a high incidence of abortions, twinning and of calves born deformed, reduced milk yields,
sore and cut teats, stampeding, marked lack of thrift, and
want of sexual capacity in the bulls – were too
pronounced and varied to be accounted for by natural
causes (as was suggested by the defendants) or bad farm
management. The most credible explanation offered for
the ailments and abnormalities in the cattle was the toxic
emissions from the factory.

Mary Hanrahan, as resilient as ever, welcomed the judgement with
the contentedness of a woman, in her late sixties, who had suffered
and watched her family experience great pain and hardship. 'If we
never get a shilling damages I am happy that we got our name
cleared, that we are not crooks.'

3 Killeagh: Power and Effluent

This is the power of the future
and the future marches on
and they call in all their favours
all their political gains
while the spills fill the rivers
and settle in the plains

Jim Page

Time has stood still at Lower Fanisk bridge, where the confluence of the Womanagh and Dissour rivers is redolent of east Cork country, picture postcard Ireland. Looking north east over the bridge a grey mottled British Army pillbox, an innocuous relic from the Tan War, guards the south-eastern edge of Dinny Walsh's land. A few miles away in the Community Hall in Killeagh the serenity is being shattered. 'Ye have pow-lut-ted the U-ni-ted States. Ye have pow-lut-ted Germany. Well I can tell ye, ye are not going to pow-lutt us here, in Ireland. Ye can take your pow-lut-tion back to the U-ni-ted States, where ye belong', the ageing farmer, his voice straining with emotion, his east Cork accent harsh and pronounced, was heard to proclaim. Sean Landers' well-chosen words would be prophetic. He did not know it at the time. Like many of his neighbours he was afraid, and the people to whom he addressed his tirade were not forthcoming with information to ease his fear.

It was the Monday night of the August bank holiday, 1988. Representatives of the IDA, Eolas and Merrell Dow, a US pharmaceutical company, had come together with the local community in the small room at the side of Killeagh hall to explain why a factory for the drug company should be sited a few miles up the road, within view of the fishing village of Youghal.

If Tom Kennedy, Merrell Dow's main man in Ireland, was affected by Landers' angry outburst he did not display any visual emotion. In the manner of American chemical engineers turned businesspeople he remained and would remain mute about the subject, content to remark that his company was in the community hall as guests of the Killeagh/Inch Council, who had initiated the week-long nightly meetings.

Merrell Dow had just acquired an option on 90 acres of Dinny Walsh's land, flat gradually sloping ground sandwiched between the main Cork to Waterford trunk road to the north and the gently simmering Womanagh river to the south. For many people in the area, particularly those with a republican tradition, the invader was back, dressed in different clothing, bringing a new threat. 'We fought for the Land League, we fought the Brits, and there's no way those yanks are coming in here with their polluting factories', was the war cry of one old man.

On 25 July 1988 the Killeagh/Inch Community Council sent letters to its parishioners informing them that Merrell Dow had applied for planning permission to construct a factory at Fanisk, roughly two miles from Killeagh village. The letter stated that the community council had 'arranged a series of meetings to take place over the coming weeks in connection with the proposed plans'. But it was clear to the locals that only the people within the jurisdiction of the Killeagh/Inch Community Council would be invited and only on specific nights. 'Some of the people who are closest to the proposed site were not even invited to the meetings and people down wind of the site were not invited', said John Beecher, who lived on the hilly ground overlooking Youghal, to the east of Killeagh.

It was also clear on Monday night that Tom Kennedy of Merrell Dow, Ken Macken and David Kelly of Eolas, who co-authored the Environmental Impact Study (EIS) on the factory, and Pat Howlin of the IDA and the community council itself were unaware of the groundswell of opinion that had grown against the factory and, according to one objector, 'bedlam broke out'. The major objectors, who subsequently formed themselves into the Womanagh Valley Protection Association, claimed that approximately 200 people attempted to cram into the community centre on the opening night.

'To say there was a great deal of tension in the hall is an understatement', said Joan Vaughan, whose house, like Beecher's, sits on the high ground north of the proposed site.

The attempts of the Killeagh/Inch Council to assuage the fears about the plant were, said the objectors, the desperate actions of 22 community councillors who had got themselves into something they had no experience of. Yet the community council, particularly chair Paddy McGrath, should have known better. On 11 May he received a letter. If he had been unaware of the community's concern about Merrell Dow before he read the missive, its contents quickly changed that. The author, writing on behalf of the people 'who have already expressed grave concern' about the Merrell Dow factory, stated they were 'conscience bound' to furnish 'some of the frightening information that we have received concerning such plants'. The letter went on to criticise political interests in Midleton, east Cork's principal town, and Youghal:

> It is obvious that such people have done absolutely no research and have no authority to welcome a life-threatening plant into our locality. From the literature we have received, and given to you, it is clear that Merrell Dow Corporation has a very questionable record ... It is our belief that so far the people of Killeagh have been given a very one-sided view of this proposed plant – namely that it will bring employment to the area, but how many people from Killeagh are qualified to work in such a plant? To date nobody in authority has mentioned that this plant brings a great deal of risk with it and it could totally change the whole agri-social structure of the locality. We stress that we are not a bunch of selfish agitators trying to prevent our children or the children of the locality from getting employment. The fears and worries we have will affect everybody, not only the people living in the parish of Killeagh/Inch, but surrounding parishes as well.

It was a further two months, and after Merrell Dow had lodged its planning application with Cork County Council on 15 July, before McGrath reacted. He commissioned an independent report from the Resource and Environmental Management Unit at University College Cork. When the August bank holiday meeting came around, the report wasn't ready.

Joan Vaughan recalled, mimicking Kennedy's mid-west American drawl:

> After we got over the fact that we didn't have the UCC report and were assured that it would be available the next week a man commenced by telling us he was Tom Kennedy from America. With the aid of an overhead projector he explained about Merrell Dow, what its products were and where they were made.

The locals were in fact making it easy for Kennedy. The room was heavy with tension, anger and frustration. The meeting continued with Macken and Kelly of Eolas speaking in favour of the factory. The meeting gradually assumed the elements of decorum the officials had longed for at the beginning. Amidst the chaos Macken stood up first and began to talk to the crowd who jostled for space in the tiny room, poured out of windows, and listened with a patience that didn't seem possible earlier.

Joan Vaughan explained:

> Dr Macken began to tell us about Merrell Dow's state-of-the-art technology and how they had never seen anything like it before. He went on to tell us how clean it was, how the wonderful incinerator worked – he didn't name the make of the incinerator, he just said it was state-of-the-art – and then he introduced Mr Kelly. He spoke about the water supply and then said his greatest worry was that Merrell Dow was setting such a high standard with this plant that it would be difficult for other Irish plants to live up to it.

If the majority of the people at the Monday night meeting were annoyed by what they saw as the patronising attitude portrayed by the representatives of Merrell Dow and Eolas they were much more angry about the manner in which the meetings were arranged and conducted. John Beecher subsequently complained in a letter to the *Cork Examiner* that he had been excluded from the meetings.

> I was informed that I was not invited, that it was not a public meeting and only those on a particular list were invited to come. On inquiring I was informed I was not on any list because I was not in the community.

Beecher felt, however, that he had 'a moral right to put a few searching questions to the "team"'. Despite the prohibitive arrangements, the objectors, including Beecher, successfully managed to ask a few searching questions. Macken was asked if the Institute for Industrial Research and Standards (IIRS) had done a similar report for the Merck Sharp and Dohme factory. One of the objectors moved towards Dr Macken, and spoke.

'Do you think the man who did the report is proud of this?' A photograph, which showed the emaciated and dying body of farmer John Hanrahan's dog, was held up.

Dr. Macken was silent for a moment. Then he spoke. 'It's ten years on,' he told them, 'everything is much more advanced. What happened there could never happen here.'

The objectors were not deterred and, according to Joan Vaughan, they switched their anger towards Kennedy:

> We asked Mr Kennedy about [Merrell Dow's] products, Agent Orange [used by the US government in the Vietnam War] and Merbentyl Syrup [which Merrell Dow removed from the market after it was believed to have caused the death of two children], and did his company tell the American government that they were going to poison the soldiers in Vietnam as well as the Vietnamese? He couldn't give any answer.
>
> Then we asked him about California, where six people ended up being sterile as a result of what happened in one of their chemical factories. He told us he knew nothing about it. We asked him about their antagonism with the [US] Environmental Protection Agency and we quoted [former] Dow chairperson, Robert Lundeen's comments that said, 'We play our cards close, maybe because we have a high regard for the value of technical information. We don't back down easy or compromise. We are perceived as prickly, difficult and arrogant.'

Kennedy told them all that had changed, that they were no longer like that. 'By the end of the week,' an objector joked, 'he was almost apologising for the Dow side of the Merrell Dow Corporation.' Finally in spite of the earlier antagonism the meeting ended on a reassuring note. If Merrell Dow did what it was supposed to do and if Cork County Council monitored the factory like it was supposed to, nothing could possibly go wrong. The objectors were mollified but they were not convinced. They wanted to know more.

On the Wednesday night several objectors attempted to attend the third meeting, according to John Beecher:

> to ensure that the other side of the case was presented to the local people – and not just the company's story. They were

refused admission to the hall by members of the local community body. They were told they already had an opportunity to make their case and that the meeting was for other people to attend. It seemed that those behind the project were hand-picking the people they wanted at meetings.

Margaret Browne said at the time:

> What I find alarming is that all of us are going to be the closest people to a pharmaceutical plant. Now we know their history right round the world and the only bit of information we can extract, really extract, from them should be done in a little tea room in the back of Killeagh hall for two hours on a Bank Holiday Monday, and that is going to affect us and our children and their children for generations.

Margaret Browne, who with her husband Michael runs a dairy farm and guesthouse, was approached by Merrell Dow and an offer for some of their land was made. Following consultations the offer was withdrawn. After initial inquiries at several farmlands in the area, Merrell Dow finally purchased an option on 90 acres from Dinny Walsh, for a reputed figure of IR£600,000. At more than IR£6,000 an acre this was three times the price for agricultural land in the area. Comparisons with the higher cost of development land cannot be made because no precedent was set in the area.

Anthropologist Adrian Peace, who devoted a book to the campaign, remarked how quickly the Womanagh group organised itself to challenge Merrell Dow. 'The group had to anticipate the realistic, if daunting, prospect that the County Council would authorise construction of the factory, regardless of the opposition already making itself heard', Peace wrote:

> If Merrell Dow was to be stopped the Womanagh Valley residents closest to the site had to commit themselves to the long haul. In anticipation of this, they took several crucial decisions. Since they knew that the development proposal would soon come before the council, and thus by law be available for public examination, they determined to seek out scientifically qualified advice. This would spell out more clearly what the consequences of the factory's construction might be, and would put them on a more

informed footing for mobilising opposition. They also decided to try to recruit some media support, although hitherto they had been unsuccessful in getting attention from even local newspapers. Group members based these strategic decisions on a close reading of the social context which they well knew, while also recognising their collective limitations. Since the protection of their own interests could be realised only through the harnessing of a broadly based constituency of support – unlikely to materialise easily in a bourgeois code – the Womanagh Valley group set its sights on bringing such a constituency into being.

Among the support it garnered was the service of Rory Finegan, an independent scientist, who agreed, in the words of Peace, 'to translate the environmental impact statement into lay language and to extract from its tables the statistic information' relevant to the protesters. But Finegan did more than this. According to Peace, 'he simultaneously provided a political interpretation, and political signposts for the future. He spelled out a scenario of catastrophe for the entire Womanagh Valley and beyond, should the chemical plant be built.'

Another was the author of this book, who was contacted by Maureen Forrest on behalf of the Womanagh group because of a feature he had written on the fall-out from Hanrahan's court battle with Merck Sharp and Dohme. According to Peace:

The way Robert Allen had covered the Hanrahan affair suggested to the Womanagh Valley objectors that he would be a useful ally. When he arrived in Killeagh at their invitation, he had a fund of knowledge to share with his hosts. He was well-informed about the operation of the IDA in Dublin; the economic relations between the IDA, overseas corporations, and the Irish government; and the more informal politics which made these relationships so impenetrable to uninformed outsiders. In other words, the cosmopolitan, Dublin-based journalist provided the peripherally situated grassroots group with a map of metropolitan-based power which their struggle would have to take into account. Like Rory Finegan, Robert Allen was no mere commentator on the emergent conflict, but a significant figure in its political configuration and a producer of political text.

That text was a feature in *Magill*, Ireland's current affairs magazine called 'Power and effluent', published in September 1988. Peace wrote:

> Allen's article entered into the general circulation in photo-copied form to be widely read and discussed; the journalist had provided the opposition movement with precisely the coverage they had hoped for. Without notable polemic, it established a clear opposition between the objectors' reasonable concerns and justifiable anxieties on the one hand, and on the other hand the secrecy of the management, the corporate's poor environmental record, and the total compliance to Merrell Dow's demands by the IDA, Eolas, and the County Council. This was a compelling image of provincial people with an entirely just cause, fighting off a predatory multinational corporation with no other concern but the maximisation of profit.

Merrell Dow's parent was Dow Chemical, who are known in the United States as a small-town company. It has been part of the company's policy as well as its history to take over an area and to make the resulting township dependent on the company's existence. In Midland, Michigan, where Dow was founded by Herbert H. Dow in 1897, the vast majority of the population work for Dow. Unfortunately for Merrell Dow, their attempt to sow the seeds of such a fertile existence in Killeagh was spurned by the majority of the community. For months after the August meetings in Killeagh, Tom Kennedy insisted that 'the information meetings had been organised by Killeagh Community Council', thereby abrogating himself and his company from any criticism about how the meetings were conducted. Yet from Merrell Dow's world headquarters in Cincinnati, Bill Donaldson explained that he believed the meetings had been open to anyone who wanted to attend them. The IDA, in Dublin, also insisted that they were public meetings. Kennedy later said he believed nobody was shut out or locked out of the meetings:

> The reason I say that is that the programme for the community meetings were effectively set up by the community council. They invited people to attend one night and the whole area within three miles of the site was split up into different sections. Everybody was invited. There were people who were there and who wanted to come back in

and the community council decided they would like to keep them out until everybody else was in.

There was probably no way Kennedy could win with the objectors. They had researched Merrell Dow's history meticulously and they were determined that the company would not build a factory in Killeagh. The presence of a chemical factory in the agricultural heartland of east Cork was unacceptable to them. Despite Merrell Dow's promises the farmers of east Cork were not convinced that agriculture and the chemical industry could coexist. Their reason was selfish.

The modernisation of Irish agriculture, which had coincided with the policy of economic expansion in 1958, was designed to enhance production for the export primarily of meat and dairy produce. Subsistence farming was discouraged as the state introduced grants, loans, subsidies and technical support while encouraging farmers to modify and expand their farms for the practice of monocultural farming, which they were told would increase their profits and raise their standards of living. This policy of industrial agriculture did not work for everyone and many farmers went under, unable to find the right balance between expansion, output and their loan repayments. Those who survived knew they had worked hard for their prosperity, and in east Cork they were not about to allow the state to impose a development on them that would threaten everything they had toiled for and everything they stood for. The farm families of Cork, Peace observed:

> are engaged in socially constructing the identities of their communities, defining the boundaries between them, effecting the linkages which traverse such boundaries, and, in the course of all this, articulating the qualities of rural life which are accorded most value. This is not to suggest that farm families force their cultural emphases on others. Store owners, publicans, and the owners of fishing boats share the same normative emphases. But farming families carry more cultural weight than most, and theirs is the quintessential property of land. In sum, the identity of community in County Cork is a petit bourgeois construction, and when it comes under threat, it is the members of this class which rally to protect it.

The farmers of east Cork practised industrial agriculture (mostly live-stock and sugar beet) so the decision to allow Merrell Dow to plan a factory in this industrial sector was a further indication that the state was prepared to sacrifice agriculture in favour of manufacturing every time. Joan Vaughan was among those who immediately under-stood this. 'What went wrong in Midland can go wrong in Killeagh. The difference, my friends, is that we have 1,500 dairy cows grazing within a mile of the plant. And that is a very big difference indeed.'

The Dow Chemical Corporation is known primarily because it was one of the producers of Agent Orange and napalm, which were used to horrific effect in the US war on Vietnam, and which subse-quently caused deformities in children born to American and Australian veterans. Dow was forced to pay huge compensation in legal settlements that are still ongoing. In the 1980s Merrell Dow was criticised for its attitude to the environment and the health of the populace around some of its factories. It had a running battle with the US Environmental Protection Agency (USEPA), which had to take it to court to achieve access to its factories. Merrell Dow made it clear that it wanted nobody, particularly the USEPA, to gain access to its operations.

In 1983 the company announced a $3 million programme to allay fears about dioxins following reports, denied by Dow, of dioxin contamination and apparently high rates of an unusual cancer among women in the Midland, Michigan area. It is believed that the programme was never started. Three years later Dow's Midland factory was in the news again when 30 million gallons of diluted chem-icals were swept into the Tittabawassee river after 13 inches of rain had fallen over 30 hours. The flood had taken up partially treated and untreated fluids from Dow's wastewater treatment plant in Midland.

Merrell Dow intended to build a manufacturing facility at Killeagh to produce Terfenadine, a non-sedative antihistamine for the treatment of hay fever and related allergies under the trade name Triludan. Bill Donaldson described the drug as the 'flagship of the company'. It was also manufactured at the company's facto-ries in Italy and the United States. Merrell intended to produce Triludan in bulk powder form and export it to the United States for 'formulation' as a finished product. During the 1970s and 1980s the IDA had been attempting to persuade foreign companies to complete their production processes in Ireland. Donaldson said in August 1988 that the company had plans to extend the Killeagh factory to include formulation.

Ever since the local community first heard that Merrell Dow was coming to Killeagh it felt excluded. Several people in the area recalled seeing small plane and helicopter activity over the region in the summer of 1987 but, until the link with Merrell Dow and the Eolas environmental impact study was mentioned, few thought any more about it. It had been believed that Merrell Dow would take its factory to Kinsale, in west Cork, or to the Ringaskiddy industrial area, south-east of Cork city.

Then word got out that a meeting had been set up in the Youghal Chamber of Commerce building between Pat Howlin (of the IDA), Paddy Linehan (Chair of Youghal Urban District Council), Michael T. Murphy (Youghal Chamber of Commerce) and four nominated representatives of the Killeagh/Inch Community Council. A month later, on 29 April 1988 a second meeting was held in Youghal. This time Tom Kennedy met the four councillors from Killeagh and the two from Youghal. On 9 May Denis McCarthy, then Cork Regional Manager of the IDA, discussed with councillors from the Midleton electoral area and TDs from east Cork the plans for the factory. McCarthy and other senior IDA officials in Cork had, according to a report in the *Cork Examiner* on the previous Saturday, maintained a 'discreet silence' about Merrell Dow's plans for a IR£30 million factory for Killeagh. (The estimate was later revised to IR£60 million.) The meeting in the IDA's Cork office finally brought the matter into the open. Merrell Dow would apply for planning permission to build a 'major manufacturing facility' in east Cork. Yet it would be another three months before the people most directly affected by the facility would be invited to put their case.

In the meantime Merrell Dow began to make plans. Adverts were placed in the local paper for two jobs and a meeting was set up for 11 July between Kennedy, Kelly and Macken and the local deputies Michael Aherne, Paddy Hegarty and Ned O'Keeffe. Four days later Merrell Dow lodged the planning application, which included the Eolas environmental impact study, with Cork County Council.

On 19 July Merrell Dow finally moved its operations closer to Killeagh. A meeting was set up with the entire community council, the local Irish Farmers' Association representatives, the local Garda sergeant, the local clergy and representatives from the nearby Imokilly Co-op (the largest employer in the area). Out of this meeting came the 'Information Week' for the residents of the Killeagh/Inch community. It was decided that everyone in the community would be invited and to give everyone a chance to hear

Merrell Dow's plans different regions would attend over a period of five nights.

A letter from one of the growing number of objectors had been sent to the national and local media. It was published in full in *An Phoblacht/Republican News* and the *Cork Examiner* published an abridged version. It stated that 'while jobs are to be welcomed in this job-starved area there are certain other important considerations to be taken into account'. The letter went on to list four items about Merrell Dow's history and operations and then asked:

Merrell Dow's history
Given the unscrupulous records of both parent companies of Merrell Dow, where profit comes before any moral concern for people or the environment, can we really welcome them open-armed into our midst, and can the people of Killeagh, Youghal, Castlemartyr and the surrounding areas believe that their operations here will be guided by any different motivation or accept any assurances – from Merrell Dow, the County Manager, the IDA or any other source – that the safety and health of workers, the community and our children (born and unborn) will even be a consideration on their agenda?

The people living in the vicinity of the proposed plant and those who work on the land or fish off the nearby coast, have a right to know the answers to certain questions about the proposed factory:

1. Exactly what products will be produced?
2. What chemicals will be used in the production process?
3. What processes will be in operation?
4. What are the arrangements for the storage and disposal of waste? Is it to be pumped into the nearby river, and from there into Youghal harbour, polluting what has recently been listed as the second cleanest beach in the twenty-six counties?
5. What precautions are to be taken to protect the safety and health of workers and prevent the pollution of the environment? One accidental spill at this factory could put in jeopardy the jobs at the nearby Imokilly Co-op creamery, which is, after all, the biggest employer in the area.
6. How does the IDA and the County Council propose to monitor pollution controls at this factory?

Jobs yes, but not at the price of our health, or that of the environment. Instead of attracting in more multinational companies to take even more profits out of the country, why does the IDA not encourage more native industry, and industry without such potential for damage and destruction as Merrell Dow and their likes.

Finally the objectors had a chance to talk to Merrell Dow directly and put these questions to them, but it was in a climate of acceptance for the corporate. While one politician said that Merrell Dow would be welcome in his own back yard and a Killeagh community councillor said that it would be 'a very good thing for the area' the initial few objectors proceeded with their campaign undaunted. Information about Merrell Dow was sought, letters were drafted to experts, and very slowly a picture of Merrell Dow's history began to emerge.

Then there were the conspiracy theories. One objector began to realise that happenings over the previous few months might have been connected with the Merrell Dow application. The nearby Glenbower Wood lake had been drained, according to Cork County Council, because the dam was dangerous. It occurred to the objector that there might be a link with the proposed factory. An expert was sought and asked to examine the dam. He said there was nothing wrong with it. The Womanagh group feared that the lake would be refilled and held by a larger, stronger dam. They believed this water would be used to flush Merrell Dow's effluent in the Womanagh River when the tide was low.

On 13 June a letter was sent by the Womanagh group to Rory Finegan with a request that he compile a report on Eolas' environmental impact study. Slightly less than a month later, on 8 July Finegan met with the objectors and on 18 July he examined the planning application and the Eolas report at the offices of the Cork County Council. This was three days after the application was lodged.

Finegan described his report, which was written in the form of an objection to the planning department of the local authority, as a 'synthesis of views and information expressed by Killeagh area residents, combined with observations made on and around the site of the proposed factory during the month of July and a careful examination of the planning application'. The objectors had had Finegan's report in front of them for well over a week before the Killeagh 'information' meetings started.

Although few of the objectors realised the significance at the time, Finegan's report had touched a very sensitive nerve. The corollary of the report was simple. The Eolas environmental impact study was inadequate or, as one objector said flatly, 'it isn't worth the paper it's written on'. There was more to that statement than the objectors knew at the time.

Ten days before Merrell Dow lodged its planning application, on 5 July the Minister for the Environment, Padraig Flynn, announced details of how he intended to implement a new EC directive on Environmental Impact Assessments (EIA). Merrell Dow's environmental impact study (EIS), conducted by Macken and Kelly, would be the first to be tested under the strict EC legislation. The Environment Minister was in no doubt about what the directive meant. 'It highlights the crucial need to give adequate attention to the environmental consequences of development and sets out an effective mechanism for considering these consequences', he said at a press conference. On 4 July 1988 Flynn's department issued a press statement detailing instructions issued by the Minister to local authorities on EIA. Three days earlier J. Ryan, Assistant Principal Officer Planning and Policy Section, issued a circular to all local authorities stating that the EC Directive 'should be operated as and from 3 July 1988'.

The directive, as refined by the Department of the Environment, was unequivocal. New industrial developments had to be assessed for potential environmental damage and the views of the public and relevant bodies were to be taken into account before a project could commence. Yet although the directive states that the public should be told about the EIS, which should be made available to them, and that the local authority should 'invite written submissions and observations in relation to environmental aspects of the development', many in the Killeagh community were adamant that this was not done. It was not until 12 October that Padraig Flynn, Minister for the Environment, announced the 'detailed regulations' which would give 'full legal effect to the EC Directive on Environmental Assessment'. He stated that they would be in place before the end of the year.

Joan Vaughan, who became Chair of the Womanagh Valley Protection Association, said:

> That Eolas report is actually the property of Merrell Dow, because when we asked Cork County Council for a copy

they said they were terribly sorry but they couldn't give me the report. 'You will have to get it from Mr Kennedy.' So I went to the meetings in Killeagh and in front of 200 people I asked Mr Kennedy for a copy and he said he couldn't give it to me because, he said, it contained his company's trade secrets. He implied that his competitors were incapable of writing out the report from the County Hall.

Eventually copies of the EIS were made available to the community which had to collect them personally from Kennedy's office in Cork city and hand over IR£15 per copy.

In his report Finegan described the effect the effluent would have on the region. 'The estuarine area and foreshore into which the Womanagh river would convey the liquid waste products from the factory is classified as a Wetland of International Importance for Waterfowl and Wading Birds.' He contended that these areas were entitled to statutory protection and the location of a pharmaceutical factory would contradict that. The factory, he stated, would:

> damage agricultural, residential and tourism values; degrade the quality of air and water, result in chemical fall-out and consequent damage to property and health, contribute to 'acid rain' with resultant damage to crops and Glenbower Wood, pollute the rivers and coast and endanger the Wetland of International Importance.

The UCC report, which the Resource and Environmental Management Unit stated was based 'entirely upon the technical details' of the Eolas EIS, in contrast appeared to give the factory a clean bill of health. 'If the recommendations are carried out as described, the proposed plant will cause minimal impact on the environment', it concluded.

Killeagh is a small village 23 miles from Cork on the N25, the trunk road that links Cork with the passenger terminal at Rosslaire, via Youghal and Waterford. The village can be driven through in a few minutes along the N25 which runs north-east and then turns sharply to the east at a junction beside the Saint John and Saint Virgilius Catholic church. In 1988 the population of the village was around 300, having risen from 298 in 1971 to 317 in 1981. To the north-west where the village merges unobtrusively with the country-side is Glenbower Wood, described in the East Cork Development

Plan as 'an important regional amenity, which has the potential to further enhance Killeagh's seasonal tourist trade'.

The proposed factory was to be sited less than two miles to the east of the village, off the long stretch of road from the church. In a four-mile radius of the site in 1988 there were 3,400 dairy cows, producing 3.5 million gallons of milk annually. Most of the holdings in the surrounding townland in 1988 were large, between 200 and 400 acres. In 1988 there were 1,000 acres of milling wheat, 4,000 acres of malting barley, 5,000 acres of vegetables and 8,000 acres of sugar beet (then the highest concentration of sugar beet in Ireland before Monsanto started trials elsewhere with genetically modified sugar beet). The people of the region depended almost exclusively on farming, fishing and tourism for their income.

Merrell Dow planned to pump its effluent into the Womanagh river, less than a quarter of a mile from the Fanisk Old Bridge, where the Dissour river meets the Womanagh. The effluent would then have been carried via the Womanagh, which is affected by spring tides, into the sea at Youghal Bay.

In the week before Cork County Council granted planning permission, subject to 27 conditions, for the factory, the Womanagh group intensified its campaign, meeting the local IFA, the Imokilly creamery and cheese-making co-op and government Press Secretary P. J. Mara. The local branch of the IDA voted unanimously to object to the factory. The Killeagh resolution was subsequently passed by the IFA's national council. The lobby against the building of the factory increased throughout August and September to include other groups involved in tourism and fishing in the area.

On Monday 22 August the Planning Department of the Cork County Council said that 30 objections had been received. By Friday 26 August, when the County Manager, Patrick O'Dowd, agreed to pass Merrell Dow's application the objections numbered over 80. The Womanagh group immediately announced that it would appeal the decision to An Bord Pleanála.

The campaign grew vocally as the massive number of objectors, other than the Womanagh group, became known. The fishing people in the south coast village of Ballycotton gave their support. A meeting was planned for the village. The Irish Sea Anglers Association, several small factories in the area and Myrtle Allen, who with her family runs Ballymaloe House, a hotel and catering college attracting students from all over the world, added their vociferous objections.

For the first time a proper open and public meeting was held in Killeagh to discuss the proposed factory. Approximately 400 people packed into the Killeagh community centre. As the meeting began it was explained that the local IFA, who chaired the meeting, had asked the Killeagh Community Council if it would like to share the meeting and the platform. It had declined. Merrell Dow, the IDA and Eolas had been invited to attend, it was announced. The corporate had also declined the offer. The IDA and Eolas did not reply and did not turn up. It was the same at subsequent meetings in nearby Gortroe and Ballycotton: no multinational, no semi-state body representatives and packed halls.

Fianna Fáil Deputy Michael Aherne sat at the back of the hall during the Killeagh meeting until someone asked if any elected representatives had bothered to turn up. Would he be prepared to support the majority, who are opposed to the factory, someone asked? He couldn't answer.

Bob Bickerdike, an ageing Independent councillor for Youghal, said that it was not good enough for public representatives to sit on the fence. 'There is no such thing as neutrality where these companies are concerned', he said.

'It's an act of suicide against nature', someone else said.

Aherne was questioned again. 'A lot of people have made up their mind with a lot less information. Why, with a lot more information, can you not make up your mind?'

The packed halls in Killeagh, Gortroe and Ballycotton were told about Merrell Dow's history: how it and its parent Dow Chemical deliberately obstructed the EPA. 'If the US government can't get anything out of Merrell Dow, what hope have we?' asked one objector, who referred to the company's intransigence and its contempt for the local community. 'We are entitled to know everything about Merrell Dow, yet they have never told us anything about the potential dangers.'

'Merrell Dow will happen over my dead body', said one man at the Killeagh meeting.

'If you allow those cowboys to come in here, you are a crazy people', said a priest who explained that he worked in the developing world.

As a result of the three meetings, over 1,000 signatures were collected. The following week a deputation from the Womanagh group delivered the signatures personally to the offices of An Bord Pleanála in Dublin. It was going to be a long battle and the community was ready for it. Peace could see the determination to win in their actions and words:

> The crisis surfacing in east Cork exemplified the enduring opposition of interests between those who had economic and political power and those who had not. Yet the latter were not really powerless; their locally based social power, latent in their everyday lives, could be drawn upon to support the opposition movement. It soon became clear that the judgements of ordinary residents were to be accorded paramountcy, and this would provide the charter for political action.

While all this was going on Bill Donaldson, speaking again from Cincinnati, told the *Cork Examiner* that another site could be found. The IDA immediately reacted and stated that Merrell Dow was determined to fight to remain on a site it took more than two years to find. An IDA source told the *Cork Examiner* on 8 September:

> They wanted to base the plant in an area which projected a good, bright, clean image. They are treating objections in a serious manner, but they feel they've gone to great lengths to address the fears of the objectors and are disappointed that the views of reputable experts are being ignored.

As the objectors waited for An Bord Pleanála to decide the appeal, the community split that many had feared manifested itself as a jobs versus the environment battle. From Castlemartyr, the Killeagh Pro-Industry Group was set up by Breda Prendergast, an occupational health nurse. She told a reporter shortly after the group was formed:

> Does anybody really think we would be in favour of a factory that would destroy our own environment? We must live here too but we are convinced that once the guidelines are followed, the plant will cause no damage to the environment.

An Bord Pleanála had received 21 formal third-party appeals and four objections (from people who simply wanted their views recorded). Merrell Dow had also lodged an appeal against the 27 conditions set down by the local authority. Late in October the planning board announced that an oral hearing of the objections would take place in Cork County Hall on Tuesday 6 December.

On the morning of Friday 16 December a press release from the World Environment Centre in Washington DC found its way to the offices of the *Cork Examiner*. It announced that the Dow Chemical Company would be awarded the 1989 gold medal for International Corporate Environmental Achievement. It stated that Dow had been 'selected from a number of corporate nominees by an independent international jury'. It referred to Dow's Open Door policy 'that helps the public better understand (sic) the company's environmental concerns and solutions'.

The press release had been faxed from the United States on 13 December, yet it didn't reach the *Examiner* offices until the Friday, the final day of the oral hearing. Consequently the *Evening Echo* ran the story beside its report on the hearing which, ironically, was a negative piece from Merrell Dow's point of view.

It was a shrewd and well timed piece of public relations. The *Evening Echo* report was headlined 'Impact study condemned'. The objectors thought it was one of the few accurate assessments in either the *Echo* or the *Examiner* during the eight-day hearing that reflected the objectors' side of the debate. For most of the hearing Merrell Dow's PR firm was firing on all cylinders, getting the best possible coverage for its clients. It was to be a quite sizeable bone of contention among objectors to the factory that Merrell Dow was able to dominate the media so thoroughly.

When Dominic Hegarty, a senior inspector with An Bord Pleanála, initiated proceedings just after 10.30 a.m. on Tuesday 6 December he unwittingly set out a schedule which Merrell Dow took immediate advantage of.

'I will ask the representatives of Merrell Dow to briefly describe their proposed development. This is in no sense to be construed as presenting their case. It is merely to set the scene for the hearing at large', he said and added that he would hear the agreed appellants (objectors to the plant who had paid An Bord Pleanála IR£36 to be heard at the appeal) first:

> I am slightly departing from my normal thing in that I normally hear the Planning Authority. I feel, however, that since the main thrust of the evidence for the development will come from the developers I should take them next and after that I should hear the Planning Authority.

It was a bad start.

Colm Lopez, a shopkeeper from Youghal opposed to the factory, jumped to his feet. 'Is it proposed to hear the objecting parties once and Merrell Dow twice? Merrell Dow is speaking first.'

'If you listen to what I say,' Inspector Hegarty stressed, 'I want Merrell Dow to show the people at the hearing what the development is and show us when the people refer to things like a process building or a formulator [sic] building – it is not evidence.' He insisted, 'It is a description of the development. They are setting the scene.'

Approximately 15 minutes later, following a protracted debate about whether certain witnesses would be called or not between Sean O'Leary, Barrister at Law, representing the local authority, and Dermot Gleeson, Senior Counsel, for the Womanagh group and others opposed to the factory, H. Fred Plagens, Chair of Merrell Dow, did what the inspector had asked him not to do.

'I am just asking you to describe the development, not to make a case for it', said the inspector.

Philip O'Sullivan, Senior Counsel, for Merrell Dow, interjected. 'This witness has prepared a statement. He is actually going to be my general introductory witness.'

The inspector was insistent. O'Sullivan said it was a brief statement. The inspector allowed Plagens to continue. 'Sorry, maybe I was premature. Carry on and I'll stop you again if I think I should', he said.

O'Sullivan then explained that most of what Plagens would say would be relevant. 'If you feel that this witness is becoming irrelevant just indicate that I will tell him to skip a paragraph or whatever. I have a draft of what he is going to say.'

So did the press. Merrell Dow's PR firm had handed out copies of the statement. Less than half an hour later the reporters from the *Echo* were filing their story on the morning's proceedings. Plagens' speech was given prominence, under the heading 'Ireland was initially rejected' and ran for ten paragraphs. There was no mention of the inspector's discussion with Plagens and O'Sullivan. Neither was there any mention that after Plagens was approximately four minutes into his speech he was stopped by the inspector:

> Sorry, can I interrupt you. Really I was quite right originally. This isn't what I want. I just want you to describe the plant. You can give me all that again if you want to but

really, Mr Lopez will be complaining to me that we are giving you a second platform.

Plagens continued for several minutes, ad-libbing this time. He was then questioned by O'Sullivan. 'Merrell Dow', O'Sullivan said, 'is prepared to make what it considers would be a considerable concession in the light of written appeals and objections.' O'Sullivan suggested that it was the right time to inform the planning board about the use of high sulphur fuel. The inspector said he would take the amendment if it was not too lengthy and if Gleeson had no objections.

'I have no position on this,' replied Gleeson, 'but I would like to know about all the amendments fairly soon, all the amendments.'

O'Sullivan said he had four paragraphs which related to amendments. He then added that considering the inspector's requested guidelines it might be better to deal with them in one go. The inspector nodded an almost inaudible 'okay'.

After this confusing beginning the hearing got under way. There was no evidence that Gleeson was provided with the amendments Merrell Dow had suggested. It was to be a problem that would arise later in the hearing, when the US company would be accused of duplicity. There was no doubt in the minds of the objectors that Merrell Dow had won the first round, despite the impressive array of witnesses who had presented themselves in opposition to the proposed factory.

The first day of the hearing naturally attracted the largest attendance, approximately 350 people filling the Council Chambers on the top floor of the County Hall. The inspector sat in the County Chairman's throne, flanked by Don Menzies, a chartered chemical engineer, to his right and a Bord Pleanála secretary, to his left. The developers occupied, with members of the Eolas team, the seats to the inspector's right. To his left sat the local authority witnesses, mostly from the planning department. In front of the inspector, below him, sat the various legal teams. Further behind them in the council seats to the left and right sat the appellants (the objectors to the factory). Along the aisles at the two sides of the chamber sat, variously, more objectors largely from fishing and farming backgrounds, the media, Merrell Dow's PR team, representatives from the numerous Irish-based chemical companies, representatives from other local authorities and people simply interested in the events. These would have included the Hanrahan family: John, his wife

Selina and his mother Mary. For most of the eight-day hearing they made the three and a half hour round trip from their farm in Tipperary.

During the opening three days the inspector heard from the objectors and others concerned about the location of the proposed factory in an agricultural and maricultural area. Keith Sargeant, speaking for An Bord Fáilte (the Irish Tourist Board), was among a number of witnesses who questioned the Eolas EIS and its implementation under the 5 July EC Directive on Environmental Impact Initiatives. He said the controversy over the Directive was not the concern of the hearing:

> but An Bord Pleanála should note that the terms of any EEC directive represent the lowest common denominator of standards agreed by member states of the EEC, i.e. an environmental directive cannot be passed down to member states from Brussels unless it has been formally agreed by the Council of Ministers (with responsibility for environment in the member states). Ireland cannot afford to allow the EEC standard on environmental impact assessments to be applied in anything less than the manner intended.

The following day James Rogers, manager of the Southern Regional Fisheries Board, put a case for continuous biological monitoring. He said that the Fisheries Board felt this was of utmost importance because 'it must be assumed that sooner or later something will go wrong on the site'.

'We will not earn public confidence if we base our monitoring simply on information provided by the company', he added and stressed that did not imply any mistrust of the company. A few minutes later he explained why he felt this was an imperative request:

> In my present position, for the last six years, I have had very great experience, unfortunately, of my pollution control staff being impeded, ostensibly for safety reasons, at factory entrance gates and in many many instances they are impeded ... for so long that their subsequent inspection of the effluent handling area is virtually a waste of time.

Rogers said that the Fisheries Board's assessment was that the developer should 'ideally, be limited to the provision of appropriate and immediately accessible monitoring facilities'. He added that an independent agency should be funded to 'check and calibrate all of the gauges, meters and sampling devices and to carry out analyses of effluent composition and environmental impact'. This, Rogers implored, should 'be recognised as the ideal option' but one that should be proceeded towards 'whether in this case or in subsequent cases'.

He also said that the public should 'have access to the on-site monitoring data, in so far as it relates to the composition of the effluent being discharged to the river'. He concluded: 'I would feel it to be entirely unacceptable that such monitoring data should be denied to the public.'

Rory Finegan was the most dominant of the witnesses for the objectors. Representing Ballycotton Fishermen's Association, Ballycotton Deep Sea Anglers' Centre and Youghal Fishermen's Co-op Society Limited as well as the Womanagh group, Finegan prepared the principal objectors' first independent report on the Eolas EIS. Initially Finegan had stated that the proposed factory would:

> damage agricultural, residential and tourism values, degrade the quality of air and water, result in chemical fall-out and consequent damage to property and health, contribute to 'acid rain' with resultant damage to crops and Glenbower Wood, pollute the rivers and coast and endanger the Wetland of International Importance.

For three hours Finegan emphasised these points and his argument that Killeagh was not a suitable location for the proposed factory and that the Eolas report was an 'unreliable document'. Merrell Dow, he said, was 'the sort of factory which should locate in an area properly zoned for such enterprises, with appropriate industrial infrastructures, following the completion of properly conducted environmental studies'. It was the crux of the objectors' argument.

John Taylor, an Irish fresh water ecologist based in Canada who spoke for the Womanagh group on the first day, was among a number of observers who felt that the objections to the factory were genuine, the very real fears of people who perceived a very real problem. 'It is farcical, crazy, to site a chemical plant in a food production area', he said. He continued:

You have a river that produces salmon, major agriculture, mussel beds and a Wetland [of international importance]. Any one of these things should persuade a government to tell Merrell Dow to set up elsewhere, instead of allowing a community to spend money on something that is patently ridiculous and wrong for the area. In contrast Canada would pay millions to expand such a mussel bed, as the one in Youghal.

Day three concluded the Womanagh group's evidence and the submissions of their major witnesses. John Connolly, a former chief fire officer with the Department of the Environment, was scathing in his criticism of the Cork County Fire Service, of how it would deal with a fire or explosion at the proposed factory at Killeagh.

Among other points, he said that its officers had 'no proper operational instructions' to deal with a fire or explosion in chemical factories, that the Cork Fire Service was 'not adequately trained in operational fire fighting let alone in tackling major chemical fires and that no effective arrangements were in force to guarantee ten or more fire brigades at the scene of a major chemical fire'. He added that 'no agreements are in force with neighbouring fire authorities to ensure adequate back-up'.

He was also critical of Merrell Dow's attitude. 'It is painfully clear that Merrell Dow see no useful contribution from Cork County Fire Service. Did they base this on information from other chemical plants in the Cork area?' he asked.

The failure of the [Cork] chief fire officer to ensure adequate supplies of fire fighting water for his firemen leads me to believe he does not intend to commit them to attack a major fire in the proposed chemical plant.

If the go-ahead is given for the development it must be on the understanding that, in the event of a major fire, explosion or chain of explosions, the affected areas of the plant will burn uncontrolled over a period of time, scattering the products of combustion to the winds.

Connolly concluded with a rhetorical word on the Whiddy Tribunal, which criticised the chief fire officer involved for not informing higher authority when he knew that the bye-laws were defective and 'it was conceivable that something might have been done about it'.

Richard Crinion, of the Veterinary Department of University College, Dublin, said that the 'extreme close proximity of the factory to dairy herds on all sides would allow no room for error, over the life of the factory'. He said that because cows were very sensitive, a pollutant could gain entry into the food chain, via milk, within a short period of leaving the factory. While many safeguards had been laid down in the planning permission to protect the environment, he said, 'there is no specific mention of farm animals or their safety'. He proposed eleven conditions, principally a baseline study of animal health, crops and pasture and soil over seven years.

Another Dublin based university lecturer, Paul Dowding of the Environmental Services Unit at Trinity College, criticised the Eolas EIS and requested that monitoring data be made available for public inspection. 'They do not contain industrial secrets and there can be no reasonable grounds for withholding them from third party inspection', he said.

Among his summary objections to the proposed factory were that a new EIS should be produced for any new process proposed by the developer and that this should be made available to the public and other interested bodies. He said that 'the emission and environmental monitoring to be carried out by, or on behalf of, the county council to protect local amenity is deficient'. Dowding, an expert in air pollution who also gave evidence during the Hanrahan/Merck case, was also critical of the structure and procedures in the planning application which, he said, would 'lead to undue risk of local environmental air pollution'.

The objectors had laid out their case. They didn't want Merrell Dow; the factory should locate in a suitably zoned area, but if the community had to be subjected to it, they wanted environmental controls and conditions never before built into the infrastructure of a planning application for a chemical factory in Ireland. Some objectors believed they were winning. Michael Browne did not. When Adrian Peace remarked after the morning session of the third day that it looked good for them Browne was reticent. 'That's right, you're quite right, we scored some fine points in there against the bastards', he told Peace.

> The morning was ours all right but don't you feel ... can't you sense in all this ... that somehow it's all slipping away from us. We've done all right, y'know, in getting it to a hearing and that. And we all know that all of east Cork's

right with us, right behind us. But somehow, I don't know about all this, somehow in here y'know now, it's all slipping away, just slipping away right out of our hands.

Merrell Dow and the Eolas EIS had taken a verbal hammering during the opening three days. There had been two specific scientific arguments: the quality of the air and the water from an ecological point of view. In his submission Dowding had demonstrated that the effects of the air emissions would have a local impact, that any emissions would not be dispersed and instead, for a significant part of the time, would fall onto the surrounding countryside. The treatment of the water quality issue in the EIS was shown to be insufficient and cursory. Taylor stated that the major criticisms stemmed from 'a poor reporting of method' and 'use of inappropriate methods, lack of data for various requirements and confusion over the accuracy of calculations presented in the EIS'.

Day four began early, just after nine. Plagens, just as he had done on the first day, took the stage and then stole the show. 'I would now like to discuss four specific areas of the project proposal which have received some comment,' he announced, 'the need for a baseline study, the use of high sulphur fuels, concern over environmental monitoring data, and indemnification for damages.'

Merrell Dow, in a matter of moments, upstaged the objectors and demolished most of their arguments against the factory. There was no immediate, discernible reaction from the objectors in the council chamber. Gradually they drifted outside into the lobby or down to the second floor, to the County Hall canteen, for refreshments. Some felt they needed it. 'They didn't just offer the minimum that would satisfy people', said one of the Womanagh group's experts. 'They offered a superior set of adjustments.'

Plagens, in offering what the media headlined as 'major concessions' had cancelled most of Taylor's and Dowding's evidence. 'We believe it will be responsible and helpful if we fund a comprehensive baseline environmental study', Plagens said, adding that it would be an independent study that would 'include a complete audit of flora and fauna at the site and surrounding areas, yielding information against which future studies can be compared'.

'I have heard expressions of concern regarding the sulphur dioxide emissions which would result from the burning of high sulphur fuel in our process boiler', he said, and added that Merrell Dow would use low sulphur diesel fuel. This effectively meant that sulphur emissions from the proposed factory would be cut by 85 per cent.

Having dealt with the scientists' arguments, Plagens turned to the community's fears about the factory. He said:

> Merrell Dow will establish a local community environmental consultative committee soon after planning consent is obtained. We will invite delegates from various bodies and groupings to participate. This committee would meet regularly and would have access to all environmental monitoring data and information resulting from the baseline study mentioned earlier. By forming a local community environmental consultative committee we are providing an opportunity for direct citizen involvement in monitoring our activities to ensure compliance with the planning consent.

Perhaps wary of the Hanrahans' victory over Merck Sharp and Dohme, Plagens said that Merrell Dow would pay compensation 'if a professional agriculturalist or veterinarian retained by one of our neighbours were to believe that observed ill effects had been caused by our operations'. He added that Merrell Dow 'would request the regional Department of Agriculture diagnostic laboratory in Cork to investigate the cause of the ill effects'. Plagens said Merrell Dow would agree to 'abide by the conclusions of that body as to causation and pay damages if warranted'. He said the same procedure would apply in the event of crop failure or animal mortality.

'These ideas are offered as an initial good faith effort to resolve our neighbours' concerns.' Plagens said that Merrell Dow were confident that with the implementation of these initiatives their investment 'will be right for Merrell Dow, right for the Killeagh/Youghal area of east Cork, and right for Ireland'.

Merrell Dow had, many objectors believed, prepared a clever publicity stunt. It was the belief of several objectors, on hearing that Merrell Dow had taken 34 rooms in Jury's Hotel in Cork, that the company had brought its own experts with it. 'Merrell Dow', said one observer, 'would never have allowed a document such as the Eolas EIS to be exposed to the public view without an internal review of its weak points.' The argument was that Merrell Dow's own experts would have picked out the same faults, inaccuracies and inconsistencies as the Womanagh group's experts. Tom Kennedy, Merrell Dow's Managing Director in Ireland, later acknowledged that their 'experts in the US studied the Eolas reports' but he said that they gave favourable opinions of it.

The objectors' evidence appeared to be scientifically strong and emotionally vocal; Merrell Dow were now matching that performance with the slick professionalism expected of corporate capitalism. All their witnesses' statements had been prepared in advance; copies were made available to the inspector, to the various legal teams and to the press. It looked good.

Plagens had been followed in the witness chair by Peter Langford, a chartered engineer with Ove Arup and Partners Ireland, which was commissioned by Merrell Dow to evaluate potential sites, and Gerald McCarthy, an architect and town planner. Tom Kennedy and Jerry Martin, Dow Chemicals' Director of Environmental Quality, followed. Ken Macken, who co-authored the Eolas EIS with David Kelly, was the sixth witness. Merrell Dow's legal team then presented another independent environmental consultant, Michael Bailey of Envirocon in Dublin, to validate Eolas' findings.

Despite the pace set by Merrell Dow's witnesses, Bailey came to the stand behind the company's own schedule. Many of the objectors were still mulling over Plagens' remarks and lunch was beckoning. The inspector, who had been unusually quiet for most of the morning session, asked Bailey, a few minutes into his submission, whether his evidence referred to the new sulphur figures or the old ones.

These are current, Bailey told him.

Dermot Gleeson, senior counsel for the Womanagh group, immediately jumped up. He asked Bailey when he had learned about the new figures.

There was a pause. Bailey looked over at the bench where the Merrell Dow team were seated. One of them, in the back row, got out of his seat. They stared at each other for a matter of indeterminable seconds. Bailey finally replied: '24 hours ago.'

A few people in the chamber laughed. For others it was more serious. It was the first chink in Merrell Dow's armour. Bailey's prepared submission was ten pages long and included a further six pages from the Foras Forbartha report on *Air Quality in Ireland* (November 1986). The submission was extensive and well thought out.

Although the inspector and Gleeson took Bailey's word that he hadn't known about the figures until the day before, there were many in the chamber whose conspiracy theories were working overtime. Later a scientist attending the hearing remarked that if Bailey had prepared his report that quickly he was a genius.

Several objectors and one of their experts were beginning to believe that Merrell Dow had come to the hearing with two distinctive plans. Two days later their theories gained even more credibility. The *Sunday Tribune*, in an interview with Plagens, reported that the 'concessions' had been 'prepared before the hearing began and were intended as part of [Plagens'] opening address to the appeal on Tuesday until he was restricted in his remarks by planning inspector Dominic Hegarty'.

Merrell Dow had, on day four, seemingly responded to the evidence presented by the Womanagh group's expert witnesses and those of other independent objectors to the factory. But it was obvious to the objectors that what Merrell Dow had done was to fall back onto one of its plans: the one that had been prepared before the hearing began in case events turned against it. After all, Philip O'Sullivan, on the first day, had spoken of an amendment regarding the use of high sulphur fuel. The objectors accused Merrell Dow of duplicity and in his summing up Gleeson brought the matter up, that Plagens had not intended to talk about the concessions on the opening day, and that O'Sullivan had cleverly avoided the issue.

'I want to say something about the mode of disclosure of the compromise proposals', Gleeson told the inspector on the final day.

> Mr Plagens told us that he intended, on the first day of the hearing, to offer one set of the compromised proposals and that when the compromised proposals were finally put, after all the objectors and appellants had been heard, they were different and more responsive proposals.
>
> I utterly reject it. Anyone and everyone who was present in this room knows that what Mr Hegarty said to Mr Plagens was an invitation to outline the project, not to argue for it, not to advocate it, but to outline it; and it was entirely within the scope of the inspector's invitation that Mr Plagens could have disclosed any modifications he wanted and if he felt he couldn't or if he was confused by the ground rules that were being laid down by him, there was nothing stopping his legal advisors from communicating these modifications either by standing up and saying that the proposal is changed, or by passing a note across this not very large desk, and saying that the proposal is changed.
>
> It was not just a choice for the developer to tell us that the proposal was changed, it was incumbent upon them as

a matter of fairness to tell us that the proposal was changed. In my view it is entirely reprehensible that they should have permitted my witnesses to troop across the stage, as it were, and give their evidence, while the Merrell Dow representatives sat there knowing that my experts were handling a proposal which was now, in parts at least, in some details – to what extent I do not know – abandoned or modified.

That was a piece of unfairness and I reject and complain about it. The proper conduct of this hearing clearly depended upon my experts having the opportunity of being able to speak about the proposal as it was now known to be to the developer.

O'Sullivan, in his final submission, refuted Gleeson's comments but he admitted that the original four concessions 'were altered and amended, in the course of the following days'. O'Sullivan said that it was not his intention to impose a difficulty on his legal colleagues and apologised, but he added, 'I think to suggest this was some Machiavellian scheme to undercut the experts of the appellants is going a trifle too far.'

Conspiracy theories and Machiavellian notions were prevalent throughout the homes of east Cork since Merrell Dow announced its arrival. One of the most enduring of these, which gained considerable credibility during the hearing, was the belief that Merrell Dow was tied up with the government's plans for a national toxic waste incinerator in east Cork.

The objectors were baffled why Merrell Dow had gone to such lengths to come to Ireland unless there was something else in it for them other than grants. Tom Kennedy repeatedly said that Merrell Dow had been invited to Ireland by the IDA and the major attractions were 'an educated English speaking workforce, a politically stable environment for business and financial incentives'.

Following protracted and failed negotiations between government and local authorities since 1976 to establish a toxic dump, Padraig Flynn, the Minister for the Environment, told a Cork conference on waste disposal in November 1988 that incineration was the long-term answer to industry's toxic waste problem in Ireland. The objectors were convinced that the national incinerator was linked to Merrell Dow's application to build a factory in east Cork.

During a meeting of the Youghal Urban District Council, while the Bord Pleanála hearing was in motion, the disused Cork–Youghal railway line was debated. The objectors feared that the line was not being abandoned and that it would be reopened when the chemical industries came in. Although the Youghal UDC's reasons for wanting the line back were commercial, Iarnrod Éireann's Cork Regional Manager, Paudie Lynch, confirmed the objectors' fears at the UDC meeting. He said that if the proposed industrial development in Killeagh takes place 'there could be a spin-off for the rail line'. It wasn't until the shortlist of tenders for the national toxic waste incinerator was drawn up in September 1989 that the conspiracy theory was proven groundless. Merrell Dow was not on it and at no stage had it been involved.

The objectors' conspiracy theories were further amplified during the hearing when it was learned that in a letter from An Bord Iascaigh Mhara (fishing board), the Youghal Fishermen's Co-op's application for a licence had been delayed 'due to an objection by the IDA, since your site is positioned opposite a proposed or existing industrial outfall'. The letter was dated 26 February 1986. This was brought up during the hearing and near the end the Youghal fishermen were told that their licence (to grow mussels) would be granted.

The objectors were convinced that all these events were linked, particularly when Jerry Martin and Tom Kennedy, at the Bord Pleanála hearing, refused to give any specific details about the incinerator they proposed to use at Killeagh. This was despite the fact that the Eolas EIS referred to an incinerator with specific features. Yet in cross-examination Martin told Gleeson that 'the incinerator had not been completely designed'. Then, later in the cross-examination, Martin revealed that the incinerator had not been purchased.

Gleeson asked him if there was a short list. Martin confirmed there was and after further questioning said that it 'was probably less than six' but that he hadn't seen it. He eluded to the inspector that it was a confidential matter and that Tom Kennedy 'would be more than happy to share [the information] with the Board who [we] have quotes from'.

When Gleeson came to cross-examine Kennedy he asked him if he would like 'to disclose the qualifications of the six people who will design and/or choose the incinerator'.

'Well, they are certainly qualified engineers, based on their experience and their education.'

'So', Gleeson said, 'the extent of their qualifications, which you wish the Board to be informed of, in relation to the incinerator designer/chooser, is that they are all engineers, is that right?'

Kennedy said: 'Fine, yes.'

It was the objectors' contention that the debate about the incinerator was crucial, particularly, they stressed, as it was the incinerator in Merck Sharp and Dohme's Tipperary factory that allegedly caused the Hanrahans' ill-health and the deaths of their cattle.

It will probably remain a matter of debate among those who attended the hearing whether Eolas escaped with its credibility intact. Although the testimonies of several witnesses had weakened the credibility of the Eolas EIS, the specific criticisms were about the water quality and the fact that the report did not assess the potential impact on dairy cattle and on crops. 'Dairy farming is, in the long term, the most economically important, taken together with the other farming enterprises of fruit and cereals, the most environmentally sensitive activity in this neighbourhood and what has happened here?' Gleeson asked rhetorically in his final submission. 'It has been ignored by Eolas.'

On Monday 27 February 1989 An Bord Pleanála upheld the decision Cork County Council to grant planning permission to Merrell Dow to build their factory. Laying the foundations, however, was still a long way away. The Womanagh group immediately instructed its solicitor, Tom Menton, to seek a judicial review of An Bord Pleanála's grant of permission on the grounds that the EIS had not been properly implemented under EC legislation.

Despite the very strong scientific arguments put forward by the objector's experts, An Bord Pleanála had ruled that:

> The proposed development would not be injurious to the residential and visual amenities of the area, give rise to a public health hazard, militate against the development of agriculture, damage aquatic life or be otherwise contrary to the proper planning and development of the area.

The board, however, stipulated in one of its conditions that Merrell Dow should commission from an independent body a baseline environmental survey which would cover 'freshwater, brackish and marine organisms in the Womanagh river and estuary and an assessment of the terrestrial environment on and around the proposed plant'. The reason for this, stated the planning board, was to 'provide baseline data to assist in the monitoring of atmospheric emissions and effluent discharges with a view to protecting amenities of the area and protecting public and animal health'.

The Womanagh group did not believe such a study would make any difference. An Bord Pleanála appeared to believe that a short-term baseline study survey would allay the fears of people who perceived a very real problem. The Womanagh group and others opposed to the factory stressed that the battle lines were just been drawn when they heard the board's decision. 'A battle had been lost, the outcome of the war had yet to be decided', said Colm Lopez. 'It's a five hurdle race. There are three more to go and all we need for victory is to jump one of them. That can be achieved', he insisted. The oral hearing, he stressed, had been a 'joke'.

Their specific criticisms of Merrell Dow had not been addressed by An Bord Pleanála. The hearing, many of the objectors agreed, had been a cosmetic, political exercise, yet at no stage during those early days of December did any of the objectors believe that the board would turn down Merrell Dow's application. It seemed that to win, to get rid of Merrell Dow, they would have to go all the way to the High Court, to the Supreme Court, to Strasbourg. Gradually too the political mood towards the environment, toward the agitators, to the general public who sympathised with the plight of the communities fighting Merrell Dow, the IDA and the government was changing.

The next hurdle, the High Court, was shackled by the establishment to the system, believed many objectors. A contentious debate raged among the numerous objectors over whether they would receive satisfaction in Dublin's Four Courts.

Yvonne Scannell, Trinity College, Dublin law lecturer and specialist in environmental matters, succinctly put the objectors' case against An Bord Pleanála's decision in perspective. 'As I see it,' she told a seminar on environmental issues in Trinity College in March 1989, 'the good environmental lawyer will advise clients on how to make their environmental impact assessments litigation proof, or will identify procedural or substantive errors which may justify an action for judicial review of a decision on a project.'

Although she was not referring specifically to the anti-Merrell Dow lobby's judicial review it was obvious that the multinational, An Bord Pleanála and Cork County Council would be vindicated by the High Court, if the Womanagh group's lawyers could not identify any errors. In a letter to the Womanagh group, Rory

Finegan warned them not to put all their eggs in one basket when they challenged Merrell Dow and An Bord Pleanála's decision in the High Court. Merrell Dow's EIS, the Womanagh group argued, had not complied with the EC directive on environmental impact assessment, which it seemed, had come into force on 3 July 1988. Finegan and others who had investigated Ireland's obligations under article 189 of the EC Treaty (the implementation into Irish law of EC directive 83/337/EEC) were convinced that the Womanagh group had put all their eggs into the wrong basket.

Scannell explained:

> On July 1, 1988 the Department of the Environment issued circular letters (PD 111/8/20) and an internal minute (PD 111/8/21) to the secretaries of government departments. It was claimed that these administrative measures were inadequate to implement the requirements of the directive. In my opinion, neither the circular nor the internal minute could constitute the proper implementation of the directive.

The objectors' case was further weakened when the EC Commission confirmed that it had begun enforcement procedures against Ireland for failure to implement the directive. Existing Irish requirements on environmental impact assessment were, argued Scannell, 'confusing and unpredictable'. Furthermore Scannell believed that the directive was 'not binding on developers who are not required to submit EIS's under our planning legislation'. Merrell Dow's development, however, was bound by article 28 of the Local Government (Planning and Developments) regulations, 1977, particularly Article 3(b) which applied to any development with a capital cost of IR£5 million or more. Merrell Dow's development had been originally costed at IR£30 million. Scannell, however, pointed out that it was arguable:

> that if an environmental impact study submitted under Article 28 of the 1977 regulations does not contain the matters which the directive states must be contained, and does not spell out the effects on the environment as prescribed by the Directive, the decision to accept it as being in compliance with Article 28 is vulnerable.

But, she added with some caution, it all depended 'upon the attitude of the courts when presented with a challenge to an EIS under

Article 28'. She further stated that certain projects carried out in accordance with Article 28 did comply with the directive.

The argument from the objectors was clear, that Merrell Dow, the county council and Eolas had not consulted the local community. Scannell, again, put this in perspective:

> Existing Irish requirements place the responsibility for the EIA on the developer, whereas the directive envisages an assessment procedure involving the provision and publication of information on the part of the developer, and collecting of information from the public and others, and the arrival by the competent authority at a decision to grant or withhold consent for the developer. This is clear from the preamble to the directive which says that 'whereas the assessment must be conducted on the basis of appropriate information supplied by the developer, which may be supplemented by the authorities and by the people who may be concerned by the project in question'.

Scannell was again circumspect in her assessment of the legal complexities the Womanagh group's case was based on:

> Provided sound and informed professional judgement is exercised it is unlikely that the courts will readily strike down a decision on a project subjected to the EIA on the grounds that it does not comply with article 3 of its national equivalent.

Throughout the campaign against Merrell Dow the objectors were convinced that every move they made was countered by political inertia and dogma. Scannell concurred on the matter of the High Court appeal:

> The decision on whether or not to give consent to a project for which an EIA has been prepared is essentially a political rather than an objective scientific one and it is not a decision which ought to be taken by the courts.

Scannell's paper proved to be correct in virtually every respect. When Justice Barron delivered his judgement on 27 July 1989 – 377 days after Merrell Dow had submitted its planning application to

Cork County Council – the inadequacies of Ireland's environmental law were glaringly apparent to the objectors, disconsolate that the duplicity of Cork County Council had, once more, been to their detriment.

> While the applicants had to put their case on a narrow legal basis, they still sought to rely upon the merits to show the importance of matters which they regarded as being omitted from the environmental impact study. In my view, once it is shown that the planning authority (Cork County Council) and therefore the respondent had jurisdiction to deal with the application before them, then the question of the rights and wrongs of the application was a matter for them. Any other approach would be to turn an application for judicial review into a further appeal. I have no jurisdiction to do that. So my failure to refer to the evidence adduced by the applicants or to its importance as indeed my failure to refer to the Eolas reports or their importance or to any other matter of fact dealt with by the respondent is not to be interpreted as disinterest or lack of concern for the position of the applicants, but is dictated solely by the nature of the proceedings before me. Accordingly the relief sought will be refused.

Justice Barron had thrown the issue back to the politicians, where the objectors argued it had been all the time, except that most of the elected representatives had chosen to side-step it. With the Womanagh group determined to appeal it to the Supreme Court and take it further to Strasbourg if necessary, it was time for the politicians to listen to the objectors' evidently strong arguments. The polls, by Youghal resident Geoffrey Buckley and by the Research Bureau of Ireland, had shown that the majority of the people in east Cork and west Waterford were against the siting of the factory in Killeagh. A new battle plan was needed.

It was the end of July 1989. Events in America were beginning to influence the times ahead. On 18 July Dow Chemicals and Marion Laboratories announced the signing of 'a definite agreement for the combination of Marion Laboratories with Merrell Dow'. The objectors had begun to reflect on the events of the months between February – when An Bord Pleanála upheld the council's decision to grant Merrell Dow planning permission – and

July when the High Court refused to overturn that decision. It seemed that the county council and the IDA had won their battle to bring Merrell Dow into the lush green fields of east Cork. The IDA it appeared, was concerned only that the continuing protest was damaging Cork's hopes of securing further development. Subsequent events showed and the IDA knew at the time that such comments were pro-industry propaganda. The people of east Cork had been presented with a *fait accompli*. Warning that Cork's industrial future was in danger was, said many objectors, nothing less than blackmail. Padraic White, the IDA chief executive, accused them of emotional behaviour and said that they should 'engage in genuine and open dialogue'. It didn't go down well at all with the objectors.

Anthony Summers wrote in a letter to *The Irish Times* in March:

Above all, the opposition [to Merrell Dow] resents being patronised. We are not children, and this is not the Third World. These particular peasants obtained their knowledge by consulting experts world-wide, and rapidly raised IR£60,000 – and most of that in the immediate neighbourhood – to hire prestigious legal counsel.

The lofty officials involved should be advised that this has become, for many of us who live hereabouts, a matter of civil rights. In the decade of Chernobyl, Bhopal and farmer Hanrahan's dead cows, it is right to be dubious about assurances from Merrell Dow.

Meanwhile ... in the deafening recent silence of our local elected officials, Mr White would do well to start listening to the sound he finds so distasteful – the voice of the people in the area. Whether he listens or not, they live here and he doesn't. A majority, we believe, oppose the factory scheme. And they are going to fight.

The High Court's decision to grant a judicial review of An Bord Pleanála's decision later that month was at the time seen as a minor victory, another hurdle vaulted, but among the growing mass of objectors there was dissension about tactics. The Concerned Citizens of East Cork and West Waterford argued that a professionally run media campaign was an essential tactic. Others, many of whom subsequently formed Citizens Against Merrell Dow, wanted to take the battle onto the streets, with regular public meetings and demonstrations around the country. The Womanagh group wanted Merrell Dow and the government to 'start listening to the people because they will decide the issue'. How the people were going to do that suddenly became a problem. Tom Menton, the Womanagh group's solicitor, advised caution. There should be no demonstrations until all legal remedies had been exhausted, he stressed.

The chemical industry, in the meantime, was watching events from a relatively safe distance. The decision to grant the High Court appeal had, said Professor Alan Myers of UCC, 'implications for the chemical and pharmaceutical industry' but he said it depended on how they responded. 'They are probably looking over their shoulders but they might wait until they are forced to do something, because it costs money.' Interestingly, in the wake of Professor Myers' comments the industry began to announce that it would spend more money on environmental control and on a public relations campaign to allay the fears the public, especially those in east Cork, had about chemical factories. Surveys by the *Cork Examiner* and the *Sunday Tribune* revealed that the major chemical companies would spend between IR£40 million and IR£50 million up to 1992 on environmental control.

As the objectors waited for the High Court to hear their appeal, Merrell Dow garnered support from the pro-industry lobby. The Killeagh Pro-Industry Group welcomed Merrell Dow's Director of Human Resources, Gerry O'Malley to one of their meetings and heard him state that the company did not expect the building of the factory to be 'unduly delayed by the court case'. Michael T. Murphy, president of the Youghal Chamber of Commerce, stressed that industry was needed in east Cork and that the jobs were crucial, and his views were echoed by Sean Murphy, the county chairperson of Muintir na Tíre (People of the land), who said he hoped to see the foundation of an east Cork pro-industry group. The Muintir philosophy that industry was essential in rural areas to stem the flow of emigration, he said, was linked to the role of community councils. (It was the Killeagh/Inch Community Council that had initially welcomed Merrell Dow.)

As Merrell Dow opened up an office in Youghal on 3 April and employed a local woman to staff it, Tom Wall of the Irish Congress of Trade Unions delivered a paper at a seminar in Cork and said that the ICTU welcomed Merrell Dow 'but would have preferred it if the company had set up in Ringaskiddy, the designated site for such industries'.

In the letters pages of the media, notably the *Cork Examiner* and *The Irish Times*, the debate on the chemical industry became an almost daily occurrence throughout the months of March and April. Patricia Cockburn was one of several local people who had hitherto not added her voice to the public opposition to the factory. She responded to a letter by environmental consultant Michael Bailey in *The Irish Times* and his remarks that the objectors were ignoring all professional scientific assessments, and that there would be no pollution of air, land or water. It was a question, Mrs Cockburn wrote, 'of which scientific experts you decide to believe'. There is also the question of employment.

> Most people in Youghal and the surrounding seaside area, 70 per cent of whom voted in a poll against the building of the factory, know very well that existing tourism creates far more jobs than even the management of Merrell Dow says that they will provide. It is obvious that nobody will want to bathe from a beach that might contain the effluent of pharmaceutical factory. Whether the water is polluted or not, the mere whisper of pharmaceutical effluent will send visitors elsewhere.

A letter from John Caffrey, who criticised *The Irish Times's* environmental correspondent for aligning the paper with the opponents of Merrell Dow, brought a 'chuckle' from the Womanagh group. Margaret Browne replied to state that 'to our frustration' the reporter, Frank McDonald, 'hardly wrote anything about this crucial issue at all' until recently. Jill and Bruce Bell wrote that they were puzzled by:

> Mr Caffrey's notions about the people of this region. We too elect a government and pay taxes. We also have families, cherish hopes for our children's future and are faced with the realities of unemployment and emigration. To claim that we would preserve east Cork from any taint of industrial development is complete nonsense; jobs are needed here more than in most areas of Ireland, but not 90 jobs which might threaten the livelihood and health of us all.

The Bells further stated that the objectors 'did not speak in ignorance or out of prejudice'. Anyone with commitment, they wrote, 'can, as we have found out, organise a pressure group. It is the very ordinary people here who have done so, and who have grappled with concepts of pharmaceutical factories, incinerator technology, boiler stack emissions, dye tests and much else.'

On the same day, 20 April, Neil Buckley, the Director General of the Federation of Irish Chemical Industries, wrote in yet another letter to *The Irish Times*, that:

> All industrial sectors are capable of inflicting serious damage, both in an ecological sense and in a human sense. The fact is, however, that shipping or aviation or agriculture, have not come to a halt because of unpredictable accidents in those areas. The public seems to be prepared to accept the risks involved in a huge range of activities. Are they prepared to accept the chemical industry?

Buckley had unwittingly perhaps hit the nail firmly on the head of his own industry. The letters to *The Irish Times* and other papers said as much: the majority who wrote in did not want the chemical industry in Ireland. Buckley, in later paragraphs, also identified two of the major problems that had repeatedly arisen in two decades of struggle between communities and the chemical industry.

> A concerned public must have reassurance. The industry is prepared to deal with any reasoned argument and any reasoned group of people who wish to know more about the industry and its operations and products. But, the public will not always believe a chemical company or indeed, any other industrial on its own. That's why local authorities in particular, have enforcement obligations. On occasions the industry has been accused of being non-compliant with local authorities. The industry will not defend non-compliance. The industry welcomes full implementation of environmental controls. If the suggestion, however, is that individual companies should make data available to every member of the public or every concerned group of people, we reject that. It would be impossible to carry on business in any sector if enterprises had to deal directly with every single concerned party.

Unfortunately for Buckley and the chemical industry, that was exactly what the communities wanted. Enforcement of the existing legislation was virtually non-existent. And the question of monitoring data was a thorny one. If the data was being compiled by the companies and by the local authorities, was cost the only reason it wasn't being made available to the public? Where the public was concerned there was no reason why it shouldn't be made available, especially if the companies had no indiscretions to hide. If, in fact, the chemical companies around Ireland never emitted any toxins into the air or into water then there was no problem. The communities, however, had only the local authorities and the industry itself to allay such fears and it has well been documented that the public did not trust it either. A week later Jim and Anne Enright put the argument in perspective:

> If aviation accidents were as frequent as the emissions of noxious odours in the Cork Harbour area, then aviation would have long ceased. If ships sank at the same rate there would be no ships now. Conversely, if the chemical industry succeeded in reducing its emission rate to the rate of the enforcement of environmental controls and planning regulations on the chemical industry, by local authorities and national government, nobody could have any complaints.

While the correspondence fuelled the debate in the media's letters pages, in east Cork it became clear that the area's vets were refusing to participate in the baseline study of animal health, one of An Bord Pleanála's conditions. Merrell Dow had announced that it would be conducted on six dairy farms, three beef farms and one stud farm and on 28 March had told the Killeagh Council that the public's views on the entire study were welcome. The farmers thought otherwise and by the middle of April several vets were confirming that, as farmers were refusing to allow their animals to be used for testing, most of the practices in the area had decided to abide by their clients' wishes.

Charles Haughey, the leader of Fianna Fáil, made arguably the most obvious statement about the conflict when he said on *RTE*, 'I do not know the solution, but I am determined that we shall find an answer' as the debate was elevated from the letters pages into the political arena to become a controversial election issue. A few days earlier, on 2 June, a group of objectors had delivered a copy of the MRBI study – which revealed that 56 per cent were against the factory with 29 per cent in favour – and a petition signed by 10,000 local residents calling for the project to be stopped to Haughey's Kinsealy home. By the weekend, following a packed public meeting in Youghal which heard the views of the major political parties, Haughey said that the Merrell Dow controversy was a test case: 'We have to try and reconcile the need for industrial development with the protection of the environment', he said, telling members of the Concerned Citizens of East Cork and West Waterford that he would personally look into the issue. It was a promise the objectors were not prepared to let him forget. Less than three weeks later the objectors heard their appeal against Merrell Dow had been turned down. 'It has to be one way or the other', Joan Vaughan insisted as she confirmed the Womanagh group would appeal the decision to the Supreme Court. 'Merrell Dow are not acceptable to us.'

On Monday 7 August the Womanagh group, insistent that something be done by their elected representatives, invited politicians to view the site of the proposed factory. Merrell Dow had said it would begin site construction work as soon as it accepted tenders for the work. Joan Vaughan, perhaps offering an ironic *fait accompli*, said the groups were particularly anxious that the public representatives saw for themselves the rich farming land the company had chosen for its factory and the Womanagh river where, the group told the politicians, the company would discharge 100,000 gallons of effluent a day. It was a view the group hoped many more would see in the coming months as several objectors threatened to prevent construction of the factory. 'I think there are now more people opposed to the factory,' said Colm Lopez, 'and I think there is an element in east Cork who will take up civil disobedience to overcome Merrell Dow. If people sit on the road singing "we will overcome" it is only living proof that democracy has died in Ireland.'

It was a view many of the objectors shared and some were inconsolable in their view of the future. 'Merrell Dow are taking my livelihood away from me', Lopez, who at the time ran a multi-provisions store on the main road at the back of Youghal strand, said.

> This summer the beach has been full because of the hot weather and that beach provides my livelihood. Merrell Dow are taking the beach away from people like myself who make a living from tourism, as they are taking the land away from the farmers and the bay from the fishermen. What am I supposed to do so? Sit around, draw the dole and look at the eyesore up the road. There are a lot of angry people about, angry with the politicians for lying. All we are getting from them is waffle. I don't think the politicians of Ireland

have the guts to stand up to people with money. When Ned O'Keeffe [one of two Fianna Fáil TD's in east Cork] recently insulted the protesters, in my opinion that is what the politicians of Ireland think of the electorate, that they are used simply for marking election slips.

(During the heat of this battle it was rumoured that Merrell Dow had offered incentives to some protesters, including Colm Lopez. 'They offered me a job running their canteen for a guaranteed five years, and IR£5,000, and I know I wasn't the only one.' Lopez is now working as a taxi driver in Youghal.)

Throughout August the protesters intensified their campaign, charging on three fronts in the courts, in the media and in public halls. Street demonstrations would follow, the protesters insisted. At another meeting in the Youghal community centre on 21 August the newly elected Green Party deputy, Roger Garland, told over 500 people that 'Merrell Dow can and will be beaten.' This industry, he declared, was not welcome anywhere in this country. Other deputies, in different ways, affirmed in their statements that the democratic wishes of the people should not be ignored. Two days later Merrell Dow agreed to the opening of a book of protest at their Youghal office and one by one the objectors signed their names under a simple declaration: 'We the undersigned, totally reject Merrell Dow's proposed plans to build a pharmaceutical factory in east Cork, or anywhere in Ireland.' The company's general manager, John Oberlatz, told reporters that he would listen 'to the citizens as long as we are in Ireland' and when asked how long that would be, he replied, 'About 50 years.'

It was for many objectors an arrogant statement, which appeared to confirm their belief that the company 'had declared war on the community'. The Youghal meeting earlier that week had sought a mandate from the community for direct action against the company. The sporadic pickets of the previous months would be replaced by concerted action, including a hunger strike at the site to prevent the bulldozers moving in. Mary Harney, the Minister of State for the Environment, had earlier told the Womanagh group that there would be no direct intervention by the government. But, behind the scenes and away from the controversy, both the company and the government were looking for a way out of the conflict that would save face. The first indications came with the news that Marion Laboratories' majority shareholders had agreed to Dow Chemicals' cash offer of $2.2 billion for their shares at $38 each on 25 August. Merrell Dow was to become Marion Merrell Dow, Inc. Coincidentally Oberlatz and Kennedy had met with O'Malley and Harney at the offices of the Department of Industry and Commerce on the day before, and while some of the residents knew that the government were in consultation, the contents of the 24 August meeting were not generally known.

Events suddenly escalated. In the United States a meeting of the company's senior executives agreed that the Killeagh project should not proceed. In Cork, information about the company that would begin site construction was hard to get; something was happening. In the United States, a few days after Merrell Dow's meeting with the government ministers, a decision was made by the company's senior executives. The Killeagh project was to be scrapped. A week later on a dreary autumnal day, the first Monday in September, the objectors were told the news; suddenly everything was extremely sunny, but the controversy hadn't ended.

Six days later in the wake of the celebrations by the objectors, the *Sunday Tribune* revealed that Charles Haughey had demanded that the company delay building its factory 'until all legal avenues of local protest' had been exhausted and until a new environmental protection agency had been established. This ultimatum, the paper claimed, had been delivered at the 24 August meeting. A government politician told the paper that the Merrell Dow conflict was 'a huge political problem'. The people of the area 'were determined to fight it all the way. All it would have taken was a few people in jail or on hunger strike and we would have had real problems.' The following day Industry minister Des O'Malley refuted the story. The company, he said, had 'been agreeable to his suggestions' but that no ultimatum had been given. However it was revealed that O'Malley had asked the company to wait until after the Supreme Court hearings and until the EPA had been established before turning the sod in Killeagh. Merrell Dow, according to Fred Plagens, could not agree to this but he told *The Irish Times* he could not confirm that this had been said because he was not at the meeting. The government and the company have remained vague about what was actually said and agreed upon at the August meeting. The IDA and Merrell Dow also remained adamant in their stance that it was a 'business decision' that had precipitated the departure from Killeagh and not the objectors' demands. But that didn't matter to the objectors: Merrell Dow was gone and victory was theirs.

When the Hanrahan family successfully appealed their action against Merck Sharp and Dohme in the Supreme Court in July 1988 it was said that this David and Goliath struggle galvanised the east Cork community into massed opposition against Merrell Dow. Some observers claimed that the initial arrogance of the company and the insouciance of the IDA and the local authority rubbed a lot of people up the wrong way. Critics of the campaign against Merrell Dow said that the rich farmers funded the Womanagh group, which in turn was able to lobby the media, environmentalists and politicians and challenge the company at the Bord Pleanála appeal hearing and in the High Court. The impetus for the campaign was at once much more simple and much more complex. At the kernel of the struggle was a grassroots resistance to successive governments' dependence on corporates to improve the Irish economy, provide good well-paid jobs, stem the flow of emigration and favourably redress the nation's balance of payments.

East Cork had all of Ireland's indigenous industry in plentiful supply: agriculture; dairy farming augments the country's numerous cheese making processes and organic produce is the speciality, with fish, at many restaurants and hotels; mariculture and tourism (An Bord Fáilte claimed in 1989 that foreign tourists to Cork and Waterford contributed IR£80 million per year and seasonal employment in tourism is as high as 8,000). 'Ireland is a package,' An Bord Fáilte stated in an April 1989 report on developing Irish tourism, 'and any doubts about its image abroad would affect the national tourism potential and thereby threaten the livelihood of many of the 100,000 or so people associated with the industry.'

In August 1988 Youghal Irish Transport and General Workers Union secretary Nicholas Parker had issued a statement advising against any concerted opposition to Merrell Dow:

> The east Cork region is crying out for new job-intensive industries and should current developments lead to a decision by Merrell Dow not to set up operations in Killeagh it would have seriously adverse repercussions for the region's future industrial prospects.

The IDA said the factory would have generated at least IR£4 million a year in relative terms in the form of wages and raw materials. Approximately 300 construction jobs were lost to an industry where the take home pay was as high as IR£250 a week in the late 1980s. Merrell Dow would have spent IR£15 million on construction, and both the IDA and the company said that a Cork firm would have been given the tender.

On the afternoon of Monday 4 September 1989 the Concerned

Citizens of East Cork and West Waterford sent a one-page statement to the media. A few lines from the end it said:

> It is absolutely vital that more jobs are created for the people of our region, and we urge the government to bring in industry. But it must be clean industry, compatible with the existing farming, fishing and tourism. The people will welcome sensible development with open arms.

When the Progressive Democrats' Mary Harney had visited Killeagh she told the objectors that 'the matter had been handled badly'. It wasn't the first time and it appeared it wouldn't be the last either. The relevance of the community opposition to Merrell Dow to Irish life and politics was never recognised, and much of this has to do with the positions Irish academics, journalists and writers take towards the state's economic and industrial policies. According to Peace a number of social anthropologists have argued the need for ethnographies on the impact of globalisation on local communities. Peace's study, *A Time of Reckoning*, is such a book and in his conclusion he makes two politically cogent points.

> The first is that whereas political economists tend to portray transnational corporations as having untrammelled power to dominate local contexts in their search for profit, this is rarely achieved in reality. However inexperienced or vulnerable populations might appear, they often prove willing to contest the unequal terms which foreign enterprises try to impose.
>
> The second point is that however modest the results of such ethnographic investigations, their detail provides a challenge to those macro sociologists and political scientists who try to account for the complexities of local level community action with *a priori* analytic labels and categories. This is a recurrent tendency in the literature on social movements, frequently erasing the intricacies and refinements of individuals constructing their own projects of social action.

Did Merrell Dow give up because of the community opposition? At the time the IDA said it was a business decision. In 2000 Padraic White, IDA managing director between 1981 and 1990, said: 'Local hostility to the project was so great the proposal was abandoned.'

4   Cork: Poison Harbour

It is a matter of public opinion – we're trying to police the operations of these plants and I think we do it to a satisfactory degree, to accepted standards. We won't go out of our way to change the standards, that is where public opinion comes into play and I would hope that it is informed public opinion.

Iain Maclean

Cork harbour has always had a colourful history. Oppression and resistance are bywords that echo down the years and can be heard in the shoreline villages almost as old as the harbour itself. For centuries the harbour was the Irish home of the British naval fleet. Today Camden (Meagher) Fort stands stoutly as a monument or monstrosity, depending on your political view, to the wayward insecurity of the British authorities who commissioned the monolithic feat of architecture and engineering to protect the fleet in the years when maritime firepower was limited and enemy ships needed to navigate the narrow channel into Cork harbour to launch an effective attack. The British had every right to be paranoid. In those days their entire fleet was anchored in Cork. The fort was ambitious and took years to build. By the time it was completed naval warfare had rendered it obsolete. An enemy had no need to negotiate the narrow mouth of the harbour and be subjected to heavy bombardment from the fort. It could anchor off the coast and lob shells freely onto the unprotected fleet. It never happened and the fort is a reminder of how wasteful warfare can be. But the fort, derelict and impressively embedded into the side of Camden Hill on the harbour's west side, is still there, its ownership transferred in the 1980s from the Irish Department of Defence to the local authority.

Cork and its harbour achieved perhaps its first strategic significance during the height of the Elizabethan wars when the city was virtually destroyed. Swiftly rebuilt, by the eighteenth century Cork harbour became the centre of a maritime economy which boosted 'a cash economy tied to that of England by trade, traffic of people and growth of credit', that, the historian F. S. L. Lyons wrote, epitomised 'an outward looking community which was a part, even if a peripheral part, of a wider world'. Although Lyons referred generally to Ireland's maritime economy which existed 'mainly along the eastern coastal fringe from Belfast to Cork (with offshoots in Limerick and Galway)', Cork harbour served a dual function as a strategic deep water port adequate for both commercial and military vessels. Until Belfast became Ireland's premier port in the mid to late nineteenth century, overtaking Dublin in volume of trade, Cork harbour's southern most position made it irresistible. Even after the British withdrew following the war of independence, the British demagogue Winston Churchill lamented the loss of such a strategic port during the early naval skirmishes of the 1939–45 war.

The present port of Cork is a sheltered deepwater harbour with its seaward limits extending to an imaginary line drawn between Power Head on the eastern approach and Cork Head to the west. Like most Irish estuaries, Cork is secluded and deeply indented. To reach the port on the river Lee in Cork city a vessel must navigate twelve miles from the harbour entrance around Whitegate to the east and Ringaskiddy to the west before reaching a long narrow channel that opens out between Passage West and Marino Point. A sharp turn west brings shipping traffic past the Douglas estuary and Little Island to the north and finally past the Tivoli docks to the port of Cork.

To the sailor entering the harbour for the first time the view on a clear day hints only of heavy industry, the Whitegate oil refinery prominent on the eastern shore. The view, from the top of Camden Hill on the western shore, is clearer – a magnificent panorama of the harbour, that, on a dull day, hides from the visitor the factories of controversy. Spike Island, with its Irish-style penitentiary, is in the foreground, Currabinny Wood obscures most of Ringaskiddy and Monkstown on the western shore but Cóbh to the north and Whitegate are visible. Camden Hill is on the rise above Crosshaven. On a crisp, cloud-free day the chemical industry's presence, plumes willowing into the air, is unavoidable, yet below in the village of Crosshaven the view is free of industry, idyllic almost, Currabinny Wood obscuring those less salubrious sights of the harbour.

Out in the sea, slow-moving commercial shipping provides further evidence of the industrialisation of Cork harbour – and of the chemical industry. In November 1988, as the harbour's communities began to put pressure on Cork County Council to do something about the pollution from the chemical factories in their midst, volunteers aboard a Greenpeace ship, the *Moby Dick*, challenged the operations of one of those chemical corporates. The Greenpeace activists chained themselves to the anchor of the Pfizer dumpship *Roches Point* as it cruised out of Cork harbour into the open sea, where the chemical company had permission from the Department of the Marine to dump an annual load of 1.1m tonnes of organic waste, 15 miles off the Irish coast. Greenpeace claimed that this was 'the largest sea dump operation in the north east Atlantic' and they regarded it as a 'major environmental problem'. Greenpeace argued that 'in the context of the Irish government's wish to be involved with the North Sea Conference declarations', the Pfizer sea dump operation contravenes both the spirit of the precautionary principle and the North Sea states' acceptance as matters of principle that 'as from January 1, 1989, no material shall be dumped in the North Sea unless there are no practical alternatives on land'. The Greenpeace action in November 1988, staged ostensibly to protest against the dumping operation and to emphasise that Ireland should concur with the January 1989 directive, also heralded a Greenpeace preliminary report on water pollution in Cork harbour and the offshore sea dumping. Although the report dealt with industrial effluent and domestic sewage it was Greenpeace's revelations about Pfizer that upset the industry and not surprisingly the company itself.

Hugh O'Connor, Pfizer's managing director at the time, accused Greenpeace of 'reckless behaviour' and of illegally boarding the *Roches Point* for 'publicity purposes alone', which contributed 'nothing whatever to the point at issue'. O'Connor said he was:

> completely satisfied that sea disposal is an environmentally attractive mechanism for dealing with our particular type of non-toxic organic waste. Environmental concerns would only arise were the capacity of the receiving area of sea inadequate to accommodate the volume of material disposed. We know that this is not the case with our operation and independent surveys have confirmed it. In such circumstances disposal at sea represents the most natural of all possible mechanisms for recycling this material and sensational behaviour by Greenpeace cannot alter that simple fact.

Was this 'most natural of all possible mechanisms for recycling this material' chosen, Greenpeace wondered, because it was the cheapest? The Pfizer Chemical Company provided the answer themselves. A Pfizer Europe inter-office memorandum, dated 29 March 1977, highlighting a Ringaskiddy effluent study, was sent anonymously to Greenpeace. In its Cork harbour report Greenpeace announced:

> The leaked document clearly indicates that sea dumping was chosen because it was the cheaper option and could be considered in Ireland because of the 'unadvanced state of legislation'. Information Greenpeace obtained this year [1988] from Pfizer in the United States indicates that the alternative production process for the production of citric acid entitled *The Citcon Process* is not only available to the company but produces a saleable item – a food supplement for cattle and horses.

The 1977 Pfizer study highlighted the problem the Ringaskiddy factory had with its effluent. At maximum output per day the factory would need to dispose of 80 tonnes of liquid effluent and 3 tonnes of solid effluent per ton of critic acid produced. 'The BOD load alone is equivalent to the total BOD load generated by a population equal to the whole of the Republic of Ireland', the report stated, and added that it was a 'major environmental problem'.

An Taisce certainly saw it that way in 1972 when Pfizer applied for outline planning permission to discharge 136,000 kg of effluent per day into the harbour. This was ten times the amount originally agreed in 1969 when Pfizer started building in Ringaskiddy. 'They were producing an equivalent BOD of two and a half million people', Philip Mullally, Cork chair of An Taisce, recalled. The conservationist organisation, which had a high profile in Cork in the early 1970s, also believed it would damage marine life but, as Mullally stressed, it would have pre-empted the harbour's capacity to take industrial effluent. The council, however, gave planning permission and An Taisce appealed. During the four-day public hearing in October 1972 Pfizer claimed that the costs involved in treating this effluent – a capital cost of IR£13.3 million and annual running costs of IR£1.1 million – would make it uneconomic to expand production in Ringaskiddy, and threatened to pull out of Ireland if it did not get their way. Mullally said:

> Pfizer's were very hot and very sore about it because their managing director had a very high profile. He identified

strongly with the Chamber of Commerce, the trade unions, the bishop, that sort of situation and he made us out to be bad boys.... There were three of us in An Taisce, Maire Mulcahy of University College Cork, Eamon Dalton, the chief engineer in the Cork Corporation and myself, who decided that it was an issue that should be tackled.

In 1970 Pfizer had commissioned a Boston, USA, company of consultants to survey Cork harbour, to gain data that could be 'used as a guide in locating trial positions for a future Pfizer outfall discharge point' and to study the harbour's assimilative capacity. Mullally learned about the report, obtained a copy from Pfizer, and then 'discovered serious flaws in the reasoning':

We effectively reduced [the survey] to incoherency. There were serious flaws in the logic of some of the conclusions they had drawn, even from their own information. The hearing got under way in the County Hall and we were given permission by the [planning] inspector to carry out our own defence. It went on for several days and during the process two thing happened. Firstly, the city authorities decided to disown Eamon Dalton and make it clear that he was acting in a private capacity, which was correct. Secondly, there were screaming headlines in the *Echo* and *Examiner*; 'Pfizer Pull Out – Jobs Loss' and 'Threat By An Taisce To Jobs', the usual stuff. That was denying the fact that Pfizer had made an IR£30m investment already, so we rubbished that as complete nonsense. The argument was about protecting the environment – how much were Pfizer going to pay? So we positioned ourselves as having a serious professional input and secondly as taking the underdog situation, taking on the giant Goliath of Pfizer. So the publicity began to swing against them, particularly when the government acted and even after the Pfizer managing director, Platt, claimed he would drink the water from the Pfizer effluent.

During the hearing An Taisce accused the local authorities and the corporate of collusion which would reduce planning permission to a mere formality and 'would reduce the people of County Cork to the status of fools'.

1972 had been a bad year for Pfizer. It had attempted to inciner-
ate its toxic effluent, from its Organic Synthesis Plant (OSP), but this
led to objections from residents in the Monkstown area, who
complained about thick black smoke and noxious fumes, and it was
discontinued after a couple of months. Pfizer's Ringaskiddy effluent
study of 1977 recognised this and described the incineration as 'oper-
ationally unsatisfactory'. There was, the study revealed, a 'practical
alternative, using a cocktail of bacteria especially developed for
organic plant effluent', which it called 'bio-oxidation'.

Greenpeace have argued that Pfizer could easily have abandoned its sea dumping operation, before being forced to by legislation, and adopted other methods. Bob Edwards, the Greenpeace
toxics campaigner in Ireland, also questioned Hugh O'Connor's
statement that the Pfizer biogas project, converting its waste into an
energy source, owed 'nothing to any environmental concerns at sea
disposal and everything to our desire to reduce the very substantial
cost of that operation'. The 1977 study clearly showed why Pfizer
used the sea dump operation:

> In the case of our existing methods of effluent disposal, i.e.
> Citcon at Groton, Weston (bio-oxidation) at Southport and
> sea disposal at Ringaskiddy, the choice is clearly in favour of
> sea disposal as the future method at Ringaskiddy as both the
> capital cost and annual running costs, both on a cash and
> book basis, are less than half of the other two alternatives.

Pfizer is now the dominant chemical corporate in Cork harbour and
its threat to pull out is hardly remembered. But one corporate did
pull out, after a long and bitter battle in the years when the chemical industry was facing opposition everywhere in Ireland.
Raybestos Manhattan came to Ireland in the mid-1970s desperate
to escape tough new legislation and regulation on the US asbestos
industry.

While Raybestos Manhattan, IDA and other state officials
denied that Raybestos's move to Ireland was an example of the
export of hazard, connected with the difficulties faced by producers
of asbestos products in the United States, the former economic
attaché for the US Embassy in Ireland, Kenneth McGuire, said that
while market factors may have been important considerations for
Raybestos, the relocation factor probably cannot be entirely
dismissed in the Raybestos case.

In this environment the IDA's handling of Raybestos was discreet. In September 1975 the IDA announced a IR£4 million investment by Raybestos Manhattan for its advance factory in Ovens, County Cork. From the beginning the IDA trod carefully: the planning application for the site appeared in the *Irish Independent*, a national paper, rather than the *Cork Examiner*, then a local paper, and the application did not specify that the factory would be using asbestos. The IDA regional manager said the factory would be 'clean'. Planning permission was granted on 22 December 1975, close enough to Christmas for no one to have been paying much attention, and the period for appealing the planning permission was over before local residents discovered Raybestos Manhattan would be processing and emitting asbestos, a highly toxic pollutant and confirmed mass killer.

In his action in the High Court against Raybestos Manhattan, Patrick McFadden sought a declaration that planning permission granted to the IDA by Cork County Council for the Raybestos factory was bad on the grounds that the newspaper notice setting out the IDA application was defective insofar as it failed to fully disclose the purpose of the factory. During the hearing in November 1977, counsel for Mr McFadden said:

> The manner in which the planning application was brought by the IDA led one to believe that it was a calculated effort on the part of the IDA to deceive the local people so that they would not be aware of the nature of the application and would not cause any trouble. The planning notice had been published in the *Irish Independent* which was not circulated in the area. It should have been published in the *Cork Examiner*.

Having lost the opportunity to oppose the construction, local opposition first focused on the factory's dumping plans. Much of the initial opposition came from Beverley, an upmarket housing estate on the southeastern side of the factory. On 15 July 1976, Ovens residents objected to a planning application by William O'Brien Ltd, a waste disposal company, for an asbestos dump in a quarry at Knockanemore, a mile from the Raybestos Manhattan factory site. When Cork County Council's planning committee met later that month it agreed to hold further consultations with local residents. In August Raybestos announced a change in its proposed dumping method: instead of dumping wet asbestos, Raybestos announced it would encapsulate the asbestos waste in concrete pellets. At the same time the company announced it would spend IR£225,000 on installing a special air filter in the factory.

The council gave permission for the dump, the residents said they would appeal and Raybestos decided to abandon the Knock-anemore dump 'in the interests of community harmony'. As a result the IDA began what was to become the first step in the desperate local search for a toxic dump site.

On 1 December 1976 the IDA applied for permission for an asbestos waste dump on land owned by it at Currabinny. Opposition also began to mount among concerned locals, an opposition which manifested itself both individually and through the Ringask-iddy Residents' Association, formed two years previously without thought of involvement in any controversy over previous planning applications for industrial projects in the area. While the population could understand trading off pollution for jobs, they saw no advantage to the locality in being the site of a toxic dump. Concern was also focused on the fact that Ringaskiddy School was within 400 yards of the planned asbestos dump site.

By February 1977 the opposition to Raybestos developed on two fronts: in Ovens against the factory, in Ringaskiddy against the dump. The opposition to Raybestos was unusual in that it involved the formation of an autonomous women's group, in which up to 30 women became involved. This women's group was set up because of dissatisfaction with the lack of action by the male-dominated Ovens committee. One member of the group said: 'We were very frustrated that nothing was being done in the local area against the factory.... The men's committee was waffling on twice a week and doing nothing.' The women's group's orientation was towards action: 'There was no way we could beat them in the courts. We felt we could only do it through local pressure, using the media and direct action', a member of the group recalled. The group picketed IDA offices in Cork, Cork County Council's headquarters and the Raybestos site, and then went to Dublin to picket the US Embassy and the Dáil.

Opposition continued to grow, but on 28 February 1977 the council voted 27 to 17 to grant planning permission. In response to the decision the Ringaskiddy Residents' Association issued an eight-point plan of opposition:

Eight Point Programme
Having considered all the developments relating to the

planning application for an asbestos waste dump at Barnahely, Ringaskiddy, Co. Cork, we outline here under an
Eight Point Programme to ensure that this is not imposed
on the community.

1. Any approval by Cork County Council will be
   appealed to the new Appeals Authority set up by the
   Minister for Local Government;

2. Should approval be granted contrary to the majority
   decision of Cork County Council, section 4 of the
   Planning Act will be invoked;

3. Ratepayers in the above areas will withhold payment
   of rates and we will recommend similar action to the
   many other communities who have publicly supported
   us;

4. Pickets will be placed on Connolly Hall by trade union
   members resident in our areas whose wishes were not
   represented by the current action of the Irish Trade and
   General Workers Union;

5. Pickets will also be placed on the IDA offices, the
   County Hall and premises of other bodies supporting
   the action;

6. Contractors involved in the transport of the waste and
   the site excavation will also be picketed;

7. In the event of any attempt to commence dumping
   we will recommend that the parents withdraw their
   children from the National Schools of Shanbally and
   Ringaskiddy, in view of the proximity of these schools
   to the site;

8. We will take any further steps necessary to ensure that
   the wishes of the community will be complied with. We
   trust commonsense will prevail and that the Authorities
   will heed the massive number of bona fide objectors to
   the application.

On 3 March, 250 people met in the community hall under the
auspices of the Ringaskiddy group and approved the plan of opposition. By that stage the Ringaskiddy group's opposition also had
the support of Crosshaven, Currabinny and Carrigaline Community Associations, Cóbh and Middleton Urban Councils and
Passage West Town Commissioners. At the end of March however
An Taisce, Cork, decided not to object to the granting of planning

permission. On Friday 22 March, John Carroll of the Irish Transport and General Workers Union (ITGWU) called for a sworn public inquiry into the possible health hazards of the Raybestos factory, though also saying Raybestos must be allowed to go ahead. The ITGWU County Cork organiser, Hugh O'Callaghan, responded that he was convinced that the project would go ahead, though an appeal might help to quell current concern.

The decision of the council was inevitably appealed to An Bord Pleanála – the hearing taking place in June. The hearing revealed that Raybestos proposed to dump 400 pounds of asbestos in Barnahely per week. Three months later An Bord Pleanála granted planning permission for the dump, subject to 18 conditions. This finally freed Raybestos to begin production. Raybestos's planning permission for the factory was conditional on having an available and operating dump.

The local residents were bitterly disappointed with the decision. They threatened to withdraw their 186 children from the Ringaskiddy and Shanbally national schools. They continued to argue that the Barnahely site was unsuitable, because it was frequently waterlogged and flooded during winter. The Ringaskiddy group was very doubtful of the adequacy of stringent planning conditions in restraining companies' operations based on their own experience with Penn Chemicals:

> The residents are obviously very cynical about the stringency of planning conditions for industry generally in their area and yesterday they pointed out that in a nearby factory, Penn Chemicals Ltd, are in breach of the planning regulations daily since they commenced production of a new wonder drug at the beginning of the year. Mr Twomey explained that it had been specified before starting operations that no obnoxious smelling gases were to escape into the atmosphere but in the manufacture of the new drug the company he alleged had been allowing methyl mercaptan, a highly toxic gas with an extremely disagreeable odour, to escape into the atmosphere.

The campaign had already cost the locals IR£2,000 and a fighting fund was started to enable them to take a High Court case if necessary. At the end of the month, Raybestos and the IDA applied for a temporary injunction to prevent a picket on the dump site. In response to the injunction, residents of Barnahely maintained their 24-hour watch on the site. Members of the picket refused to accept copies of the injunction issued against them.

The struggle in Ovens intensified again in November when 200 people picketed the factory. Carrying pickets reading 'ASBESTOS KILLS' and 'NO SURRENDER', the protesters picketed the main road from 8 a.m. to 11 a.m. 'Our demonstration is more to alert public opinion than to block the entrance. This is not an attempt to stop production at the factory', Rosemary Cubitt of the Ovens Womens' Action Group said.

Pressure continued on the community to end its resistance, Raybestos claiming it had lost orders of IR£1 million over the previous six months, while another source claimed the corporate was suffering from a 'crisis of consumer confidence'. The financial health of the corporate was considered more important than the community's concern over the health of its children. Another legal struggle by the Ovens residents failed when the High Court refused an injunction to Patrick J. McFadden, a pharmaceutical representative of Beverley, Ovens, to refrain Raybestos Manhattan from carrying out any process using asbestos.

Four days after the court judgement, Raybestos' managing director, Ted Deane, accompanied by twelve Gardai, met a human barrier of 60 men, women and children when he attempted to gain access to the Barnahely dump, all of whom refused to accept copies of the interlocutory injunction. When the protesters refused to move, Gardai took the names and addresses of the protesters.

The tension increased further on 16 November when the IDA issued a warning that those picketing the dump could face jail for defying the High Court injunction. The IDA threatened to return to the High Court with a list of names of those defying the injunction. The statement emphasised that the IDA and Raybestos Manhattan were operating jointly in this matter. The following month negotiations between the residents and the IDA led to a compromise, allowing interim dumping at Barnahely until an alternative permanent dump site was found.

By May 1979, when Raybestos made its first attempt to dump at Barnahely, the compromise had apparently failed. Raybestos's first attempt to dump at the site was blocked by residents. On Monday 15 May, however, Raybestos's second attempt was successful when 25 Gardai brutally forced a way through a human barrier of women and children to allow Raybestos's waste onto the site. Some 200 protesters, including 80 schoolchildren between the ages of seven and twelve, had assembled at the site to block the dumping. Local people were amazed at the violence of the Gardai. Nine people were treated in hospital and one ten-year-old child was detained overnight.

Ringaskiddy Association's chairman, Ted Forde, commented: 'It's clear now we live in a police state.' The local newspaper reported:

> The confrontation was extremely violent, reminiscent of a street battle in Derry or Belfast, and introduced an ugly new element to the asbestos row. Children were knocked to the ground, screaming and crying as the Guards broke through the picket line. Women who were knocked down later said they were punched and kicked by Gardai. A man on a crutch was thrown to the ground. Other men engaged in close hand-to-hand scuffles with the Gardai.... A big rock was thrown by a man at the front of Mr Deane's Mercedes. It shattered the window but the glass held and he escaped injury.

Deane was quoted in the local paper describing the incident as 'an awful shock'. He was not the only one. Speaking at a meeting attended by 400 people in the local village hall, local primary teacher Donal O'Connor said children should not be used in future protests. 'Children have been used up to this point because we felt it showed a non-violent style.'

The acting committee, which previously had consisted of four women to each man, was dramatically changed. As the committee sat down to meet, the call went out for women to leave the hall, and the male members of the action committee to remain on. The results of the change in gender were immediately obvious. That night the main gate of the dump was destroyed, the chain link fence around it torn down and the concrete posts lining the entrance to the dump smashed. That day Raybestos had succeeded in dumping some 100 bags of waste. Some 30 sacks were taken by six cars to the factory 25 miles away and thrown into it over the main gate at 3 a.m. Other bags of the waste were thrown about the entrance to the dump. Women residents continued to picket the dump and denied all knowledge of the overnight incidents.

James McLoughlin, a senior vice-president with Raybestos Manhattan in the US, said it saw the scenes at the dump site as simply another obstacle on its rocky road to success in Ireland. While admitting that the US corporate's board had discussed winding up the Irish operation a number of times, he emphasised his gratitude and that of the board for the help and cooperation received from the Irish government and the IDA. The following day *The Irish Times* reported that 711 ex-workers of Raybestos Manhattan in New Jersey in the United States were suing the company and its asbestos supplier, Johns Manville, for $2 million each in workers' compensation and punitive damages awards. One year after the New Jersey factory closed, Raybestos Manhattan began talks with the IDA about setting up in Ireland, but a senior Raybestos Manhattan vice-president 'categorically denied' any connection between the two events.

Following the violent confrontation the dump was closed. The IDA and the residents began negotiations again which resulted in another agreement to allow the short-term use of the dump. The agreement included the arrangement that a local resident should supervise and inspect all dumping operations. But in the end the agreement only allowed the local resident to inspect the security of the chain link fence around the dump. One resident explained the factors behind the agreement:

> The agreement when it was signed was full of loopholes. First people really believed that it was going to be a temporary dump. [John] Gannon, the executive director of the IDA, was made to repeat himself to every woman man and child at the public meeting in Ringaskiddy it would be 'a matter of months not a year'. I suppose people were afraid too. We'd fought hard all day and night guarding the dump and the weather wasn't too good to us either. People offered us support, financial and whatnot, but we needed physical support, we're a very small community and in a way we were left on our own. The crunch came when they moved in the police. People didn't expect such violence and brutality. The women and the kids had been really badly beaten. One child was flung over the eight foot fence and he was in and out of hospital four times. Another child's teeth were knocked in. The county council had given permission for a 70 acre toxic waste dump in Ringaskiddy on part of the 1,000 acres owned by the IDA and there was that threat over people's heads. Part of the agreement was that if we accepted

the asbestos waste temporarily, there would never be a toxic waste dump in the Monkstown parish. But we realised later that for the IDA and the county council the dump was there to stay till they found another.

The opposition to Raybestos appeared to die down, only to return with a vengeance the following year. The first attack on Raybestos came yet again from Ringaskiddy residents, in April 1980. While the agreement between the IDA and Ringaskiddy residents over interim storage seemed to settle the dumping issue, the residents had accepted the agreement only after they had been physically attacked by the forces of the state, and the resources and energy of the community had been exhausted.

Their naiveté in believing the IDA's promise that the dumping would only be short term soon became apparent as other communities resisted proposed dumping in their areas and the Nohoval farmers began their long and eventually successful campaign in the courts. The Ringaskiddy Residents' Association monitored the dumping operation however and on April Fool's Day 1980 Michael Linehan of the Ringaskiddy group announced that he had found exposed sacks of asbestos waste at the Barnahely dump. He employed a professional photographer to photograph the exposed bags and other serious irregularities in the dumping: these included reject brake pads lying exposed on the site, as well as a container which still contained substantial amounts of asbestos.

The following day the IDA advised Raybestos to cease dumping in Ringaskiddy for the moment. The company began storing the waste at its factory site. On 3 April Raybestos denied in a statement that any irregularities had taken place. The Chief Environmental Officer for County Cork, Liam Mullins, refused to travel to Ringaskiddy to meet the residents 'to be harangued' but said he was prepared to meet the residents to discuss the alleged irregularities:

> I am quite willing to meet the residents for talks. It is obvious that we should have talks but I am not willing to be told that the talks can only take place at one location and I am not willing to accept an invitation to a slanging match. I want a sensible venue and a sensible discussion.

The following day Ringaskiddy residents upped the ante by announcing they intended going to the High Court to seek an order enforcing the asbestos dumping regulations. The Ringaskiddy group's solicitor, Charles Hennessy, pointed out that they contemplated taking proceedings 'under the Local Government Planning and Development Act, 1976, which states that the High Court may, on application from any person, by order, prohibit the continuance of an unauthorised use of land when a breach of the planning conditions occur'.

The Ringaskiddy Residents' Association also intended to meet council officials. As a result of these meetings early in June Cork County Council began steps to take legal proceedings against Raybestos for the violation of the dumping regulations. In return for the council taking proceedings against the company the residents deferred their own legal action and allowed the dump to reopen.

On 9 June, in a hearing before the High Court, new safety procedures were agreed by both Raybestos and Cork County Council. These new procedures were drawn up by the company itself, according to the council's senior counsel. Included in these procedures were the keeping of a logbook of each container load of waste, notification of the council in advance of the dumping schedule so that officials could inspect dumping operations and a prohibition on containers, empty or full, being left overnight on the dumping site.

Raybestos was found by the High Court to have violated six conditions of its planning permission. According to H. J. Leonard, who studied the impact of the chemical industry on Irish society, although:

> Raybestos officials claimed that they were strictly observing all agreed upon dumping procedures, on-site inspection provided clear evidence to the contrary. Asbestos pellets and waste brake pads were strewn about the site unburied and a large waste bin left on the site was covered with substantial quantities of asbestos dust.

The court heard that when the Deputy County Engineer inspected the dump site on 15 April, he found four bags of pelleted asbestos exposed on the site, pellets scattered on part of the site and for 70 yards along the access road and one pellet at the entrance gate to the site.

While the compromise by the corporate seemed likely to settle the waste issue for the immediate future, a new threat to Raybestos's operations entered the scene – a threat that was finally to end Raybestos's operations in Ireland. While Raybestos had succeeded in carrying on despite the intense opposition of two communities, it was unable to survive the actions of its own workers fighting the hazards of asbestos at the point of production. Little problem had been expected from that workforce: it was young, unorganised and naive. There were no older workers in the factory and therefore no tradition of workplace organisation and militancy for the workforce to call on.

Their working conditions were described as follows:

> Blue overalls, no hairnets, they didn't shower before they left work. They went from the workplace into the canteen, they sat and opened their lunch boxes in their working clothes. They went home in the evening ... and they didn't necessarily wash when they went home either. So whatever fibres were flying around they would have been carrying.

When a spill of asbestos occurred shortly before 3 a.m. on Tuesday 27 May, workers stopped work immediately. A meeting of the workers was called in the locker room by the shop steward at which it was decided that no one would return to the contaminated area. Management then asked the workers to leave the premises and pickets were placed by the 27 night-shift workers. The pickets were not passed by the 30 workers arriving for the morning shift. Speaking on behalf of the workers, one said the dust was so thick in the air it could be seen. 'This is not the first time this had occurred', he said. 'It has happened on four or five other occasions.'

On Tuesday morning, management met with Irish Transport and General Workers Union (ITGWU) officials. The officials asked the workers to lift the pickets, which they did. The afternoon shift, however, refused to go into work. A mass meeting of the Raybestos workers was then held at which workers agreed to return to work after being assured by union representatives that a safety investigation would take place at the factory and the findings would be made available as a precondition for a return to work. A Department of Labour inspector visited the factory on 28 May. According to Raybestos the inspector spent the day in the factory 'giving it a top to bottom going over'. The company also described the spillage as a minor one, and said that ten days previously an IIRS/Eolas monitoring test had found emission levels from the factory to be satisfactory. A further meeting between management and union was promised over issues still outstanding such as the pay lost by the workers while they were on strike.

This militancy on the part of the workers did not spring from nowhere. Working conditions at the factory were claimed to be atrocious. According to one worker:

> This wasn't the first time the pin in the tower blew out, it used to happen one in every six mixes. Safety is a joke ... some men don't have dust-proof overalls. They work in ordinary blue boiler suit things ... there's a poster beside one of the machines – 'DON'T DISREGARD REPLACE THE GUARD' it says ... you have to laugh – there are no guards, they were taken off the machines to up the produc-tion, they only put them on when the big bosses are coming over from the States to inspect the place – the place really gets cleaned up then. Two men nearly lost their fingers with the grinding machine. You can't wear gloves – there is no grip ... there is so much dust around the grinding machines – one of them caught fire five times during the past three months ... then there is a fellow going around with a bottle of water. That is supposed to be the sprinkler system for wetting down the dust. The dust is diabolical – at one stage you could be fired for using a sweeping brush and not a vacuum. Now it's all brushes. Two weeks ago we were given hand brushes to dust the machines in front of us. Another thing is the heat – the temperature at the presses is around 150 degrees ... you just couldn't wear a mask there.

Still, the previous spills of asbestos in the factory had not led to any action by the workers. The main reason for this was that neither management nor the union had gone out of their way to provide workers with this information. Prior to the spill in May, however, the workers were provided with information on the hazards of asbestos by the Cork Noxious Industry Action Group – a group organised by political and ecological activists drawn mainly from the anti-nuclear movement. This group distributed leaflets to the Raybestos workers warning of the dangers posed by exposure to asbestos, leafleting both in the morning and the evening to catch the different shifts. The group later took part in discussions with the Raybestos workers and continued to share information with the workers by producing a series of leaflets on the hazards of asbestos and on the need for workers to organise autonomously from the trade union in order to defend their health and safety.

The Cork Noxious Industry Action Group was a group formed mainly by activists within the anti-nuclear movement who wished to extend the opposition to nuclear power to other toxic process industries and who had organised several workshops on toxic industry and toxic dumping at the Second Anti-Nuclear Power Show at Carnsore in 1979. This group, as well as the anti-nuclear movement itself, was strongly influenced by members of Revolutionary Struggle, an extreme left-wing group which mixed neo-Marxist economic analysis with traditional republican ideology and was strongly influenced itself by the revolutionary movement in Italy and, to a lesser extent, France, at the time. There were also anarchist influences within the movement generally and in its anti-toxic outgrowth. Membership of the Cork Noxious Industry Action Group overlapped with the Cork Anti-Nuclear Group. Sue Baker wrote:

> [Both] had no formal membership, no executive or committee structures, no elected secretary, treasurer or chairperson. Members were free to engage in any activities, whether using the name of the group or autonomously, and to adopt any tactic (violent or otherwise) as they saw fit. The only condition was that those involved opposed nuclear power (CAN) or toxic industry (CNIAG), terms loosely defined.

The continued operation of the factory had been undermined because the anarchists refused to accept that it was possible to work safely with asbestos while the workers wanted answers. The workers, placed in a situation where they could trust neither management nor union, entered into an uneasy alliance with the anarchists' group, engaging in a series of discussions and meetings over the summer of 1980. The residents had few if any contacts with the workers. Given their portrayal by trade unionists as rich members of the bourgeoisie who were concerned only over the value of their property, they did not expect a sympathetic reception from workers. When the anarchists became involved the residents, according to Sue Baker, 'did not wish to be associated with the militant and national campaign against toxic industry and FDI (foreign direct investment) that was beginning in Ireland'.

The issue erupted again when asbestos spilled in the factory over the first weekend in June and Raybestos management announced it had closed down that section of the factory. On Friday 6 June night shift workers again took unofficial action when a mixed material containing asbestos dust spilled. Raybestos made the factory available for reopening the following Monday, and, though no pickets were placed, the workers did not come into work. Management offered to pay the workers for the lost days if they returned to work by Wednesday morning, but at a mass meeting on Tuesday 10 June workers voted 48 to 10 against resuming work and rejecting settlement proposals worked out between management and the union until they had seen a report from the Department of Labour Factory Inspectorate. Workers eventually returned to work on Monday 16 June, having accepted as satisfactory a Department of Labour Inspectorate report at a meeting over the weekend.

However, Raybestos Manhattan had had enough. With the prospect of continuing struggles with the factory workers over the safety conditions in the factory, and with a highly suspicious community monitoring its dumping operations, the company could afford no further mistakes. The council had also now to increase its monitoring of dumping operations in response to community concerns. On 22 October 1980 Gabriel Ferrucci, president of Raybestos Manhattan's international division, flew into Cork to appear at a joint press conference with the IDA at which the company announced its intention to pull out of Ireland. It's worth noting how coverage of that particular press conference described the conflict on 15 May 1978. According to *The Irish Times*:

> On 15 May, children from the area staged a sit-down protest and when Mr Deane tried to lead waste lorries through under garda protection, the windscreen of his car was smashed by a stone. Mr Ferrucci said yesterday that he was aware 'of the inconvenience caused to Mr Deane at the time'.

Thus what happened on that day was turned upside down. The injured party becomes the American executive intimidated by the locals, rather than the local children injured by the Gardai. Nevertheless, further details of Deane's harassment were revealed. Deane admitted constant harassment and anonymous phone threats had forced him to move his wife and four children out of Cork. It is interesting to note that some ten years later the use of anonymous phone threats arose again in the Sandoz case. Here the IDA claimed the family of one of its executives had received anonymous threats by phone but strangely neither the IDA nor the executive had seen fit to report these threats to the Gardai.

Ferrucci denied that the continued dispute over the safety of asbestos had any part in the company's decision to close the factory, though he admitted that the environmental difficulties experienced were 'more severe' than Raybestos had expected, and no other Raybestos Manhattan factories were being closed down. Ferrucci blamed the closure on the severe depression in the US market for brake disc pads. He also admitted that the initial delay in bringing the factory on stream had lost Raybestos Manhattan a market opportunity in Europe. Nevertheless he dismissed the residents' protests as mere 'inconveniences' and insisted:

> The closure of our Cork plant is in no way a reflection on our workforce, on the IDA, nor the Irish government which extended all possible facilities to our corporation in the difficult times we experienced. Notwithstanding the difficulties we encountered our experience in Ireland has been positive.

Others were less sanguine. John Keegan of the IDA Automotive and Engineering Department said the lesson of the Raybestos Manhattan affair was that, while the people of Ireland supported the IDA, the same people 'were not prepared to see an industry right on their doorstep'.

Other lessons were drawn by the opposition. The Raybestos struggle was important as the only struggle until DuPont in which both workers and community activists were involved, though not, unfortunately, in alliance with each other. The struggle highlighted again the problems posed by the divisions between the community and the workers, while the role of the trade union was also highly criticized. Locally the struggle was seen as a defeat, with the workers reportedly being blacklisted for their efforts to defend their safety and health, and the communities at both Ovens and Ringaskiddy having being defeated despite their strong opposition. Nationally it showed how far the state was prepared to go to force an industry on a recalcitrant community and how, when a choice existed between the interests of foreign capital and the health and safety of both community members and workers, the state and its various organisations defended and protected the corporate.

As a final ironic footnote, in August 1982, after the showing of a documentary on Yorkshire television on the hazards of asbestos, Liam Beecher of the ITGWU, one of the officials involved in the Raybestos controversy, expressed concern over the effect on the health of the Raybestos workers of their exposure to asbestos in the factory and called for regular monitoring of the health of the 130 people who had worked in the Raybestos Manhattan factory.

It is impossible say how much Raybestos Manhattan's departure affected the political mood of the harbour communities, given that the progressive political action came from anarchist groups and not from the communities, who at each stage were reacting to events. The other chemical factories were also problematic, yet it wasn't until the late 1980s that their stink caused a political storm and reinvigorated the debate about toxic industry. For nearly two decades the residents around Crosshaven and beyond in Ringaskiddy and Monkstown complained about smells – odours like rotten eggs or smelly cabbage.

'Penn [Chemicals] have been here for 15 years and while they have got better over the past three years they were very bad for the first 12 years', Ron Holland, a yacht builder, said in February 1988. When Iain Maclean was appointed Chief Environmental Officer of Cork County Council in 1986 they opened discussions with him, according to Holland, 'about the problems and how he can solve them'. Holland had been optimistic the new man could do something, but this eventually turned to pessimism. 'The companies say the smells don't make you sick but after a couple of hours it can affect you', Joanna Holland said, her concern for their two young children manifest because they had always been subjected to the smells. 'It's ridiculous to live that way if it makes you ill and we never know when it is going to happen. It depends on the wind direction. It's not consistent but it can be every week.'

'My concern', added Ron Holland, 'is that the council have not done the job right with the factories here, so why should they suddenly get it right now', he said in a reference to Maclean's assurances that the new Air Pollution Act (enforced from 1 March 1989) was, as the environmental officer put it, 'the light at the end of the tunnel'.

The Hollands complained 'hundreds of times' to the local authority about the smells. Over the years residents' groups and individuals attempted to highlight the problem about air pollution in the harbour area, emphasising the noxious smells they claim only the factories are causing. Numerous people said they had complained to the council and to the chemical companies, yet the local authority insisted that it did not keep a register of complaints and the companies stressed that the smells were harmless. Reports in the media, local people insisted, mentioned only a fraction of the incidents since the industry came into the area in the early 1970s.

According to Kieran Keohane:

> In the Cork County Council Environment Section a file is kept of complaints made by members of the public about nuisance caused by companies or businesses within the jurisdiction of the local authority. Complaints of a nauseating smell emanating from the newly opened Penn Chemicals plant poured into the office. These complaints were so frequent, so serious and so consistent that the Environment Section opened a separate file dealing exclusively with complaints about Penn: an unprecedented move, according to the Assistant Environment Officer.

Keohane's source was S. O'Bresail, Cork County Council's Assistant Environment Officer. When the author asked the council about this file and others in August and again in September 1988 he was told none existed.

It was not until December 1988 that the smells became a national issue when, during the planning board appeal hearing against Merrell Dow's planning application in Cork's County Hall, journalists were alerted by reports that schoolchildren in Monkstown had been overcome by sickly odours emanating, parents and residents claimed, from one or both of the nearby chemical companies. On the morning of 15 December, Monkstown National School was, according to one parent, 'awash with sick' as at least a dozen children vomited and as many again were forced to go home, unable to withstand the smell that 'had clung to the village since before 9 a.m.'. Martina Donnelly, whose eleven-year-old son Rory was one of the those overcome by the stench, described the odour, which hung in the air at its most acute stage for about half an hour, as like 'rotten cabbage'. Many of the villagers said they were nauseated by the smell which hung over the harbourside village for several hours and, according to Donnelly, was not unlike other smells that had occurred occasionally. 'But never had it been so strong', she added. Later that night angry parents told local reporters that they wanted 'a full scale council investigation' by Maclean's department. 'We want to know what and who caused the stench and we want the council to find out', demanded one parent. 'We also want to know whether it was dangerous or not. It had to come from one of the nearby industrial or chemical plants and we want to know which one.'

Suddenly the 'mystery' smells were news. Liam Mullins, the County Chief Engineer, was quoted as saying that the 'culprits' would be tracked down and that the source of the smells would be known within 24 hours. Referring to an immediate investigation led by Maclean, Mullins said, 'we are moving hard in this instance and we are confident that we will have results very shortly'. When Mullins added that the council would 'not shy away from taking a prosecution' against the offender, several residents caustically remarked that the council, under fire in the Merrell Dow affair, were trying to score points. Subsequent events would prove that the council had spoken out too soon.

Less than a week later, with the story still topical in the local media, Mullins, perhaps aware that 'flushing out' the culprit was easier said than done, changed his tack; while admitting that the 'mystery' smell was being treated by the council as 'more than serious', he added, 'we have built up a credibility for monitoring and we are not going to let anyone demolish it'. It then appeared that the council's investigation had identified the 'culprit' but a prosecution was not that simple. County Manager Patrick O'Dowd said that it would be difficult for the council to prove a case against the company, which he refused to name. The council, he added, were unsure of the legal ramifications. The county manager then announced that the Monkstown 'culprit' was Angus Fine Chemicals.

As Cork County Council subsequently discovered, it was one thing to claim that Angus was the 'culprit' and another thing to prove it. The issue became more complicated several months later when workers from Penn Chemicals sent documents, which included information on the day of the Monkstown 'incident', to the county council, enclosing comments of their own. The same information and further comments were anonymously sent to one of the harbour residents. The problem, it appeared at the time, was an open grid on a pipeline leading into the estuary. The Monkstown community were not so sure that the council had identified the right company. Stefan Antosik, the newly appointed General Manager of Angus, 'while denying responsibility' confirmed that his company had met with the council 'about the odour problem' in general and that they were 'working together'. He added that his company would 'provide a percentage of the funds to ensure the grid is covered'. O'Dowd concurred. 'We are working with a chemical company [in Ringaskiddy] in an effort to solve the odour problem. Our view is that this is a nuisance and the company has to get it right. We believe they are working positively towards a solution.'

Reading media reports about the mystery odours in isolation confused the issue for many residents. What was causing the smells? Was it the release of gases from Angus and Penn? Was it the IDA owned industrial sewage outfall or was it Angus's Bio-plant, which was uncovered and giving off an odour, according to Angus manager Stefan Antosik, 'not dissimilar to mercaptan'. The company eventually covered the Bio-plant and the problem of the sewage outfall was also solved, with the aid of IR£200,000, of which IR£80,000 was contributed by Angus, but not before screaming headlines accused the IDA of being the 'culprit' of the mystery smells.

When the 'sickening smells' returned before the residents of the lower harbour had time to recover from New Year hangovers, O'Dowd, in a further statement to the media, tried to allay their fears that the smells were dangerous or toxic. 'We are happy about the safety of residents', he told a *Cork Evening Echo* reporter on 2 January 1989. 'I believe the odour is more a nuisance than a threat to health', yet O'Dowd later told another reporter that there had been 'four major incidences' in two months and that the complaints by residents of 'rotten cabbage' smells were being investigated.

Maclean, who had been getting on with the job of investigating the 'culprit' or culprits, announced, five weeks after Mullins had promised action 'within 24 hours', that prosecutions were imminent. 'I would hope to have the enquiries concluded and follow up with suitable legal action within the next week', Maclean said. On 21 February the *Cork Examiner* revealed that the council was to take an 'unprecedented step' and prosecute two chemical companies under the Air Pollution Act, 1987. For nine weeks the media had focused with as keen an eye as possible on the residents' complaints of chemical pollution yet it was the council manager, the council engineer and the council environmental officer who were quoted. Some residents felt their side of the story was not being presented. The pro-industry line was clear, and they noted an editorial in the *Cork Examiner* on 22 February:

> People living in the Cork harbour area will breathe a sigh of relief at the news that the County Council are set to crack down on industrial pollution by taking action against the chemical companies which are alleged to be causing problems. For far too long, local residents, school children and visitors in the harbour area, which embraces some of Cork's finest scenic and tourist assets, have had to endure noxious smells. The claim, sometimes put forward by State agencies involved in job creation, that such odours are not dangerous in themselves, does not justify the situation. Nobody wants to live beside a neighbour who persistently causes a nuisance by releasing unpleasant odours into the atmosphere. Living with the ever-present fear that some toxic gas may also be carried on the wind can be a psychologically damaging experience.

The council, the editorial continued, had a 'difficult task of policing such industries' and with limited 'resources and manpower' the watchdog role is increasingly difficult. Local people, the leader writer added, were in the firing line of industrial pollution and it was they who were usually first to raise the alarm 'if something goes wrong at a factory. In extreme cases, that kind of warning can be too late.'

But the sting in the tail of the editorial indicated clearly where the allegiance of the paper lay. 'By and large, the chemical industry in this country operates responsibly. Indeed some companies which have been identified as causing problems, have gone to considerable lengths and cost to rectify them.'

Maclean said that the council were aware that mercaptan gas had been released into the air by both companies and he agreed with Stefan Antosik that the gas, 'while strong smelling is not harmful'.

Stefan Antosik said that methyl mercaptan was harmless in small quantities; the amount he said was emitted into the air around Cork harbour. It is not harmless, he added, in a confined area.

> You would need to be subjected to 200 parts per million over an eight hour period for it to be harmful. Outside you would need extreme weather conditions, 10,000 times more than is being emitted for it to be medically harmful.

Methyl mercaptan is indeed harmless at low concentration but reports stressed that high concentrations could lead to respiratory illnesses. Learning this and knowing what the foul odour was called did not make any difference to the Monkstown parents and their children or to the residents in Ringaskiddy and Crosshaven. They wanted the council to take action against the chemical industry and they wanted the smells stopped. Then an ally no one thought about appeared.

Workers in Penn had more to fear from methyl mercaptan. Main doors in the factory were kept closed which, claimed some workers, did not allow fresh air into the working areas. 'The absence of fresh air means that fumes emitted from processes in the plant take much longer to disperse. This has obvious and incalculable effects on workers' health', was how one Penn worker described conditions in the factory.

The concern of the Penn workers came into the open in April 1989 when they sent information to Cork County Council about what they alleged was the company's breach of the air pollution laws, including their own observations and comments about the December emissions:

The reaction started at 7.22 hours [on 15 December 1988]. In an normal batch, this reaction starts with a heating up period of approximately half an hour and continues with a controlled addition over two and a half hours approximately. During this reaction, mercaptan gas is given off. This is either scrubbed in the scrubber or burned in the incinerator, whichever is on line. However, this particular batch took nearly six and a half hours because of problems associated with it.

The problems started when the incinerator went off line and the mercaptan gases were diverted to the scrubbers. Unfortunately, there was no flow to the scrubbers and the gases went through quickly pulled by the general extract fans, and [were] pumped out into the atmosphere virtually untreated.

This was discovered when a supervisor in Penn (off duty at the time), Brendan McCabe, who lives across the bay, came over at approximately 09.45 hours and complained of a wicked smell of mercaptan. This smell could only have come from Penn as Angus lies to the east of him and the wind was from the south.

In the next few weeks, the batch sizes of cets isothious-rea (the process involving the mercaptan gas releases) are going to be doubled in size with the introduction of new vessels. This is a cause of great concern for us because even with the batch sizes we have at present we regularly have leaks and emissions, within the plant. Yet, no modifications as far as we know are being made to the scrubbers and incinerator to cope with the increased gases being released. How is something that is barely adequate at present going to be sufficient with the introduction of increased batch sizes?

Another cause for great concern will be a major process change which will be taking place shortly. This involves the release of hydrogen sulphide gas into the general extract from the using of crude BMEP within the main plant building. We have serious reservations of the ability of this scrubbing method to deal with this highly noxious and dangerous gas.

Following protracted consultation with their legal advisors, Cork County Council finally decided to start prosecutions against Angus and Penn. The Crosshaven and Carrigaline doctor Mary Dunphy, whose anti-nuclear and anti-toxic campaigns had given her a high profile among the community, was delighted. 'It's the first time the authorities have taken seriously the pollution being perpetrated by those companies in this area', she said.

Maclean, confirming that it was the first time he had attempted to prosecute anyone under the new Air Pollution Act, was, nevertheless, cautious. It had taken his department over three months to build what he described as a 'reasonable case' against Angus and Penn, yet he was uncomfortable and admitted, three weeks before the prosecutions were due to be heard at Carrigaline District Court, that he wouldn't be surprised by the outcome. 'I've had better cases and lost and poor cases and won. Hopefully we'll be successful.'

Both companies were being prosecuted under sections 24 and 29 of the Act which state that 'the occupier of any premises shall not cause or permit an emission from such premises in such a quantity, or in such a manner, as to be a nuisance' and 'as soon as practicable after the occurrence of any incident which may cause air pollution notify the relevant local authority of the incident'.

Surprisingly, to the wonder of residents and critics of the chemical industry, it was Penn that pleaded guilty to the charge of failing to report an emission of mercaptan lasting 60 minutes on 30 December 1988 to the council. The company was fined IR£1,000, the maximum allowed on a summary conviction under the Act. Maclean said he would have been surprised if the maximum fine was imposed, admitting before the case that he was 'relatively philosophical' about the legislation. 'If the convictions are being loaded on a company you have a good case to shut them down, so it has an increasing momentum. Anyway,' he said, 'the fine is not as hurtful as the publicity.' He had been wrong on one count but he had been right about the publicity. 'I don't think the rest of the industry is as bad as this pair', he said, noting that the council's action could be viewed as a warning shot which should not be ignored by the chemical industry.

The management of Angus thought differently. While Penn took the punch, Angus decided to fight back. The case against it was adjourned for six weeks to 31 May 1989. The council alleged that Angus had breached section 24 of the Act on four different dates, 15 and 16 December 1988 and 7 and 8 January, and had breached section 29 on 31 January. Angus's legal team argued that the company had immunity against prosecution and Justice Carroll adjourned the case once more, for a week, when he said he would fix a date for the hearing of one of the five prosecutions. On 21 July at Mitchelstown court the protracted legal battle between the council and the company was prolonged when the judge reserved judgement and referred both parties to the High Court in the autumn. The High Court subsequently referred it back to the District Court and when it was finally heard Angus received a statutory fine.

While all this was going on Angus committed to a IR£5 million investment on environmental control to 1992. Antosik said that the company's research and development programmes included projects designed to eliminate or reduce pollution from their manufacturing processes. 'All new processes are evaluated for environmental and safety impact', he said. 'Projects have been terminated because they were deemed unacceptable from an environmental/safety risk and existing processes are continually evaluated by chemists to reduce waste.' Penn had already announced that it would spend IR£4.8 million on the installations of an additional incinerator and a continuous monitoring system plus the expansion of their waste treatment plant. The company also agreed, as part of its new environmental package, to fund 'whatever independent monitoring Cork County Council finds necessary to carry out'. The two companies subsequently commissioned the Resource and Environmental Management Unit of the University College of Cork (UCC) to carry out external monitoring at chosen locations in the lower harbour.

The new dawn for the chemical industry and particularly Angus and Penn did not improve the lives of the lower harbour residents, some of whom wondered why all this spending should happen while the Merrell Dow controversy was going on and why it had not been part of the companies' original investment. Others wondered why the council had not prosecuted the companies earlier. Surely, several residents remarked, mercaptan had been released, and in large quantities, on more than the few occasions the council alleged. And what about the incident at Angus which workers claimed had nearly caused an explosion? Workers told of how 'toxic' substances were released into the air from the Chemical Two building in Angus after a fault in a reactor. One worker overheard two supervisors remark that the factory was 'five minutes from going up'.

The incident was one of three occasions when Angus admitted it was responsible for major emissions since it had begun operation in July 1986. Stefan Antosik dismissed the claims that the factory had been 'five minutes from going up' and said that the accident, which resulted in the release of methyl mercaptan 'for about five to seven minutes' after a shaft had snapped on a badly constructed reactor causing a chemical reaction, overheating and a failure in the system, had always been under control. 'There was never a safety problem, only a odour problem', said Antosik. 'Every process we have goes through a hazardous analysis to see what can go wrong and every process is approved by the county council.'

'We have genuine fears concerning the obnoxious smells from the chemical plants in Ringaskiddy', Angela Morrissey said when she founded Responsible Industrial Development for Cork Harbour (later known as RICH) with several Crosshaven residents in the winter of 1988:

> It is impossible to get information regarding the content of the smells. We know that mercaptan is being emitted but our concern is what is coming out with it. There are two obvious varieties of smells in the harbour; one is that of rotten cabbage and the other is a gas smell which to the layperson appears to have ammonia in it. It is particularly offensive because it can cause people to cough.

RICH's objectives were concise and they believed indicative of what people in the harbour area felt about the chemical industry. Over 100 people attended their inaugural meeting to agree 'that existing industry in the harbour operate to the highest possible standards' – though it would be a further year before anyone in authority would admit that some of the industry were not operating to these standards – and 'that future industrial development must respect the rights of people whose livelihood is dependent on our natural resources. We want jobs. We don't want pollution.' Yet it was symptomatic of the problems facing small communities in their struggle against 'toxic' industry that Angela Morrissey and Anne Oulsnam – RICH's two principal protagonists – did not believe when they started that they had the clout to extensively lobby councillors, local politicians and TDs and they were unsure and inexperienced in their dealings with the media.

Mary Dunphy and her husband Sean – also a doctor – were different. As chair of the Irish Medical Campaign for the Prevention of Nuclear War, Mary Dunphy was known to the media as a 'good person for quotes' and when the Dunphys announced that they had recorded rare tumours in the respiratory systems of six patients under 35 between 1985 and 1988, the story made front page news. Patients attending their practices in Crosshaven and Carrigaline reported high incidences of asthma, colds, coughs, flus, headaches, nausea and skin and eye irritations which, with the tumours, the Dunphys believed were linked to chemical pollution and probably toxins from the harbour factories. Illnesses like those documented by the Dunphys are not uncommon all over Ireland yet the villagers in the lower harbour appeared to have suffered disproportionately from respiratory-related ailments.

A short time after the Dunphys made the claim about the tumours, six other GPs, doctors Walsh, Canniffe, Cantillon, Murphy, Martin and Scully, questioned the Dunphys' assertions. The GPs sent written statements to O'Dowd, the County Manager, who said he was 'reassured' that they had discovered no unusual cases of tumours in patients under 35 among six years of their own medical records. 'What the doctors told the county manager seems to be the traditional orthodox belief but the fact is that many members of the public think that the illnesses are precipitated by smells from chemical plants in the harbour area', Mary Dunphy said in her initial response to the media in February 1989. She continued:

We were specifically looking for the problem. We have been primed for years to look for a problem and we expected a problem. I enquired internationally and I asked what would we start see happening, and I was told that if we saw asthma turning up in increased numbers in our small area, then there was something radically wrong, and that's what is happening.

'Suddenly this report appeared out of thin air, to the effect that a six year retrospective study had been carried out by six doctors in the area showing no increased cancers', Sean Dunphy recalled.

We contacted a number of the doctors and one of them stated to us that he had received a single phone call with a single question about lung cancer, a second doctor said he had not been communicated about this at all and a third said they had looked at some of his files. So when we contacted the doctor who was supposed to have carried it out he admitted that it was for a non-medical source.

The postscripts to the affair came firstly when *The Irish Times* journalist Dick Hogan interviewed three of the doctors almost seven months later and discovered that their initial caution, as it had been reflected by the media at the time, had been replaced by concern. 'Dr Dunphy's findings, startling though they may be, must be weighed against those of her colleagues', Hogan wrote. 'However, one of the six, Dr A. J. Walsh is concerned about the smells. He has noticed that patients who leave the lower harbour area improve, but then disimprove when they come back. He told *The Irish Times* he was aware of unusual colds and coughs.'

Dr Larrie Martin, Hogan wrote, concurred but warned 'against hasty conclusions'. Dr E. B. Canniffe told Hogan that the six doctors had made their statements 'to allay fears in the locality and because of the lack of evidence'. All the doctors agreed that only a major health study would provide the answers.

To many residents it was not surprising that Mary Dunphy should attempt the survey without state funding, and be forced to use an international organisation, Rosalie Bertell's Canadian Institute of Concern for Public Health. What did surprise householders in Ringaskiddy, Crosshaven and Carrigaline, where volunteers distributed 3,000 copies of the survey, was its comprehensiveness.

'It's too intimate. She'll never get people to answer those questions', was a common remark when people read the 20-page survey. Yet there was a spiritual, almost instinctual, reaction, that participation was crucial to the future well-being of those who lived in the lower harbour area. Many residents, vocal and non-vocal about the chemical industry, frightened because they did not know, as one person put it, 'the extent of damage being caused to our health' believed that only a comprehensive health survey would prove that irreparable damage was being inflicted on an unfortunate, sometimes wretched, community.

On a visit to Cork in October 1988 Rosalie Bertell put the debate in a perspective that was decisively pro-people and fundamentally anti-industry. She announced at a public meeting organised by the Medical, Biological and Geological Societies of UCC, that:

> There is no such thing as a safe level for most of these chemicals. Only one per cent of those being used have been tested for their effects on human health, and no tests have been carried out on the effect they can have after they have interacted with each other, as must happen in the Cork harbour area where there are many chemical plants all emitting chemical waste.

Before Dunphy and Bertell could announce the results of their survey an unexpected salvo came from behind the barricades at Leinster House, where the government ministers in the forefront of the industry versus the environment battle were tentatively emerging. Padraig Flynn, the Environment Minister, in a lengthy almost unprecedented speech on industry and the environment from a governmental department, did not name Mary Dunphy but it was obvious who he was talking about. 'There have been claims about the incidence of cancer in the harbour area which are quite improper, coming from an individual doctor, who knows that anecdotal evidence should never be presented publicly as objective fact.'

Mary Dunphy defended her claim about the cancers and said she had not released specific details because she did not wish to break her patients' confidentiality. 'I didn't wish to distress the people involved because it would be obvious immediately who the people were.'

It wasn't the communities who were distressed, it was the state and the chemical industry. When UCC graduate Kieran Keohane reported in *The Ecologist* in August 1989 that successive Irish governments were in collusion 'with toxic industries in keeping people uninformed and suppressing disquiet' the IDA and the Federation of Irish Chemical Industries (FICI) responded swiftly. 'That type of statement is unfair and does not reflect the true situation here', an IDA spokesperson said. Neil Buckley, the director general of the FICI, in a letter to *The Irish Times* on August 21 1989, wrote that:

> the chemical/pharmaceutical industry rejects outright that Ireland is a dumping ground for toxic industries. The industry is proud of its life enhancing and life saving products. The author of the article referred to in your issue (of 11 August) would have done well to check the facts in Ireland before making unfounded assertions from Canada.

Yet Keohane had checked his facts and his sources were, in a pro-industry sense, impeccable. *SCRIP* is the internal journal for the chemical industry. In 1985 it published *Ireland: An Investment Opportunity for the Pharmaceuticals Industry*. The report referred to environmental controls and in one paragraph summed up the problem of smells from Penn Chemicals:

> The population living near to Penn Chemicals cimetidine plant in Carrigaline, County Cork, initially objected to the unpleasant odour associated with the by-product of cimetidine, methyl mercaptan. The company subsequently made a significant investment in measures to control this problem and has, as a consequence, developed considerable expertise in this area. Penn believes the smell is now at an acceptable level, although concedes that it still receives the occasional complaint.

Keohane was able to show in his research for his thesis that Penn received more than the occasional complaint throughout the 1980s and that the communities in Ringaskiddy and surrounding areas did not agree with the company that the smell was 'at an acceptable level'.

An interesting postscript to this debate came in a letter on 13 September 1989 by Keohane to the *Wall Street Journal* in response to a letter by David O'Sullivan, Executive Director of Ireland's

United States Council for Commerce and Industry. O'Sullivan had responded to an article on Merrell Dow in Ireland by columnist Alexander Cockburn, whom O'Sullivan claimed had 'engaged in a flight of fancy, never once allowing facts to get in the way of good copy'. There was not one recorded case of pollution by the chemical industry in Ireland, O'Sullivan wrote. 'Ireland's strict environmental protection laws ensure that these industries operate safely and cleanly.' Keohane didn't agree:

> between 1985 and 1987, while a graduate student at UCC, I conducted extensive research into the activities of the (largely US) chemicals and pharmaceuticals industry in Ireland. My study focused particularly on environmental pollution associated with the industry, with relevant Irish industrial development policy, and with the legislative and administrative framework which controls such development.

Cockburn's 'flight of fancy', Keohane argued, was 'factually accurate' and it was 'untrue to allege that Ireland's environmental legislation is strict and that it ensures protection'. In many respects, Keohane wrote, 'it is lax and fundamentally flawed, and under resourcing and influence brokerage at local authority level conspire to prevent regulations from being implemented'. Keohane was not as ignorant as Buckley believed or wanted the public to believe. In *The Ecologist*, he wrote:

> Local authorities have repeatedly failed to prosecute pharmaceutical companies for regular persistent breaches of effluent and emission levels. Public objections to proposed developments are stonewalled, or has been the (Merrell Dow) case more recently rejected out of hand. The state is deliberately slow to implement European Community legislation on environmental and employee protection and on corporate privacy, and when forced to adopt this legislation ensures that it remains ineffective.

This may now seem a little hard on former governments, and without much feeling and understanding of the bureaucratic incompetency and centralism inherent in the Irish system in those days, yet Keohane's remarks were based on extensive research. And he was not the only one to reach these conclusions. 'Essentially I think the view in

Dublin is that the people of Ireland cannot be trusted to manage their own affairs locally', was how Philip Mullally of An Taisce saw it.

> That's the flawed thinking; we've been very bad at restructuring; we continue a form of parliamentary democracy (the Dáil) that is unsuited to ourselves. Since they were de-rated and failed to get control the councils have been centralised, because they have no financial stability. They've had to move into areas of planning – one of the few areas where a council or a councillor can exercise any power. The real power is money and they don't have the spending of money. There is a complete failure to enhance local democracy. By and large, senior officials in county councils are excellent people and they're put into a ridiculous situation. They are certainly beholden to the Department of the Environment and the centralised thinking, without consideration for the planning of their areas. I feel they have taken on the role of developers – pro-development because that is what their elected representatives want.

Keohane's thesis, produced at UCC and completed in 1987, focused on the attraction of Ireland to the corporate chemical industry and why the communities became dependent on the companies. For his case study Keohane chose Penn Chemicals. He claimed that SmithKline Beckman, Penn's parent company in the US, deliberately selected Ireland because it 'needed an active ingredients plant to manufacture their new product cimetidine. [SmithKline Beckman] knew that such a plant would produce a large amount of hazardous waste including a noxious gas – methyl mercaptan. They knew that such a plant would be environmentally problematic.' Keohane also claimed that 'the environmental problems caused by Penn' prompted local people to enter 'the political arena'. He interviewed 'at length' a number of people from the communities affected by Penn, and he came to the conclusion that all the people he spoke to became 'involved with the residents' associations specially in response to the problem caused by Penn'. There was also, he discovered, 'a high degree of critical political awareness', which he believed was derived from a conscientious position:

> All felt that they had a serious, justifiable grievance which initially they expected they would be able to get sorted out satisfactorily. Their experience over the years didn't match

their expectations. Now (1987), people felt that at worst their interests weren't catered for at all, or at best that their interests came a poor second to more powerful interests like 'big business' and politicians. Everybody felt that they were in a 'no-win' situation and while there is a general consensus of resignation it is by no means passive. Most people are quite angry that they have been treated in such a cavalier fashion.

Keohane wrote that he was 'struck' by the extent to which the lower harbour residents were 'familiar with the structure and the mechanics of the county council and the IDA, how much people knew about existing and forthcoming environmental legislation and of government and IDA industrialisation policy'. He added that he was surprised by 'people's ability to offer incisive criticism and comment on these subjects', yet as he discovered not everyone wanted to fight the chemical industry, and while many residents resigned their lives to the problem of pollution, others simply decided their only choice was to leave.

Those who had no choice decided something had to be done, and this included Penn's workforce, which was becoming more militant by the day. Nearly three months after the Penn workers had sent the information and comments to Cork County Council they decided to send the material, with further comments, to one of the harbour residents:

Since this letter to (the council) containing information on breaches of Air Pollution Act by Penn Chemicals and major process changes involving chemicals responsible for these breaches, three things have happened which directly relate to the letter in question.
1. Penn Chemicals were fined in connection with the incident on 30 December 1988.
2. The scrubbing capacity of the mercaptan gases has been increased.
3. Our fears in connection with the process change involving the release of hydrogen sulphide gas into the general extract scrubber have been quickly realised in only the second batch started.
This happened over a period of three and a half/four hours on the night of Tuesday, 16 May and the morning of

Wednesday, 17 May. During the distillation step from RV302 the excess H_2S and hydrochloric acid reacted violently every time steam was put on the vessel. Not only was this cloud of gas pushed out through the vent in the general extract but also through every suspect flange in the general extract. The pressure involved was so great, the cloud of gas was so bad that it covered half the site on a number of occasions. The company fire brigade was on duty for the duration of these emissions, spraying water on them to keep them under control. We don't think there were any complaints because the wind was blowing it out [of] the harbour. However, we did inform the Council as we considered it a potentially very hazardous situation. They said they would look into it.

The workers then decided to write a letter which they gave to a local journalist. In the opening paragraph, the letter stated, that not enough attention was being given to the 'sort of jobs' being created by the chemical industry in Ireland and the 'sort of working environment and conditions employees are subjected to'. Employment, the letter stressed, is the only positive factor involved in the chemical industry.

Among the major problems facing the workers every day they turned up for work was the intransigence of their union and the power of the Penn management. The workforce, the letter stated, had been divided by management.

Short term financial inducements and pressure from management prompted half the workforce to sign away their basic rights. The result of this is that the union's ability to negotiate on health and safety matters (of which we have a great concern about) has been severely weakened. Co-operation and communications at work have suffered which increases the health and safety risks for all workers.

The safety committee set up under the health and safety legislation, designed to protect workers, is now heavily imbalanced in favour of management. This undermines the whole purpose of the committee as it is supposed to have a proper and fair representation of all interests. At present there is only one person on a committee of ten representing employees still negotiating through the union.

Recent pressure from the County Council on the company concerning environmental problems has, ironically, been a bad blow for us. Main doors are kept closed at all times to contain smells. Access to emergency fans, which we had used to clean fumes from leaks and emissions, has been banned. Floor space has been filled in to facilitate new, more intensive production methods. A combination of these three factors has led to a serious deterioration in the quality of the air that we breathe. In fact what the company is trying to do is contain their problems instead of trying to solve them.

We have every reason to be concerned because the statistics speak for themselves. Eight years ago there were approximately 22 operators per shift. Now, because of health reasons and unfair pressure from management, the numbers are down to 15.5 per shift. 'Who's next?' a now famous line conjured up at a dispute a few years ago has a very true and frightening ring to it now.

We hope that this letter will throw some light on the jobs, that because of their relatively high remuneration, are thought to be the answers to all dreams ... perhaps it will only be the beginning of a nightmare.

One Penn worker said they were working in fear, that workers were being pressed to sign non-union agreements and that there were a lot of cover-ups:

We want to get the place cleaned up. Conditions are deteriorating. You see people leaving because of ill-health and it's only a matter of time before your number comes up. It just happens all of a sudden. You try not to think about it and try to be safe but it's what other people do that puts you at risk. The ventilation is wrong and the equipment you wear is no good.

Any time Iain Maclean comes down they make a complete fool of him and lead him a merry dance, hurrying him and showing him just what they want to show him. They send him over to Angus when the problem is in Penn. Penn are the biggest culprits because they are using the biggest quantities.

The same was true for local residents who phoned up to complain about the odours. Angus is causing the problem, they were told. One resident who phoned Penn was told the odours were coming from Angus, He asked to speak to someone in charge and was put through to one of the chemists. 'It can't be Angus', the resident said. 'They're shut down at the moment.'

Throughout 1989 the management of Penn was worried about the workers' increasing dialogue with the world outside the factory. Veiled threats were made to some workers, that such behaviour would not be tolerated, that any worker leaking internal Penn documentation would be suspended, or worse, sacked. For some workers it was too late, time was already running out. In the middle of November an inter-office memorandum was sent to the *Cork Examiner*. The memorandum, dated 13 October 1989, referred to the 'tremendous environmental activity' in the local area and in the media, which is 'likely to be heightened with the proposed submission of a planning application to Cork County Council by Sandoz'.

> As recently as this morning we have had an important meeting with the Cork County Council during which they strongly emphasises (sic) that they will not be able to tolerate any more odour incidents over the next few weeks. They made strong reference to the recent incident we have had which involved the Bio-Plant approximately two to three weeks back. Specifically they requested from the company that the incidents of odorous, liquors being allowed to enter the Bio-Plant will not reoccur again. They also referred to the incident of 3 May which resulted in an extremely bad emission of H_2S from the exhausts of Building 120 Scrubber Stack and also the incident of 30 December last for which we were prosecuted for not notifying them. Overall their view is that the type of incidents we have appear to be primarily due to operational deficiencies, including human error. The purpose of this memorandum is to highlight the importance of our environmental control procedure over the next few weeks and in particular of ensuring that any liquid waste being discharged to the Bio Plant is not odorous.

The memorandum concluded with a request that each foreman 'ensure that on each shift that this procedure is clearly understood by everybody'.

It wasn't until 17 November, about a week after the workers had sent the memorandum to the *Cork Examiner*, that the paper wrote a story about it but only as an addendum; the headline read, 'Chemical plant to make its monitoring data available'. Penn managing director, Dr Reg Shaw, was quoted:

> Access to relevant information is an integral part of any meaningful communication with the public. We feel the most effective and immediate course of action would be to make monitoring data available. We as a company have decided, therefore, to make our monitoring data public. We are currently exploring with the Federation of Irish Chemical Industries and with the IDA the development of an appropriate mechanism through which to communicate this data.

The story, which ran to 20 paragraphs, had no byline. Some workers wondered why the paper had waited a week before publishing details of the memorandum, and when it did, why the news that Penn would release its monitoring data took precedent over the information contained in the document, which to them was much more relevant. The workers weren't impressed. They had a different story to tell about the reasons why 'operational deficiencies, including human error' were causing problems in the factory, why working conditions had deteriorated and why they were concerned about their health and safety.

> Pressure is brought on workers to clock in for their next scheduled shift after having an accident so that it will not be shown as a 'lost time accident'. Workers can then get time off sick without it showing as a lost time accident.

Penn's management had responded with what appeared to be a positive gesture to the people around the lower harbour; to their workers they issued a warning, whoever had leaked the memorandum would be sacked. The workers, however, had decided to take precautions and prepared a ten-point affidavit about the 'deteriorating industrial relations and new practices' in Penn, which are causing 'grave concern'. Health and safety were the crucial issues, particularly the 'increasing amount of carcinogens' being used in the processes 'without adequate information to workers on the risks associated with these substances'.

Every year blood samples are taken from all workers. These samples are sent to the United States for analysis. The test reports that come back to the workers are from basic tests that are routinely carried out in Ireland. We believe that this testing may be linked with the increasing number of carcinogens used in the plant.

As the year drew to a close some workers decided it was time to bring the conflict into the open. Their union would have to take action. On 18 October 1989 a letter, with a brief history of the 'situation that has developed in Penn Chemicals in the past two years', was sent to all Services Industrial Professional and Technical Union (SIPTU – then ITGWU) branches in the country. On 10 January a further letter was sent to all members of the executive of the Irish Congress of Trade Unions (ICTU).

In view of the forthcoming review of the working of the Programme for National Recovery (PNR), it would seem appropriate to remind one of the situation that exists in Penn Chemicals. In September 1987, 44 out of 92 Section Members signed individual work contracts with the company, despite Union and Congress advice to the contrary. The first phase of the PNR was introduced in December 1987, but in March 1988, the management awarded pay increases in excess of the terms of the national plan, to those who had signed individual work contracts. A subsequent claim in the Labour Court on behalf of those who had remained within Collective Bargaining, the majority of the Section membership, failed because the court was not prepared to recommend an increase in excess of the terms of the national plan. Given that the plan was in its infancy at that time, such reticence might be understandable, but it does not alter the fact that the formal company/trade union agreement, 1974, had been ignored in this instance. The national plan, negotiated in good faith to promote stable industrial relations and economic growth was, in this instance, used to perpetuate an injustice. Where this happened once, it can all too easily happen again.

The letter concluded that 'those who needed the advice of the ITGWU and Congress officials remained within collective bargaining and maintain that stance to this day', confident that collective bargaining was best for them, that the Labour Court would 'not feel itself constrained by the PNR' and confident that the 'power and influential Trade Union organisation in this country will not allow such an injustices to go unchallenged. To do so would to undermine the very fabric of unionism.'

Five days later the Penn SIPTU branch sent a letter to all the unions affiliated to the ICTU.

We are employees of Penn Chemicals, Currabinny, Carrigaline, Co Cork. Penn Chemicals is a subsidiary of Smith-Kline and Beecham. Our principal product is a drug for ulcers, called Tagamet. It is the second biggest selling drug in the world. We manufacture 50 per cent of the total production of that drug for world wide distribution. We are the loyal members of SIPTU Cork Number Two branch, who have, on the advice of the ICTU and our own union remained faithful to the collective bargaining system. Our fellow trade unionists in SIPTU have ignored that advice and instead have opted for a system of individual assessment.

While we are constrained by the severe pay restraints incorporated in the PNR, our fellow workers in SIPTU have no such restrictions. The wage differential at present is IR£30 per week, not including bonuses or overtime. We do exactly the same work as these people, very often working side by side in the control room or on the factory floor. Working 12 hour shifts together, days and nights, relieving one another for breaks. Any problems that arise during a process are solved by combined co-operation, both groups of workers labouring strenuously, side by side to ensure that a first class product is achieved. With pollution being such a sensitive subject in these times, it is only by conscientious efforts on our behalf, that we ensure a satisfactory result is achieved. Why management adopt such a cruel and cynical attitude towards us seems to be bordering on the fringes of lunacy.

The minister for Labour, Bertie Ahern, has said that the best hope for the low paid workers, lay in the strength of the collective bargaining system, operating in conjunction with the system of joint labour committees. In view of what is happening in Penn Chemicals, his opinions cannot be taken seriously. The Labour Court's main function now, is the policing of the strict implementation of the PNR, even though that necessitates discriminating against workers who will not be coerced into 'signed' individual contracts of employment. By adopting such a role, the Labour Court is about as effective as a toothless tiger.

Management have used some unsavoury tactics in their endeavours to have a large majority sign. These tactics involved an initial 'signing on' fee, if workers signed on a certain date. Workers were also warned individually of perceived misdemeanours. There were also whispers and innuendo that intimidated some of the weaker members. Despite all this, their majority was never achieved. The only result was 3 years of the PNR wasted, when, without the burden of wage bargaining, solutions could have been achieved that would have given hope for long and lasting industrial peace.

By clever manipulation of the PNR, Penn Chemicals' management have succeeded in undermining the most powerful union in this country. The 1974 company trade union agreement states that conditions of employment will continue in force, until such time as all parties to the agreement reach full and final agreement on any modifications. Outside National wage agreements, collective bargaining has always been the wage determining factor in Penn Chemicals, but now management have introduced individual assessment. By their refusal to have labour court intervention on this very serious matter, they have convicted themselves.

Prior to the PNR, we always had four members of the Safety committee of ten. Because of the split, management were able to change the election method agreed with the union in 1983. On this occasion without consultation with the union, now we only have one representative on the committee, all the others are the preferred choices of management. In a chemical plant that uses so many dangerous and carcinogenic chemicals, one would have expected management to welcome a critical analysis on such a very important committee. One section of the workforce have been allowed to exceed the terms of the PNR, by such a clever move, management can exert enormous influence on the way these people elect candidates to the safety committee. This surely is inimical to the best interests of the trade union.

Since the start of the PNR, we have lost 10 per cent of our members, and production has risen by 25 per cent. Unfortunately, many left, totally disillusioned with the trade union hierarchy, not for entering into a national plan, but for allowing it to be used to perpetrate such grave injustices to workers, who would not sign individual contracts.

We have made many requests to have exploratory discussions on the implementation of the 39 hour working week, so far to no avail. At this point in time, we are not very optimistic.

The unions are to be commended for their patriotic gesture on entering into a PNR, in view of the disastrous state of the economy of this country, which has been caused by gross mismanagement, by successive bad governments. But by allowing the national plan to be used to discriminate against their own members is in our situation, a disastrous miscalculation. On its inception, had we known the consequences, we would have been forced to seek legal opinion to protect us from a national plan that is open to widespread abuse.

At the special delegate conference to be held shortly to review the workings of the PNR, we hope that our justified aspirations are supported by you, as we sincerely believe that with a little help from our friends, we can redress this very serious imbalance.

The letter was signed, Committee, Penn Chemicals Section, Cork No 2 Branch, SIPTU.

With the Penn workforce split, the workers who were still part of the union were despondent; 'sadly we are chasing our tails', they complained, because it was easy for the Penn management to 'exploit' the divided workforce.

The communities around the factories were also divided. While Kieran Keohane was able to identify an increasing degree of sophistication in their attitude to the chemical industry, the formation of the various opposition groups had not done enough to raise concern among all the people in the area. Something had to happen to unite the harbour communities, and there was only one scenario that could do that, the advent, as inevitable as the dawn, of another chemical factory.

On Monday 13 February 1989 John Conlon started a new job. He had worked at the IDA's Wilton Place HQ as a project executive in the chemicals/pharmaceuticals sector. Prior to that he had worked in the same capacity in consumer products and in the plastics area of the healthcare section of the IDA. He had joined the IDA in 1982 following his graduation from University College Dublin with a degree in business studies. His new job with the IDA, almost ten years on, was completely different from anything he had done before. As far as the IDA was concerned the job was unique. Conlon would remain in the pharmaceuticals sector but for the first time in its 40-year history he would carry the IDA flag to the community. When his superiors in Wilton Place asked him to talk to the communities and the chemical industry, with the sole purpose of bringing them together and dissolving ignorance and distrust, the industry's profile in Ireland was intangible and weak, yet Conlon wondered if it would make any difference. 'I might discover things that they don't want to know', he said of the IDA hierarchy, after a month in the job.

By then Conlon had contributed to Padraic White's key note speech to the industry and environment conference in Cork in February 1989 and attempted to talk to the communities opposed to Merrell Dow. Few people in east Cork wanted to know about the IDA initiative. It cost IR£100 to attend the conference, thus precluding interested observers from the Cork communities who would not have had an expense account to plunder. One community activist from Youghal, in east Cork, managed to strike up a deal with the organisers but he paid for the pleasure out of his own pocket. The media dutifully reported the conference and White's remarks that Ireland did not support dirty industries, 'yet there is a myth that we are a dumping ground for industries unacceptable in other countries'. Those with long memories in Cork had indeed heard it all before. In November 1980 White stated that the IDA did not 'support dirty industries' and promised that prior consultation with local groups would be a priority of the IDA's. 'The IDA will pay special attention to the volatile environmental lobby in Cork', he had said. 'Our sense of Cork is that there are more environmental groups there than anywhere else.'

Had the IDA learned anything in those intervening eight years? Anti-toxic activists thought not, but as the front line in the battle between the communities and the chemical industry extended into Cork harbour from east Cork and Conlon found people willing to talk to him, it became apparent that his brief was not simply about placating the communities and understanding their concerns.

The news that Sandoz, the Swiss pharmaceutical company responsible for the destruction of a section of the Rhine river in November 1986, was coming to Ireland broke in *The Phoenix*, Ireland's satirical current affairs fortnightly, on 16 June 1989. Operation Ramses, the code-name for Sandoz's search for a suitable location in an EC country, had 'focused strongly on Ireland' and the IDA confirmed that Sandoz had been 'to Ireland to look at various locations, including Cork harbour'. The Scottish Development Authority was in strong contention with the IDA to get Sandoz to build their IR£150 million (revised to IR£170 million when the planning application was submitted) plant there instead, so the IDA had to move fast. Some Cork harbour residents suspected that another chemical company was on the way; a few knew that the IDA had been talking to Sandoz and that negotiations had been going on for some time. It was rumoured that the *Cork Examiner* knew of Sandoz's plans but agreed with the IDA not to release the story. This has never been confirmed by either the paper or the semi-state authority. By the end of June, though, the IDA and John Conlon came clean. While his brief has included the Merrell Dow controversy it was, in effect, a smoke screen to cloud his true objective; to find out what the communities wanted from the IDA if a new chemical company was announced for their area. Conlon had managed to talk to several of the anti-Merrell Dow lobbyists and he had gleaned from them that nothing less than an open door policy would be acceptable in the advent of another chemical coming to Ireland.

The IDA desperately needed to fill in the gaps in its Ringaskiddy Industrial Park, which had been built at the cost of IR£100 million and was seen as a political white elephant. At the beginning of July, within two weeks of the *Phoenix* story, the IDA began contacting the media, community groups, local politicians, trade unionists, interested business people and An Taisce to invite them to meet Sandoz at the authority's offices in Cork. Sandoz had agreed to two days of discussions before deciding whether to apply for planning permission to build a factory in the IDA's ill-fated Ringaskiddy Park. It was an initiative light years away from the traditional, dogmatic, IDA approach to corporate investment in

Ireland. Sandoz and the IDA, it appeared in the summer of 1989, were asking for a mandate from the Cork public before proceeding with planning permission. For some community activists it all seemed to be too good to be true. To the general Irish public, seeing no evil, hearing no evil, the initiative was progressive in the circumstances. Once again it was the contrived calm before the inevitable storm.

'We're excited about the prospect of getting Sandoz to come here with this project', the IDA's Kieran McGowan enthused to the assembled reporters, while the Ringaskiddy Residents' Association patiently waited their turn to hear about Sandoz:

> Because of the size and scope of what we're talking about, it would be, if it comes, the biggest single pharmaceutical investment ever in Ireland, ever since we started. It would involve, during the two year construction period, peak construction employment of a 1,000 people, and it would involve, in terms of permanent employment when the plant is up and running, over 200 workers. It would be based in Ringaskiddy and as you know we have, for some time now, been questioned or chastised – or whatever the word is – for our lack of progress in the Ringaskiddy area. So it would be an endorsement of the policy adopted of providing services and making an investment in Ringaskiddy ...

McGowan added that the IDA were very keen to win the Sandoz project. 'We want to involve the people of Cork in a unique way', he said, emphasising that the IDA and Sandoz did not wish to present a *fait accompli* to the Cork public. 'We're doing this as part of the process of trying to win the project rather than as an indication that we've won it.'

He then announced, a little gingerly, that the IDA would lodge a site development planning application within two weeks. A few moments later, perhaps acutely aware of exactly what he had said, he stressed that the IDA's application was 'an utterly separate exercise' and that the company would still have 'to go through a full planning permission process in the normal way'. (Later when the lower harbour communities learned about the 'site development' the general feeling was that the IDA was being arrogant and as several people put it: 'How can you miss what they are doing, with trucks shifting soil?' and 'It's obviously to do with Sandoz.')

Edgar Fasel and Winifred Pedersen spoke for Sandoz, stressing that the company wanted to know in advance whether it could be accepted by the public in Ireland. The technical talk that followed was well intended, rich in content on Sandoz's history, its products and its expansionist plans, but it was poor, almost non-existent, on the matters that concerned the residents of the harbour. It didn't take the reporters long to notice that the allocated time was running out and that Sandoz had said nothing of significance to the people of Ireland. One reporter, in a brusque, genuine, tone, asked if some questions could be put.

The first question was inevitable. 'How can you assure the people of Cork harbour that you're not going to do to the harbour what you did to the Rhine in 1986?'

Pedersen answered, at first hesitant and unsure, momentarily stunned by the question, almost as if he had never expected the Rhine spill ever to be brought up.

> Sandoz are operating in the middle of cities many years without problems; ... even if this factory is dangerous we will apply the standards we have learned; ... it is a completely different unit ... we are convinced this cannot happen.

The reporter persisted. 'You're not going to tell us here that you're going to build the perfect factory, no such thing exists!'

'Would Sandoz', the reporter added, 'offer compensation if something went wrong?'

'If there was an accident,' the Sandoz man replied, 'the company would take over all responsibility', but he added, 'it's not even necessary to say that.' Suddenly he moved on to a tangent to quote how wonderfully Sandoz had dealt with the Rhine spill and how the company had been congratulated by several countries.

Then the direction changed again. 'What degree of public opposition would decide you not to locate in Ringaskiddy?'

The Sandoz man clearly did not want or could not answer the question succinctly. 'It's up to you and the public opinion to let us know if you agree with this construction or not ... if we work it out and tell you what we know about this project I'm sure we will be welcome in Ireland.' It wasn't what the reporters wanted to hear.

'If 50,000 people signed their names to a document which states that they're against you coming to Ringaskiddy, would that decide you to locate or not?'

'This is not the moment for me to give you an answer on ...'

'Well what would decide you then, on not locating here?'

'Certainly a big opposition ...'

'Can you put a figure on it?'

'No, I can't.'

'Are you aware of the Merrell Dow controversy?'

'We are, yes.'

'If you were subjected to the same type of opposition that that company is now being subjected to, would you pull out then?'

'I would say ...'

'Probably. Yes', the reporter prompted.

'That's the sort of reason why we are here.'

The floodgates had been breached. The reason why Sandoz had allowed itself to be subjected to media scrutiny may have been good public relations but it wasn't good copy. Now it was.

> What we are trying to do is build up a kind of trust. It's clear to us, there are always people who will object to everything and with this we have to deal. But if we cannot build up trust with the population here, that they think this is a good company ... we try to do everything that we can do now. If we cannot build up this trust, I mean, why should we set up a factory and operate it if we have everybody against it?

If the Sandoz executives, who were beginning to feel apprehensive, believed that the questions would get any easier they were mistaken. 'What assurances could Sandoz give to the people around the Angus and Penn factories during these discussions?'

'The public relations process', the Sandoz man replied, 'has just begun.' An information centre had been established in the IDA's Cork offices, open daily to anyone with concerns about Sandoz. 'We are certainly glad to come back and explain more to people', he said and then, almost on cue, came the promises: 'Again what we want to do over the time, really, is to build up a relationship of trust and that we can work with the people, that we listen to their concern and we try to react ...'

'Sorry, sorry', a reporter interrupted. 'If I were to ask you to give me three reasons why your plant will be safe; if I was a resident of Ringaskiddy living right beside your site, I've to ask you for some reasons as to why you think you're the safest industry coming into this country today?'

'We are using chemicals on a small scale', he replied. 'They will be processed under controlled conditions and they will be protected....' Later he said there would be a moat around the factory to contain any contaminated run-off water.

The questioning moved onto the warehouse fire that caused the spill into the Rhine. Gradually the pro-industry line from both the IDA and Sandoz began to fade. Bearing in mind the Merrell Dow controversy, another reporter began, two factories in Ringaskiddy are being prosecuted for pollution. 'You can't expect an easy ride for this action?'

McGowan replied:

> I think that we're looking at a real crossroads for us, and for industrial development in Cork town, because it's in the pharmaceutical sector, which we are, which is one of our targeted sections. [Sandoz] is a very reputable international company, it's the biggest investment ever in Cork, it is a very clean investment and we're adapting.

He added that the decision to involve the community, 'to get support in the local area' was a 'turning point for industry in Cork from our point of view'.

For over half an hour it seemed that the IDA and to an extent Sandoz had missed the point. 'But even accepting that,' a reporter said, 'aren't you putting a fairly big load on people in Ringaskiddy? After all they've suffered smells, continuous pollution, continual hazards; there's been a school which has had to be evacuated because of the chemical smells. It's an ongoing thing. Are you now making them the industrial decision makers for the future?' McGowan replied:

> Not really, no. It's a big onus on them, but rather, I suppose what we will be saying is the fact that there are 212 pharmaceutical and chemical companies in the country and most of them, as you know, have been model companies, very responsible but some of them haven't. A small number of them haven't and as a result ... they are now putting at risk a lot of very nationally desired development. What we're asking people to do is hear out what the company has to say and make the distinction between what has happened, with one or two companies breaking the law, and what is, as a general rule, an industry that we're trying to promote.

'Was this not putting people on the line?' another reporter asked. 'You are putting Sandoz' in:

> possibly the most thorny place you could choose ... you have an ongoing legal problem that's still not sorted out; you have one factory who have admitted to a pollution problem and you've got continuous reports almost every month in the same area.

'Well, it's difficult to win,' said the IDA man, 'that's all I can say.'

'But', the reporter sighed. 'Are you giving yourself any chance to win?'

The IDA man's answer was astute, at once pro-industry and anti-pollution, with a clever reference to Merrell Dow's choice of a 'green field' site as a location for its factory. 'In Ringaskiddy we've been criticised fairly heavily for not getting further pharmaceutical companies into [the industrial park] ... we've been criticised for not directing other companies [Merrell Dow] to Ringaskiddy rather than where they have gone to.'

'You are on a sticky wicket this time', the reporter remarked, sardonically.

'We recognise that it's a very important time but I hope', the IDA man said, ' ... we're doing what we're doing in an extremely open way, and I hope it will be seen that way as a responsible approach to the issue.'

'Are you saying that if you can't get Sandoz in you have little chance of getting anyone else, because of [Sandoz's] state of perfection?'

The reply was stark and whether Kieran McGowan realised at the time it was the worst comment he could make in the circumstances. 'If it turns out that we can't get Sandoz in ... it would be impossible to over-emphasise the implications it has for our continuation in pharmaceutical industry, in my opinion.'

McGowan and John McSweeney, the IDA's main man in Cork, had fielded the reporters' questions with intelligible, perspicacious, pro-industry answers. The Ringaskiddy Residents' Association was still waiting in the Sandoz information room on the ground floor. The reporters had a story; Sandoz would pull out if they faced mass objections from the community and the IDA would lose the pharmaceutical industry as an investment opportunity as a result. Yet the Sandoz executives had been unable to provide the hard information on their proposed factory and there hadn't been enough time to elicit the kind of information the reporters knew that the anti-toxic communities would demand. The IDA and Sandoz had come through, relatively unscathed. There was, however, one last scoop for the media, and McSweeney provided it.

'If the Ringaskiddy community association (sic) comes to you and demands more stringent control on existing plants, would the IDA be willing to go along that road so as to encourage Sandoz in and perhaps persuade the Department of the Environment to exert more stringent controls on existing plants?'

'It's fair to say at this point in time that the IDA's official position in the control of the environment is as follows: any company that breaks the law can be prosecuted and we will support that prosecution right up to and including the closure of the plant.'

'But to answer the question properly,' the reporter persisted, 'would you be willing to impose more stringent controls on existing plants in Cork harbour, in Ringaskiddy for example, Angus and Penn? Will it go down that road?'

'Let me just say that the controls that the IDA has with industries, the relationship is normally a money one. If a company breaks the law and is prosecuted we stop the payment of grants. The setting of standards is a position for the county council and the Department of the Environment. We cannot interfere with that.'

'But you do pack a lot of clout, and if, for example, you're going to lose over 1,000 jobs and you're going to lose a IR£150 million project, I'm sure the minister will be willing to listen to what you have to say as a semi-state body?'

'I think we're made our position extremely clear that we will support the prosecution of anybody who breaks the law right up to and including, as I said, the closing of the factory.'

'And is that what you're going to say to the Ringaskiddy community association when they come to you tomorrow?'

'As a matter of fact,' McSweeney replied, not without a hint of urgency, 'we're meeting them right now, ten minutes ago, so we'll have to wrap it up for now.'

'Sandoz are open, so it's a good thing', said Alan Tuohy of the Ringaskiddy Residents' Association, shortly after the July meeting. 'People are worried because of what has happened before so when we [the residents association] talk about it we have to know what we are saying. We are not in a position to say whether Sandoz is good or bad', he stressed, and added that a public meeting would be organised when they had more information about the company's plans for the factory.

It was clear to the people who met Sandoz over the two days that, despite the company's openness and the IDA's clarity about the problem in Cork harbour, there was much more to be done and much more to be learned before the communities could make a decision. While the Ringaskiddy group had an 'open mind' about Sandoz, RICH, the only community group invited to the meetings who were likely to give Sandoz and the IDA a hard time, responded to the IDA's 'don't object or else' ultimatum. 'You can't threaten people', Angela Morrissey said shortly after their meeting. 'This is a democracy. We want specific information to make an informed decision about the potential risks of this factory.' It was an important point, one that would stick in the IDA's throat and develop into a conspicuous issue that would dominate the events of the following months.

In the weeks after the meetings and the announcement that Sandoz wanted a 'public mandate' before applying for planning permission to build in Ringaskiddy, information about the company and its proposed factory was thin on the ground. 'There's not much talk about Sandoz', Tuohy said before the news sunk in that Cork harbour might get another chemical company. 'People don't really know what is going on', he added. 'There are a lot of people against the Sandoz factory,' said one resident, whose reluctance to be named was endemic throughout the area, 'but whether they will object is another thing. Someone in their family gets a job and that stops their opposition.'

During July and August the debate was not omnipresent in the households of the lower harbour. In the sparse and loosely populated villages of Coolmore, Shanbally and Rahene, which are closest to the proposed site, people who were willing to talk openly about the chemical industry were unsure what they should do. Many had not vocalised their opinions about the factory and the pollution, except for the occasional letter to the local papers. Some people said they had attended meetings about the industrial problems in the harbour. Others said they were worried or put off by the tactics of the groups opposed to the chemical industry. Mary Dunphy's new group, Friends of Cork Harbour, was singled out for criticism and the doctor's own motives were questioned. 'She's too headstrong', said one person. 'She doesn't give people a chance to talk, she's too radical altogether.' Yet there were others, RICH's Angela Morrissey among them, who believed that Friends would become the dominant group in the battle against the chemical industry in Cork. 'The high powered objections will come from Friends of Cork Harbour rather than from RICH,' she said, 'although we will be putting in an objection.' The feeling among the members of RICH at the time was that it was difficult to 'slam' Sandoz and that the community would be conned into accepting the factory into Ringaskiddy. It was obvious to those who opposed the chemical industry and to many of the residents' groups that the arrival of Sandoz was detracting from, almost eclipsing, the real issue.

At its inaugural meeting Friends of Cork Harbour clarified much of the local argument about the chemical industry in County Cork when they listed, among other demands, 'that no further chemical and pharmaceutical plants be located in the Cork harbour area until those currently operating have been made environmentally safe and free from noxious smells. A guarantee of safety for both employees and surrounding populations is needed.' They also requested an 'urgent' meeting with Mary Harney, the newly appointed minister of State for the Environment and called for a 'full national debate of IDA policy'. Local hospitals, the group said, should be equipped 'to investigate the presence of toxic chemicals in the local populations'.

While Friends of Cork Harbour struggled to gain a foothold and generate an informed debated about the 'real' problem in Cork harbour, Angela Morrissey and Anne Oulsnam of RICH confronted Sandoz and the IDA, sending letters to both:

> RICH is not automatically opposed to new industries such as yours coming to Cork. Rather we wish to reach a position based on an informed judgement of the balance between the potential benefits and hazards that each new industry poses to the area. At present we consider that we do not have sufficiently detailed information to make such an informed and balanced assessment of your proposals and accordingly feel that further meetings between yourselves and us would be helpful.

> You can of course expect vigorous opposition to your proposals from a number of quarters and we consider it important that you should clearly understand why. The pharmaceutical and chemical industries in the area have persistently emitted the most obnoxious fumes and with

each new plant that comes on stream the problem gets worse. Complaints to the offenders are ignored, whilst the Cork County Council is perceived as being either unwilling or unable to enforce the law on pollution control. The companies themselves are seen as indifferent, irresponsible and arrogant in their attitude to the problem, preferring to rely instead on the moral blackmail that further investment will be withheld and job losses incurred if protests continue. (We understand that one of them is now claiming that it is to spend IR£4m on pollution control – some 15 years after they commenced operations!)

Whether justified or not, the IDA are also seen as parties to the pollution problem since it was they who brought the polluters in. Accordingly, assurance from them regarding your good reputation and intentions are not going to allay the suspicions and fears of the local people who have been given similar assurances many times before, but to no avail.

In the meantime the IDA had been growing restless. Some critics of the IDA likened the Sandoz affair to Custer's last stand. 'If we succeed with Sandoz it will give Ireland an enormous marketing boost', an IDA official said a few days after the two-day meetings. 'Psychologically the other companies and countries will take notice and because Sandoz is European and the tenth largest pharmaceutical company in the world it will be seen as a breakthrough.' John Conlon made an inadvertent, prescient remark: 'If this doesn't work we'll give it up', he told a colleague in the Cork office while the meetings were going on. (After Sandoz the IDA was unable to attract any more chemical corporates to Cork.) For Conlon the excursion into the battlefield had left him a little bedraggled, but a little wiser. 'I've discovered that most people are genuine in their fears about the chemical industry, but there are also people who will object to any pharmaceutical company coming to Ireland', he said at the dusk of the July meetings.

We've been criticised for not being open about projects – for presenting a *fait accompli*; the public only know about it when the company announces their decision to locate, say in Cork. This time we're making the community a part of the process and in a structured way which would build up a trust between them and the company at the very start.

Idealistically it was a sound response from Conlon after he had spoken with people who had been objecting to the industry, as he put it, 'to get their side of the story', and to the industry itself 'to get them to open doors and build a trust between themselves and their neighbours in the community'. In the heady days of July it was an appropriate piece of IDA propaganda, no matter how well intended. The reality of the evolving events in Cork was different. The minister for Industry and Commerce, Des O'Malley, had, days before, warned the Cork people, in a speech reminiscent of McGowan's comments in July. 'It is vital the Sandoz project goes ahead,' said O'Malley, 'not just for the very substantial benefits that it brings in its own right but because of the impact a negative decision on its part could have on our future job creation drive, especially in Cork, but nationally too.'

The IDA and Sandoz toured the communities near the proposed site with a mobile exhibition, but everywhere it went, it was followed by a counter-exhibition, organised by RICH, telling people the real story behind Sandoz. On 21 August 1989 RICH urged the people of the harbour to put questions to the Sandoz and IDA representatives. 'Take the opportunity to go to the travelling PR Caravan and ask questions.'

Ask questions

1. What chemicals will be in use at the plant, and in what quantities?
2. At what temperatures will both plant incinerators operate? The recommended temperatures are in excess of 1,000C–1,200C–1,400C where even with modern technology 100 per cent complete incineration cannot be guaranteed.
3. Will provisions be made specifically for tests of dioxins in emissions in land, sea and air?
4. Will there be 24 hour on-site monitoring?
5. Will monitoring records be available to the public?
6. Will the proposed plant in Cork, which is reputed to be similar to the plant in Basel, be handling the same chemicals in the same quantities? Will the chemical processes be different? If so, would they specify the differences between the two plants?
7. Are Sandoz aware that Ireland's lack of Air Pollution monitoring means that one unit is in use for 700,000

     people compared with Switzerland who have one unit per 50,000.

8. Sandoz are investing IR£150,000,000 in Ireland. How much benefit will we as people accrue from that investment? How much of it for example is capital equipment manufactured abroad and imported into this country?

9. Do the IDA accept the statement in the Telesis Report that the chemical and pharmaceutical industry create very little spin-off in the area of sub-supply?

10. Is it true that Sandoz will be importing all their new materials?

11. Is it true that Sandoz will not be re-investing any money in this country but will be exporting all their profits abroad?

12. Is it true that they will be manufacturing an intermediary product? Do they accept that this is a high risk end of the production of their products? ·

13. If access to EC markets is an important element in their decision to locate in Ireland, whey do they intend to locate in Puerto Rico if they are not allowed access in Cork harbour?

The counter exhibition was so effective that it forced the IDA to call a halt to the tour before it had been completed. Sandoz said it would not come to Cork 'if it is not wanted' – which were not the sort of words the IDA and the government wanted to hear, and over the following four months, from September to December, they began to win the war of words in the media. And when the reporting appeared positive there was a negative sting in the tail. Two days after reporting that the communities around the proposed factory site were unanimously against Sandoz, the *Cork Examiner* presented its readers with a human interest story about Helen McHenry, one of the women who was part of the RICH counter exhibition. Described by the *Cork Examiner* reporter as 'an unemployed mother of two from an nearby local authority housing estate', she challenged a statement by trade union official Joe O'Callaghan of the ITGWU who had earlier accused a 'small well-heeled vociferous group' of opposing industry in Cork.

I'm not well-heeled – I'm unemployed. My husband is a labourer in an unpredictable job. I live with these chemical factories, and my children live with them. I want jobs but not at any cost. I take great exception to that kind of statement being made by a trade union official.

By the middle of October, when it became clear that Sandoz was going to apply for planning permission, it seemed hard to ignore the fact that a high number of people all around the harbour and in the county of Cork who were not ignorant of Sandoz were actively opposed to the factory – or so it seemed. In the week that Sandoz lodged its planning application with Cork County Council and following a meeting of the Coolmore, Rahene and Shanbally residents – who asserted that they would oppose the application – RICH, in a statement to the media, said that 'Sandoz and the IDA have now clearly broken their public commitment to respect local opinion.'

The battle lines were being drawn. The government was steadfastly behind Sandoz. The IDA was, for the first time in months, keeping its head down and its fingers crossed. The harbour communities were adamant that no more chemical companies were wanted in Cork harbour. The IDA continued to warn of the threat to industry by the objectors. The Cork Chamber of Commerce wanted people 'to give Sandoz a chance'. The company was cautious: 'We'll go elsewhere if, within a year, the situation has become really complex.' 'Sandoz', Anton Hupfauf, the company's Senior Vice-President said, 'urgently needed extra production capacity … but it did not have unlimited time available to acquire it.' On hearing that Sandoz would argue for a clean-up of industry in Cork harbour, RICH, in a tart statement, said that harbour residents were being asked to accept 'on scout's honour not only a Sandoz assurance that they themselves will operate efficiently but that they will in fact clean up the existing industries'. Considering Sandoz's record on pollution into the Rhine, RICH said they regarded such assurances as 'hollow'.

The heat from industry was turned up further when Hugh O'Connor of Pfizer 'lashed out at the media' in Cork for its 'unbalanced reportage'. In an editorial headlined 'Pollution and the media' on Saturday, 4 November 1989, the *Cork Examiner* responded, stating that it was 'extremely difficult to strike the sort of balance that will be fair to everybody'. Ordinary people had a right to have their voices heard, 'to air their views and, perhaps especially, their fears'. Some of these lobbies, the paper recognised, 'are very vocal and quite often during the debate, fact tends to be confused with opinion'.

> From a coverage point of view, the situation is not materially helped by the fact that over the past few years, and during a number of fairly major controversies, the chemical companies themselves have tended to lock themselves in rather than come out and talk to people about their operations, their own problems, their efforts, where they exist, to take corrective action that may be necessary and to help generally to allay public fear.
>
> That situation is now changing to an extent, but probably not yet enough to allow this newspaper to be totally confident about balanced presentation of views, despite our best efforts.
>
> Very simply, and it is perhaps important that our stance is well known, it is our policy to support all new industry in the area, provided it is amply proven that it will not be environmentally detrimental. That being so, we also totally support any form of legislation framed for that very specific purpose.
>
> Insofar as our own operations are concerned, and bearing in mind our duty to the whole community as distinct from any one segment of it, we will continue to publish views and opinions on all aspects of the debate, insofar as we are able to obtain these, because we believe we have a duty to inform public opinion rather than mould it.

The editorial concluded:

> If there is, or has been, any lack of objectivity, it must be remembered that this is a very emotive debate, that full knowledge is not always made readily available to us and that too often requests for comment are politely refused by those who seem to see themselves as victims of some sort of media conspiracy. It is regrettable to have to point out that this is not the case.

And then came a response few anticipated, given the depth of feeling among the communities. On 25 November 1989, 760 residents in the Ringaskiddy area (including the townships closest to the proposed site) were asked to vote on the Sandoz issue. Approximately two in five voted and by 277 to 185 said yes to Sandoz. The Ringaskiddy Residents Association who organised the vote, which attracted national television and print media, stated that they would not oppose Sandoz. RICH said that the low turnout reflected apathy towards the vote. 'Despite the massive and highly expensive PR campaign by the IDA, 40 per cent of the electorate still voted against the proposal', said Peter Murray of RICH. Less than a week later a Market Research Bureau of Ireland (MBRI) poll commissioned by *The Irish Times* showed that 51 per cent of people in Ireland did not want the state to attract the chemical and pharmaceutical industry to Ireland. The poll, carried out on 18 and 20 November, was taken from 1,000 people in 100 locations. In Munster, where most of the chemical industry is based, 49 per cent were against the industry with 47 per cent for. The poll also noted that 71 per cent believed that jobs were more important than the environment.

It was now clear to the objectors to Sandoz that the Friends of Cork Harbour umbrella group did not have the clout to challenge the chemical industry in Cork. Mary Dunphy admitted, in December, that she and her husband Sean needed to lower their profiles and allow other people to take up the challenge. Their decision, however, angered several objectors who believed that the lost time had been crucial in the months up to the Bord Pleanála hearing on the Sandoz planning application in March 1990.

Following a Greenpeace conference in Cork on 1 December 1989, which highlighted the environmental organisation's drive for zero emissions from industry by the year 2000, the various local groups and individuals opposed to Sandoz came together to form the Cork Environmental Alliance. Not everyone opposed to Sandoz allied to the new group largely because of its stance, which was to 'ensure that [the Sandoz] development as proposed never takes place'. Meetings throughout December, January and February allowed the alliance to coordinate its activities and objectives.

On Friday 16 February 1990 the Cork Environmental Alliance was formally launched in Cork's Metropole hotel with Angela Morrissey, UCC sociologist Aveen Henry, solicitor Joe Noonan, fisherman Dietmar Scharf, and yacht designer Butch Dalrymple-Smith in the chair. The alliance represented numerous individuals and seven local groups – Concerned Citizens, Cóbh Anti-Pollution Association, East Cork Harbour Environmental Association,

Friends of Cork Harbour, Midleton Area Environmental Group, Harbour Watch Cork and RICH. 'The prospect of one of the largest chemical plants ever to locate in Ireland adding its toxic emissions to the local environment BEFORE the present problems have been resolved is totally unacceptable', the alliance said, stressing that Cork was a 'vulnerable region being made the sacrificial victim of irresponsible and hypocritical industrial policy'. Cork harbour does not need 600 tonnes of effluent a day added to it, the alliance said. 'That is why Sandoz is also a national problem. National assets are being bartered for dubious short-term gain.' It was, the alliance maintained, time to choose:

> Do we choose a government policy which puts tourism at risk, threatens our agriculture and poisons our environment or one which promotes agriculture and the further processing of food, safeguards our environment and health, and preserves our reputation as one of Europe's last remaining green havens?

Advocates of Sandoz who had had it all their own way in the autumn and early winter were suddenly confronted by a challenge to their assertions that industry-starved and unemployment-ravaged Cork unanimously welcomed the Swiss chemical giant. 'The existence of this group is proof that Sandoz is totally wrong when they and the IDA claim that the Sandoz proposals are universally welcomed throughout the Cork harbour area.'

Sadly, for those opposed to the complete globalisation of Ireland, the Cork Environmental Alliance was unable to stop Sandoz. Unlike the American corporates, this Swiss corporate cleverly weaved its way into Cork society by applying lateral thinking to each problem it faced. For example, when An Bord Pleanála said it had to operate its incinerators with zero emissions, Sandoz simply re-applied four times to Cork County Council for a new licence – and got it without the conditions imposed by the planning appeals board. Derry and Una Chambers' challenge in the courts might have had a different outcome if Sandoz had taken it as a genuine threat. Instead it went ahead with construction.

The Chambers' motives for taking the challenge were based on Derry Chambers' knowledge of the industry. 'Having worked in the industry for several years I was well aware of the antics they got up to', he said.

Venting gases at night, waste being discharged illegally, etc.
Despite the impacts these activities were having on public
health, including the health of my own children, the
authorities consistently failed to take any action. I suppose
we saw the opportunity as one of putting down a marker
that the communities of Cork harbour were not going to
put up with being slowly poisoned any longer.

The Chambers based their challenge on Sandoz's failure to produce
an environmental impact statement for the development:

Our case was based on the fact that the planning authorities had failed to demand an EIS of the developers and we
claimed this was in breach of EU Directive on EIS. They
challenged our locus standi claiming we had not taken
sufficient interest in the development prior to coming to
court. We lost on this point in the High Court and also
failed to obtain an injunction halting the development.
Costs of approximately IR£250,000 were awarded against
us. By the time we reversed this judgement in the Supreme
Court (about a year later) the factory was practically built
and on legal advice we decided not to proceed with our
substantive case i.e., the EIS breaches.

Clearly there was a problem for communities opposed to hazardous
and toxic development. Every time a community thought it had
mounted a successful challenge, it realised that the state was not for
turning. If the people in Cork were unable to successfully challenge
this industry and its waste products, what hope was there for
communities in the rest of the country? Derry Chambers remained
optimistic about their challenge against Sandoz. He said, in the end,
they felt 'like the curate's egg'. Some good things had come out of
the court case, some bad, he said.

I do think the resources used in the court case may have
been put to better use but that presupposes a community
more inclined to radical tactics. The positive side of the
case was the fact that because of the attendant interest
taken in the whole Sandoz saga the IDA has failed to
attract a single pharmaceutical/chemical corporate to Cork
since.

Community opposition in Ireland to polluting industry has largely been projected through the state's own apparatus. In other words the communities have played the game by the state's rules, using existing legislation (planning appeals), the constitution (court action) and scientific expertise to present their objections. What we have seen is an indisciplined negation of this self-empowerment, in a manner which social ecologist Murray Bookchin has always been concerned about. 'These movements and tendencies are now faced with a crisis that threatens to warp their emancipatory logic into aborted, subservient, and conventional ideologies of the status quo.' Though Bookchin is referring to the more sophisticated social movements in North America, his words resonate through the community halls of Irish towns and villages which have been the principal battlegrounds of resistance to undesirable industry:

> The problem they face is the need to discover the sweeping implications of the issues they raise; the achievement of a totally new, non-hierarchical society in which the domination of nature by man, of woman by man, and of society by the state is completely abolished – technologically, institutionally, culturally and in the very rationality and sensibilities of the individual.

Tara Jones's analysis of the Sandoz campaign is pertinent to the argument that a dialectical understanding of Irish capitalist society is essential if the pitfalls Bookchin writes about are to be avoided and why 'increasing participation in the planning, administrative and legal processes' should not be the only challenge.

> No one denies the need to challenge projects through these processes but campaigns face possible major problems through opposition groups over involvement in this type of process. To begin with, these are highly expensive actions and take place in a situation where the developers and the state always have more resources than the local community. It also means that the battle is waged mainly on the state's terrain, and in the end the decisive power in these areas rests with the state. Similarly, there can often be an over-reliance on the use of the legal system to stop a development. While many communities have become disillusioned with the

planning and legal systems as a means of opposing developments, in some cases this disillusion comes too late for
successful political action in the local area to stop the development. It would indeed be wonderful if these conflicts could
be solved through rational discussion, but communities in
these cases are not dealing with rational systems that
welcome contradiction and discussion but with money and
power – or capital and state, if you prefer – both of which are
highly irrational in their operations. Thus it would be a fool-
ish community that puts all its eggs in this one basket. Paying
too much attention to the legal and planning side and not
enough to public mobilisation, information campaigns and
direct action can lead to a fatal imbalance in the campaigns.
The issue must not be simply fought and won in the forum
provided by the state but must also be fought and won on the
streets, in the homes and farms and at the mart, in a political
way as well as an expert way. If communities win the battle
on their own home turf, only through coercion and violence
will the state succeed in imposing its plans. Furthermore the
most successful campaigns have involved a combination of
legal and direct-action tactics. The opposition to Sandoz in
Cork appears to have fallen into the trap of relying too much
on participation in the administrative process.

Jones's criticism of the Cork Environmental Alliance is justified
because, as he explained, Sandoz got to build their factory, 'a situation that could never have occurred with Merrell Dow in east
Cork'. CEA's desire to be seen as legitimate and respectable in the
end backfired on them, particularly at the planning hearing when,
as Jones noted, the alliance:

> fatally undermined its case when it advanced a compromise
> set of conditions under which it would accept the factory.
> This was the dilution of the outright opposition that
> needed to be manifested publicly and no doubt lost the
> CEA credibility locally. This decision was also taken out of
> the hands of the local groups that constitute the CEA, thus
> raising issues of democracy inside the CEA. Also the CEA's
> welcome for the 'stringent' Bord Pleanála conditions was a
> major tactical error. Unfortunately one does not win these
> campaigns by being polite and respectable.

One of the major reasons that objectors to undesirable development should not become 'obsessed with the Bord Pleanála planning dance', as Jones puts it, is because the state, under pressure from industry, can change the rules. In November 1990 Dan McInerney expressed his dismay at the latitude given to third party objectors. 'The right of appeal should be removed from third parties', he suggested. Whether McInerney was speaking in an individual capacity as a property developer or on behalf of those disturbed by the dogged community resistance to undesirable development is not known, but he certainly encapsulated the sanguinary views of the IDA, industry groups and those of a beleaguered central and local government.

Less than a year later the Local Government Planning and Development Bill 1991, which was an act to amend and extend the Local Government Planning and Development Act 1963–1990, was published, with some startling proposals. The bill proposed specific changes to the appeals process, notably that the grounds of appeal should be stated in full at the outset, that the appeal be lodged within a month, that the developer comment on the appeal within a month and that it 'will be a statutory objective for the Board to determine appeals within four months'.

The Cork Environmental Alliance, in response to the Bill, claimed that it was 'a highly regressive piece of legislation'.

> Under the guise of streamlining the planning process, this Bill diminishes the input of third parties. With weakened third party appeals, the procedure would be heavily weighted in favour of developers and against the rights of individuals to democratic participation in matters affecting their own communities. The real purposes of this legislation is to deny Irish citizens the right to full access to full information and fair participation at the appeal stage in planning matters.

Michael Bailey, managing director of Envirocon, an environmental consultancy, in a letter to *The Irish Times* in relation to 'delayed' planning decisions and the Chambers' court action against Sandoz certainly saw it that way:

> The successful court challenge by the Chambers against Sandoz indicates the difficulty which faces the IDA and

potential industrial developers in attempting to placate local opposition. I am sure potential investors, both native and international, will view this latest development with great concern. They will begin to look at other countries where at least there is some limit to third party appeals and a scientific rational approach to emissions, environmental impact and industrial development.

What was curious about Bailey's letter is that there are very few countries left in the world where public concern about pollution and damage to health and the environment is not manifest in national politics. Ireland is only unique because most Irish communities haven't a clue about toxic issues. When they learn about the impact on human health from toxic substances the shock is enough to galvanise them into action, but they remain – in their own country – marginalised and isolated. Unlike many of the less-industrialised countries which have quickly absorbed the lessons that 'development at any price' has a high environmental and human cost, Ireland has successfully ignored this reality.

Until the relevant sociological and anthropological studies are undertaken, and viewed as accurate barometers of public attitude, it will remain unknown what the majority of people in Cork harbour feel about the chemical industry. According to Ron Holland there was not an anti-chemical industry bias amongst the majority of Cork harbour residents.

> It's amazing considering the shit we've had to put up with that only 40 per cent voted against [Sandoz] in Ringaskiddy. I think that showed how open people are to the possibility of helping the IDA out. There is a problem with the IDA and their attitude; the mere fact that they began bulldozing the site in front of everyone's face here before the planning permission was put through. That was an outrageous exercise and bad public relations.

Sandoz was the 'last battle' in a war the state was determined to win. The IDA's John Conlon had made that crystal clear at the authority's HQ in Cork during the early stages of the Sandoz campaign. So who knows what the impact on the chemical industry in Cork would have been if the Swiss corporate had been forced to go elsewhere for their EU factory? What was becoming obvious was that the communities of Cork harbour, including those that had challenged toxic industry, had decided they needed jobs more than they needed to protect their health and their environment. When Greenpeace protesters occupied Sandoz's toxic waste incinerator while it was under construction in July 1993 there was not much support for their action or their demands for clean technology, zero emissions and effective monitoring. By the end of the 1990s the EPA would claim that it had got the chemical industry to clean up its act, and the communities, in the end, got what they wanted – a toxic-free environment. That is the uninformed opinion. The anecdotal evidence suggests that the pollution is still evident and impacting on the health of the communities and the workers. 'All the evidence of higher rates of cancer and other illnesses are anecdotal', Derry Chambers said.

> The Cancer Register is based on place of death and 95 per cent of cancer victims die in hospital in Cork and therefore their deaths are part of the Cork City statistics and can be masked in the much larger population as statistically insignificant, whereas if the figures were contrasted with the smaller harbour populations we would have a different story.

Chambers is not alone in not believing the rhetoric from the EPA HQ in Wexford. It is his opinion that the EPA is 'simply designed to nullify citizens' input into the development of their communities and to place a veneer of pseudo science and legality over unchecked pollution'.

Only the problem of disposing of the industry's toxic waste remained and, once again, Cork became the battleground as yet another generation in Ringaskiddy found itself opposing a waste facility. The desperate search for a toxic dump, which started in the mid-1970s, became a desperate search for a toxic incinerator – in the mid-2000s.

5   Toxic Ireland: Polluted

Scientists can pretend that they can discern 'safe' levels of hundreds of different chemicals, all acting in combination. They can pretend that they can understand all the ill effects of multiple hormone mimickers on each type of cell, each tissue and each organ at every stage of development from conception to birth, through youth and puberty and into maturity, in each of the thousands of affected species. They can pretend to know these things, but they cannot ever actually know them. They are just pretending. Scientists can pretend, but in so doing they perform a great disservice, preventing decision makers from seeing what really needs to be done: we need to abandon the practice of chemical-by-chemical regulation. We need to regulate whole classes of chemicals. And the dangerous classes need to be phased out and banned.

Peter Montague

The IDA's desperate attempts to find a final solution for Raybestos Manhattan's asbestos waste were the first appearance of a problem that would continue to dog the state at the turn of the millennium. The Raybestos experience showed that the state had totally failed to consider the waste disposal problems involved in bringing high-tech and high-toxicity industry to Ireland. As Tom McNamara of the Institute for Industrial Research and Standards admitted in November 1976, 'We haven't in fact evaluated waste disposal as we should have.'

It took two more years before the state decided to begin its first attempt at evaluating toxic waste disposal in the country. On 16 November 1978 Michael Killeen of the IDA announced that the IIRS had been commissioned to produce a report on standards and procedures for toxic waste disposal.

He did this just three days after Cork County Council took the first step to set up an official toxic waste dump. The council's

Southern Committee approved a proposal to site a toxic waste dump in Nohoval. The county council had been looking for an answer to the question of where to put Cork's toxic waste since the Raybestos fiasco had started, but everywhere it looked it found community opposition. The council also came under increasing pressure from industry, the state and the trade union movement to provide a solution to the toxic waste problem. In August 1978 the President of the Cork Council of Trade Unions called on the IDA and the council to move quickly to find a dump for waste for what he euphemistically described as 'specialised industries' like Raybestos. Some indication of the council's desperate search was that it had looked at 39 other sites before deciding on the Nohoval/Oysterhaven area. When it announced its decision, council members were warned that opposition could be expected.

It manifested itself almost immediately. A member of Cork Corporation, Councillor Kiely of Fine Gael, who had listened to the meeting from the public gallery, accused the council of attempting to 'wipe out the Nohoval community', claiming the council was ignoring the existence of 1,500 people in the immediate area who would be threatened by the dump. Councillor Kiely did not believe that the decision on Nohoval had been made on purely technical grounds. 'I feel the technical study to establish its suitability is only so much whitewash. This decision is being dictated solely by reasons of expediency.'

Opposition they expected, opposition they got. Reaction in the nominated community was swift. Following the announcement that their area was to be graced by a toxic waste dump, 70 residents came together for a hastily-convened two-hour meeting to found the Nohoval and District Residents' Association (NDRA), to which an ad hoc committee of nine members was elected. The committee then met and called a public meeting for the following Monday night. Fianna Fáil's Barry Cogan, deputy for mid-Cork, attended and reported on the Southern Committee meeting, arguing that such a dump was a 'must' for Cork's industrial development. The meeting was also addressed by Jim Enright of the Crosshaven Residents' Association who spoke of the Crosshaven residents' response to attempts to dump asbestos waste in Fort Camden in 1977.

Residents had resolved to refuse council officials permission to enter their lands to test its suitability as a toxic dump. The lands of six farmers were covered in whole or in part by the proposed site. Two days later Michael Killeen – while announcing that the IDA was going to pay the IIRS to study the problem (thus admitting that the state didn't know what it was doing) – called on local people not to block the dump. The response from the community came about a week and a half later when 500 people attended the first public meeting in Nohoval to protest against the dump.

At the public meeting in Tracton on 19 February, 400 members of the Nohoval association passed a motion unanimously opposing the introduction of a toxic dump on agricultural, health and environmental grounds. The Nohoval secretary told supporters that they faced a legal battle over the siting and financial assistance was needed as well as help and support. A short film presentation on pollution in the United States was followed by addresses from a number of county councillors. Labour's Eileen Desmond, another mid-Cork deputy, promised to represent the residents' views and Barry Cogan said he would take up the residents' case and see that alternative sites and other methods to tackle the problem were investigated.

The following day the campaign won an important ally when the Irish Farmers' Association promised its full backing to its Cork members opposed to the proposed use of their land for toxic dumping. The county chair of the IFA, Ned O'Keeffe, said the IFA would bring the case to the European Court if necessary. O'Keeffe gave some indication of the cost of forcing the Nohoval farmers off their land:

> If they win and force our members off their lands, the bill just for the six farms will be well over IR£1 million. On top of that substantial compensation will have to be paid in disturbance money. No one could expect farmers and their families to simply move on from their traditional homes without being highly paid for the severe inconvenience.

O'Keeffe suggested the council should consider alternative means of dealing with the problem by dumping in Cork harbour's sloblands or by buying an incinerator. The latter alternative was immediately dismissed by council officials as prohibitively expensive.

The same month the council formally applied to the courts to enter and test lands owned by the six Nohoval farmers. In response the Nohoval association said they would fight compulsory acquisition orders 'through every court in the land'.

As a postal strike was then going on, county council officials had to deliver summonses to appear in court to the six farmers by hand. On 21 February 1979, two council officials arrived at George Kingston's home to present him with a summons. When he refused to accept it, the officials pinned the summons and an accompanying map to his front door. Ignoring a locked gate on the farm of Michael Collins and a NO ENTRY sign on the avenue up to the house, the officials pinned a notice to the farmhouse's front door.

These actions immediately conjured up visions of British civil authorities in the previous century pinning up eviction notices, and were bound to raise the ire of the local community. Chris Collins, a spokesman for the farmers and the Nohoval Residents' Association, accused council officials of adopting 'offensive and arrogant tactics which Irish farmers did not tolerate in the last century and will not tolerate now'. Such tactics were sure to strengthen opposition. One farmer said: 'We are digging in. We have no intention of letting them in here.'

The fight then became embroiled in the court system. The first two decisions, in the district courts of Kinsale and Carrigaline, found in favour of the council. At the hearing in Kinsale District Court in April, Jack Roberts, chairman of the Nohoval Residents' Association, submitted to the court a petition signed by 500 people expressing concern over the proposed dump. The council was not so lucky third time around. On appeal to the Circuit Court in June 1979, Judge Fawsett refused permission to the council to enter Nohoval lands to take test borings. When it was referred back to the District Court in April 1980 the farmers again won. Judge Fawsett ruled:

> Having considered the whole matter since the evidence was given in the present case, I am left in the position that I am not sure. Accordingly, the appeals should succeed and I am refusing the county council's application to enter on these lands, surveying and making borings.

Collins said the decision was 'a vindication of our policy from the outset that we should put ourselves in the hands of the courts.... We did not indulge in emotionalism, riots or protests and we still made our point.' Other observers claimed it was pure luck of the draw that the residents' case came before Judge Fawsett and not another judge who was sure to find for the council. Collins costed the residents' campaign so far at IR£20,000. Circuit court costs only were allowed to the Nohoval farmers. In August 1981 an appeal was heard in the High Court and in January 1983 the Supreme Court heard an appeal. For some four years Cork County Council's plans to set up a toxic waste dump were mired in legal proceedings. In July 1983 the Supreme Court dismissed Cork County Council's appeal. Collins welcomed the ruling:

> It was a great relief to the people of our area to find that we can rely on the law to protect us. We never went in for hysterical, illegal or violent conduct or protest. Our strategy has been fully vindicated. We hope this sets a headline for other communities.

He condemned Cork County Council for continuing with the case after an expert witness the council had brought in from abroad had admitted in the Circuit Court three years previously that the selected land failed all the known criteria for a toxic waste dump.

While all this was going on, toxic waste continued to be dumped in an uncontrolled fashion. The issue again came to notice, as tends to happen in Ireland, through a near-disaster. On 9 June 1980 waste dumped in a roadside drain near the Gradogue river in north Cork was washed into the river by heavy rain. The next day fish began to die in the river while the waste moved at the rate of a mile every three hours down the Funcheon river towards the larger Blackwater river. An appeal was made for the driver of the road tanker from which the waste came to come forward and identify the substance involved, so that remedial action could be taken. Gerry Keating, chair of the Munster Trout Angling Council, asked the driver, anonymously if necessary, to contact him by phone at any hour of the day or night. Samples taken from the Gradogue and Funcheon rivers were being analysed.

At this point investigators, including the Gardai, Cork County Council, Lismore Fishery Board, An Taisce and the Munster Trout Angling Council, had an open mind whether the spillage was accidental or deliberate. Anglers turned out in large numbers to transfer fish to an unaffected side stream. Fishery Board officials said they hoped the pollutant would become more diluted in the Funcheon river, which meets the Blackwater twelve miles downstream. The test results the following day showed the substance was complex, with a strong acid content. The Cork County Engineer, Liam Mullins, requested that any firm handling or producing a substance that produced a violet-purple colour in water to contact the council.

Emphasising that the disaster wasn't being treated as deliberate, he said: 'My own feeling is that it is something that might have dripped out of a tanker on the roadside without the driver knowing it.'

By Friday 13 June it was obvious that the Blackwater was going to be saved from a pollution disaster. Tests continued in an attempt to identify the chemical but the council warned it might take some time because of the chemical's complexity. On the following Monday the chemical was identified by John Palmer of An Foras Taluntais, Moorepark, Fermoy, as chromium. Noting that chromium, which was used extensively in tanning and car assembly, is a cancer-inducing agent, he said that, but for good fortune, the waste could have found its way into the water supply of one of the local towns with tragic consequences. By Tuesday it was reported that samples showed heavy traces of chromium as well as several other toxic chemicals and a considerable amount of acid. By Wednesday 18 June the Gardai had discovered the identity of the lorry driver and of the tanker's Cork owners. The 5,000 gallons of chromium had also been traced back to the Abbeyleix, County Laois area.

All this prompted renewed calls for a national toxic waste dump. In response to the Gradogue disaster, the Munster Anti-Pollution Committee announced that it would meet to draw up legislation to control the movement of dangerous substances. Gerry Keating warned:

> The public have no protection whatever – we are now talk-ing about a danger to people, not just to fish. If the chromium had been spilled into the Lee, above the city waterworks, or above any town water supply, we could have had a major disaster.

Among those who called for a national toxic waste dump was Matthew Lynch, Manager of Environmental Services with the IIRS.

> To prevent incidents such as last week's spillage, we will have to provide a properly controlled toxic waste dump to cater for those intending to dump waste. It is a matter of immediate urgency. We should not assume incidents will not happen again.

Some 40,000 fish were killed by the pollution. The waste poisoned two rivers, the Gradogue and the Funcheon. In the Gradogue the waste wiped out all life – fish, water fowl and even rats – along three miles of the river, while five miles of the Funcheon were affected. The Chairman of Fermoy Urban District Council, Thomas Phelan, said those responsible could have caused a major tragedy if the substance dumped got into the Blackwater from the Funcheon: 'The Blackwater is what we use in our tea. You can imagine what would have happened if the stuff got through. We could all have been wiped out.'

Despite appeals for anyone with information on the dumping to come forward, it required investigation by the Gardai before blame was assigned to the dumping operations of Willie O'Brien. Speaking in the High Court on 30 July 1980, senior counsel R. N. Cooke said the county council had to have extensive tests carried out to find out what had been dumped, nobody knew what the stuff was and where it came from. Thus a week lapsed, he said, before the chromium that poisoned the Mitchelstown river could be identified.

Early in July Cork County Council obtained an order under the Water Pollution Act against William O'Brien (Plant Hire) Ltd, one of its directors, Willie O'Brien and one of his drivers, John Dinan. On 30 July, Cork County Council obtained an order against the originating company, Stonearch Ltd, a company manufacturing poultry feeds in Abbeyleix.

Speaking on RTE radio that September, Willie O'Brien blamed his worker for the disaster. 'The driver made a mistake but it will not happen again', he said, regurgitating a favourite management tactic in the chemical industry, normally used to obscure the management and technical systems that allow for, or create, human error. In this case, what comment is necessary on the management structure and attitudes of a company which apparently was unable to record that a truck full of toxic waste had dumped its contents at a non-company site? The only other conclusion other than total lack of management controls was that this was deliberate company policy and such dumping by drivers was in no way unusual. Such allegations of course were made.

This practice was commonplace in mainland Europe, in North America and in countries where state policy encouraged the importation of hazard. Drivers employed by waste disposal companies frequently dumped their wastes in ditches and on roads. Some companies, like Bliss in Missouri, even sprayed contaminated oil on roads to keep dust down. The tactic of dribbling toxic waste out on roads was also a common practice that law lecturer Yvonne Scannell said was occurring in Ireland in the 1970s and 1980s. It was also reported that O'Brien's drivers often didn't know what they were carrying. The drivers 'receive a docket which registers the date, time and place of collection of the material, but not the identity of what is collected'. This was also common around the world.

A native of County Kerry, O'Brien was an entrepreneur who began his activities at the age of 18 by purchasing with his brother a truck to transport turf. They quickly moved into sand and gravel haulage and then expanded into plant hire, with their business eventually stretching from Kerry across to Mallow in County Cork. The family business was then split, with Willie working the Cork end of it and then expanding by moving first into plastic pipe manufacture, then bulldozing and excavation and then into crane hire, a business he pioneered in Ireland. The company grew to national stature, setting up its first depot in Dublin in 1966, the same year opening a Limerick depot, in 1968 opening in Waterville, and in 1970 in Galway. O'Brien admitted in 1976 that he owned 75 trucks for carrying waste, and by 1980 he estimated his firm carried 60–75 per cent of all the toxic waste in the country.

On the same day that Cork County Council obtained an injunction against Stonearch, the company that generated the chromium waste, they also applied for an injunction against O'Brien's dump at Ardarostig and Garrandarragh, Bishopstown, Cork. This dump was on a three-acre site where O'Brien stored equipment. Barrels of chemicals were reported to have been dumped on this site. Water samples taken from below the dump between July 1979 and February 1980 showed serious pollution. O'Brien's witnesses admitted that the dump contributed to the pollution of the river but said the dump was not the only cause. They agreed to do anything reasonable to remedy the problem, but did not agree to the council's suggestions for mitigation. The council wanted the dump moved 20 feet from the river bank and also wanted the dump lined with plastic or clay. O'Brien responded with the worrying argument that interfering with the dump could cause a greater escape of pollution. Patrick O'Grady, a chemical engineer employed by O'Brien, declared the tiphead was relatively well sealed and drained by the standards prevailing then. The hearing was postponed to allow Cork County Council and O'Brien's negotiate a settlement.

The response of all parties to the poisoning of the Gradogue was to recognise the existence of the toxic waste crisis and to interpret it in their own way. Matthew Lynch, of the IIRS, blamed the widespread illegal dumping of toxic wastes on the failure of the local authorities to provide adequately supervised waste sites. Taking a similar view, the director of the Federation of Irish Chemical Industries said the development of the chemical and pharmaceutical industries in Ireland were being hampered by 'primitive' toxic waste disposal facilities.

By comparison, Philip Mullally, Chair of An Taisce, laid the blame squarely at industry's door. He accused companies of contracting disposal firms to handle 'the dirty side of the business' without showing any interest in the ultimate destination of toxic waste. An Taisce called, on 26 August 1980, for the publication of a confidential report produced for the IDA and the government in 1978 that named the companies producing toxic waste in Ireland. An Taisce said the IDA was withholding the report on the grounds that it contained confidential information. The companies who had provided the information to the IIRS had done so on condition that the information not be made public. Mullally said:

> We call on the IDA to release this information in the public interest so that the problem can be tackled on a national basis. It is time for these firms to stop pretending they can carry on in a different way here than in their parent countries. This matter has become too serious for the authorities to continue turning a blind eye to a problem which is potentially a major threat to human and animal health.

Subsequently An Taisce called for a comprehensive register of waste disposal activities to be set up that would record all movements of toxic waste and be tied to an accident alert procedure, the setting up of one or more waste disposal and processing centres – even recommending potential sites to the Department of the Environment. An Taisce wanted proper, scientific and recorded disposal of wastes.

The environmental response was strongest from Cork. Gerry Keating, of the Munster Anti-Pollution Committee, produced a document entitled *The Toxic Waste Problem in Ireland – The Need for Solutions*, which argued for the need for proper management of toxic waste disposal in Ireland, citing many examples of the effects of unregulated toxic waste dumping in the United States, and called for the introduction of waste reduction at source, waste exchange, waste reprocessing, incineration and secure landfill disposal.

The Gradogue disaster continued to have repercussions throughout the country as the crisis over toxic waste intensified. Investigative reporters with the weekly news magazine *Hibernia* followed O'Brien's lorries to County Kildare where they found another unapproved dump operating. On 25 August, Kildare County Council asked the owners of Gavin's Quarry, near Kill, County Kildare – where highly dangerous toxic effluent had been dumped – to close the pit while investigations were carried out. A subsequent study by An Foras Forbartha found traces of chromium, cyanide and other heavy metals at the pit. 'An Foras Forbartha and Kildare County Council acknowledge that no one knows the precise quantity or indeed the mixture of toxins in the ten-acre dump just off the dual carriageway.' The following day another unapproved dump at another quarry in Kerdiffstown, County Kildare was discovered. There was no planning permission for dumping at this quarry, nor had planning permission ever been applied for.

In response to this distressful publicity, William O'Brien and Axxon Waste Disposal decided to take their trucks off the road. Bernard Buckley of Axxon said it would not be handling any waste for its 350 industrial clients in Dublin until either Dublin County Council or the government provided a tip for liquid industrial waste. With pressure increasing for some sort of stop-gap solution, Dublin County Council stepped into the breach. In September Cork County Council told the government it would not provide a national tiphead for toxic waste. Attention then shifted to the Dublin area, the second largest producer of toxic waste, then under threat from the closing of dumping grounds in Kildare.

At a special Dublin County Council meeting on 20 October 1980, the council decided to provide a dump for toxic waste from industry at the existing municipal tiphead at Dunsink near the low-income suburb of Finglas in north Dublin. The Deputy County Engineer for Sanitary Services, Larry Brassill, presented a report to the meeting recommending the use of Dunsink. Estimating the cost of the dumping operation at IR£90,000, with an intake of 10,000 tons, Brassill told the meeting there were 370 firms facing problems in disposing of toxic waste and between 25 and 50 had a 'major immediate' problem. Brassill argued the dump should be provided before some of the companies 'take the easy way out and dump the material'. He assured the meeting everything that went into the dump would be monitored both by the council sanitation department and by the IIRS. He also said the dumping would represent no danger to health as solid waste would be covered every day and liquid waste would filter down through the solid waste. The meeting approved the decision by 14 to 1, the dissenting voice a county councillor who was a representative of the area.

In November 1980 the council announced plans for the dump at Dunsink. The reaction from the community was immediate. On 17 November 300 people packed into the West Finglas Community Centre for a meeting in opposition to the dump organised by West Finglas Tenants' Association. Aidan Doyle, chair of the West Finglas group, warned that the waste could seep into the Tolka river and pointed out the dangers involved in toxic materials being transported through the densely populated area of Finglas. West Finglas's secretary, Brian O'Callaghan, claimed that waste chemical slurry, pesticide residues, wastes containing cyanide and arsenic, noxious organic solvents and sludges containing metals such as zinc and copper would be dumped at Dunsink. The meeting heard how the site was very close to a housing estate of 53,000 people as well as to Cappagh Hospital, while some 400 travellers lived at a serviced site one field away from the intended toxic dump. The meeting was addressed by local representatives, tenant groups and the Reverend Mother from Cappagh Hospital, who warned that patients in the hospital and young children in the west Finglas area would face serious health risks if the plan went ahead. Brendan Halligan of the Labour Party denounced the decision as one 'taken by stealth against the interests of the people of Finglas'. The meeting voted to set up a special action group to fight the proposed dump.

If the move to Dublin saw similar community opposition grow, it also saw a change in the type of campaign waged against toxic dumping. The residents of Finglas and their allies had neither the resources nor the belief in the legal system to indulge in a lengthy legal battle with Dublin County Council. The campaign resembled the resistance to Raybestos more than the legal battle in Nohoval against Cork County Council. The campaign was both creative and radical, following the success of the anti-nuclear movement – from which it received some support, making use of cultural weapons such as anti-toxic festivals in Finglas and in Baldonnel. The Finglas opposition also made use of video technology to create propaganda against the dump and to record events at the dump as evidence.

On 25 November the Dublin Toxic Industry Action Group, an outgrowth of the anti-nuclear movement using the offices of the

Trinity College Students' Union who were campaigning against a proposal by Trinity College Dublin to site a nuclear waste incinerator in Santry, issued a leaflet opposing the dump. The leaflet argued that 66,000 tons of toxic waste would be dumped at Dunsink and that the state intended it to become the national toxic waste dump. This raised the stakes in the dispute immediately. In December, city councillors expressed fears at a Corporation General Purposes Committee meeting about the Dunsink decision, with Mary Flaherty calling for a national plan on toxic dumping for fear the Dunsink dumping would be extended. The corporation's Principal Officer, David Byrne, noted that Dunsink was a well planned and well looked after dump and that every time 'toxic' was mentioned, there was hysteria. At the end of May 1982 the government announced that industrial waste would not be accepted at Dunsink.

Elsewhere in the country it was business as usual and the hysteria was no less intense. The Dunsink solution did not deal with the toxic waste crisis and community resistance to dumping continued. As the struggle continued in Finglas, other struggles flared up and died. In September 1981 200 local residents objected to a new dump in Ahenny, County Tipperary. The same month Newry and District Trades Council called for a public inquiry into dumping of chemical waste at Newry Council's dumps. The following month a 24-hour picket by residents of Loughanure, near Dungloe in County Donegal, stopped dumping by companies from the Gaeltarra Éireann industrial estate at Gweedore. When the companies responded by moving their dumping to the council dump five miles from Falcarragh, close to the source of the river Ray, protests followed the dumping and again blocked it. In October, Galway County Council sent in work crews to dig up chemical waste on the site of the former Maxan factory near the village of Oranmore, six miles east of Galway city, after receiving a report on the contamination of the site from the IIRS. A year and a half after the Gradogue disaster, the crisis was still as intense as ever. In November 1981, environmentalists and waste disposal experts claimed that the government was turning a blind eye to the illegal dumping of toxic chemicals around the country. Philip Mullally, of An Taisce, claimed that an environmental time bomb was being planted in Ireland's water resources 'which could put the public and industry at risk in the long term'. But the government was scheming.

On 3 March 1982, Peter Barry, Fine Gael Minister of the Environment, announced that a national toxic waste disposal centre would be set up on a 14-acre site near the old Potez factory at Baldonnel, County Dublin, at a cost of IR£1 million. The Minister announced that the dump would only store waste prior to export for treatment or disposal at authorised facilities abroad and claimed it would therefore be no more dangerous than a warehouse. He admitted, however, that in future a treatment or incineration plant might be provided at Baldonnel if it became economically viable. Optimistically Barry hoped the Baldonnel 'facility' would be operational within twelve months. The government also announced new regulations governing the 27 wastes listed by the EC as toxic and dangerous, but also announced that these regulations would not come into operation until January 1983. It was reported that 20,000 tonnes of hazardous waste was being produced annually in Ireland.

The same night that the government announced the dump, local organisations met to consider the implications. This led to the immediate formation of groups from the nearby towns of Rathcoole, Clondalkin and Tallaght under the banner of the Amalgamated Anti-Toxic Group. The group called its first public meeting on Thursday 24 March, in Rathcoole Community Hall. It invited Barry and all the local deputies. Hundreds of people turned up but the politicians did not attend because it was Budget Day. The group then met Ruairi Quinn, Minister for State at the Department of the Environment, who assured them that no toxic waste unit would be built at Baldonnel until a special report from Danish experts was studied by the government.

Given that the growth of popular opposition in the area had made its toxic plans highly unpopular, the state did not rush to bring its toxic plans to fruition. The local opposition was so intense that all local TDs, whatever their party, were forced to oppose the plan to ensure their own personal political survival. The state made haste so slowly that in March 1983 Matthew Lynch, of the IIRS, was moved to complain at a conference organised by the Federation of the Irish Chemical Industry:

> The proposals [for Baldonnel] were welcomed by both industry and An Taisce as being well founded and the measures were seen as urgently needed. But the only major development since then as far as is generally known has been the build-up of organised opposition to the Baldonnel facility locally. No planning application has yet been made, as will be required by law, and the proposed facility seems

years away from realisation if indeed it will ever materialise. One cannot help concluding that the project is not being pursued with anything like the commitment and sense of urgency which seems from an industry viewpoint to be required.

By May of 1984 the Minister of State at the Department of the Environment, Fergus O'Brien of Fine Gael, announced that planning permission would be applied for in the autumn, adding that it would not be a toxic dump, it would be a toxic facility. But in April 1985, after the toxic 'facility' became a major election issue locally, Liam Kavanagh, the Minister of the Environment, announced that the plans were to be 'reviewed'. Kavanagh announced that he would appoint a small expert group to make recommendations on whether the state should proceed with its plans or let private sector interests develop suitable schemes. He said that his consultations with private sector interests had established that current waste disposal services had considerably developed and 'there may well be an interest in expanding these services and providing new facilities'. This move was seen as a victory for private interests who wished to retain control of the profitable business of toxic dumping in Ireland and had reportedly put pressure on John Bruton, Minister for Industry, to allow them to do so.

The announcement was seen by some local residents as a blatant political ploy to get the issue off the agenda for the election. The following month Fianna Fáil's Charlie Haughey wrote to anti-toxic groups stating Fianna Fáil was opposed to the siting of a toxic waste transit centre in Baldonnel, that Bobby Molloy, Fianna Fáil spokesman on the environment, had announced this to be Fianna Fáil policy and this policy was supported by local Fianna Fáil candidates. Thus the Baldonnel plan began to die a quiet death of neglect and in September 1986 the local Labour deputy Michael O'Leary claimed the government had abandoned its plans for the Baldonnel dump. In 1987 the Baldonnel dump was finally abandoned officially.

With the Baldonnel plan allowed to die quietly, the state returned to its old reliable policy of standing idly by. The state's technical advisers, primarily the IIRS, and its industrial promoters, the IDA, continued with their propaganda campaign – calling for the establishment of some sort of national toxic waste disposal scheme, with the IIRS warning continually of the hazards posed by unregulated dumping. The strategy advocated by these sectors of the state was for the creation of a national toxic waste disposal centre. This strategy was accepted by the state as the ideal solution, but the state lacked the political will to impose such a disposal centre on any area for fear of electoral repercussions. The politicians in turn hoped that if they ignored it, the problem would go away.

Meanwhile the local authorities continued to provide whatever waste disposal service they had previously provided by co-disposal on their landfills and tipheads, but failed to provide nominated sites for industrial and toxic waste disposal. Any attempts that were made by the local authorities to nominate such a site were immediately met with unified community opposition. For example, even the suggestion that Raffeen in County Cork might be used as a toxic waste dump led to a packed meeting in the Hotel Glenbrook in February 1986, which totally rejected such a suggestion. This rejection was total also in that communities rejected dumps no matter what assurances regarding safety were given by local authorities. A motion was unanimously passed rejecting a toxic dump no matter what measures were taken on the site by Cork County Council.

Faced with this situation, the two strategies that had characterised toxic development in Ireland were allowed to continue. The first strategy, adopted by the more progressive elements among the corporates, especially the pharmaceutical industry, was to deal with waste by incineration on site or by exporting it. The other strategy was a continuation of the old laissez-faire dumping policy. Both strategies had led to conflict. The incineration strategy also led to failure for two pharmaceutical companies who were reported (but not named) in the Hanrahan/Merck Sharp and Dohme High Court case as having abandoned incineration. The use of incineration in Cork harbour was becoming problematic, and following the Hanrahan victory, proposals for toxic waste incinerators in the factories of both Merrell Dow and Sandoz were to be major causes of conflict and controversy.

The hazard export strategy also ran into troubles, with some companies, such as Penn Chemicals, running into difficulties over where it was acceptable for their waste to be dumped in England. Late in 1981 Penn exported potassium methyl sulphate waste (from a new process it began in September 1981) to Chemstar, a company that operated a solvent recovery plant in Manchester. Following an explosion and fire at the Chemstar factory that killed one worker, Chemstar attempted to dump the waste at the Pitsea landfill site in Essex and at storage tanks at Killamarsh, Derbyshire, but these options were blocked by British governmental pressure. West Midlands County Council blocked an attempt to dump the waste down a disused mine shaft and Tyne and Wear prevented the waste being stored in tanks in North Shields. Following these problems Penn met British civil servants and, following their advice, stopped working with Chemstar. Instead its toxic business went to Rechem to be incinerated at Fawley and Pontypool. From September to December 1981 Penn had exported 500 tonnes of this waste. There was some disagreement over the toxicity of the waste. Penn described it as 'smelly but basically non-toxic'. British government experts however said little was known about the chemical and it was 'prudent to treat it as dimethyl sulphate', a highly toxic chemical, potentially fatal, which may cause long-term damage to liver and kidneys and listed by the International Agency for Research on Cancer as a suspected carcinogen. The British experts argued that the waste should be treated or incinerated but never dumped.

The new arrangement with Rechem did not solve Penn's problems. The following March the *Craigantlet*, a ship carrying Penn's toxic waste from Belfast to Liverpool, ran aground off the Scottish coast. The container of toxic waste on board split and its contents emptied into the sea. Again there was a problem over the identity of the waste. The ship's manifest listed it as methyl sulphate salts, firefighters thought at first they were dealing with dimethyl sulphate, the Scottish Office said it was potassium methyl sulphate while Penn said it was sodium methyl sulphate.

Despite these particular problems, the hazard export strategy continued to be a widely used and successful one. As in Ireland's methods of dealing with abortion, exporting toxic waste to England continued to provide an Irish solution to an Irish problem. In 1987, Ireland exported 2,000 tonnes of toxic waste to Britain for disposal, according to the report of the British Hazardous Waste Inspectorate. This made Ireland the second largest exporter of toxic waste to England, with 12 per cent. Despite continuous dire predictions by politicians that this escape valve was in danger of being cut off, the British state had no intention of shutting down the highly profitable waste trade, despite intense community campaigns against some incinerators and toxic waste dumps.

The *laissez-faire* dumping solution continued throughout the 1980s and well into the 1990s. In August 1984 barrels containing styrene and styrol were found dumped in a stream in Tallaght, County Dublin. In April 1986 Dublin county councillors were warned that asbestos waste was being dumped secretly on council tipheads. In June 1989 Councillor Michael Martin claimed that hazardous industrial waste was being dumped at the Cork Corporation landfill site on the Kinsale Road secretly. Later that year, barrels of polychlorinatedbiphenols (PCBs) were found abandoned in Douglas, County Cork. With stories like these in circulation, the pressure for the creation of a national toxic waste dump built up. This pressure came not only from the corporates and certain sectors of the state but also increasingly from the EU. The arguments for a national toxic waste dump began to be based on the need for Ireland to fulfil EU environmental directives that required it to clean up its act while politicians used the debate about the transboundary shipments of toxic waste transport to argue for a local solution, as it was claimed that both England and France would in future refuse to handle further loads of toxic waste from Ireland.

By 1988 the pressure to establish some form of national toxic waste dump became so strong that the state was forced to move – in a different direction. In April the government announced a feasibility study with incineration, at a cost of IR£40 million, as the possible solution. In May 1988 Eolas – the incarnation of the IIRS – issued figures showing that between 4,000 and 5,000 tonnes of toxic waste had disappeared over the past three years. The bulk of this disappeared waste was believed to have been dumped illegally on waste tipheads or through the sewage system. In July 1988 Byrne O Cleirigh Engineering, a Dublin based consultancy, were appointed by the Minister for the Environment to study the feasibility of a national toxic waste incinerator. In October 1988 Professor Charles Dillon of the ESB, speaking to the Institute of Engineers in Ireland, said Ireland should get its house in order by complying with EU directives on toxic waste. Then the state showed its hand. In November 1988 Padraig Flynn, Minister for the Environment, speaking at a conference on waste disposal in Cork, said that incineration was the long-term solution to industry's toxic waste problem but he added that it was not going to rush; another study had to be completed. So while the state's study was underway, the private sector stepped into the breach.

In June 1988 a company called Hydrochlor Manufacturing Ltd was formed to build what was claimed would be 'a small hydrochloric acid manufacturing plant' in the docks area of the city. The company stated that the factory would 'combine the production of hydrochloric acid with disposal facilities for chlorinated waste solvents from the Irish chemical industry'. At first glance it appeared to be a straightforward business proposal resulting from the merger, three years earlier in May 1985, of two Irish firms, Byrne Engineering and Shannon Structures and Services Ltd, and Basic Environmental Engineering Inc. of Chicago to form Basic Shannon Combustion, who were billed as a waste to energy company. In 1987 NADCORP, the state-owned venture capital company, bought a 20 per cent stake in Basic Shannon Combustion. Limerick business people Martin Redington and Tony Stapleton were the Irish partners in Basic. On 7 June 1988 Redington and Stapleton joined with Eamon Mulhall, another Limerick man, to form Hydrochlor. Investment in Hydrochlor came from the state agency Shannon Development, Basic Environmental Engineering of Chicago (who are an incineration design company) and Partyka Resource Management of Massachusetts (a toxic waste broker). The management of Hydrochlor had, said the company, 'the benefit of 20 years experience and expertise in the design, manufacture and running of sophisticated waste recycling and thermal converter systems'. The company also claimed that the factory 'while small' would be 'one of the most modern and technologically up-to-date anywhere, with microprocessor monitoring and control systems'.

It all appeared to be very grand. To some Limerick people, among them local IFA man and agricultural consultant David Thompson, there was more to Hydrochlor than met the eye. The key to Hydrochlor was the simple fact that it would operate an incinerator and would be taking in chlorinated solvents. The Limerick Environmental Health Protection Group was swiftly formed to find out more about Hydrochlor. Thompson drafted letters and under the group's banner started a debate in the Limerick and Cork papers, leaflets were composed to inform and advise the Limerick people of Hydrochlor's plans, public meetings were planned, advice and information was sought from Earthwatch, Greenpeace and other sources. By November 1988 Limerick Corporation had received 400 objections to Hydrochlor's planning application.

Hydrochlor's planning application stated that it expected to process 9,000 tonnes of chlorinated and non-chlorinated solvents to make 6,000 tonnes of hydrochloric acid per annum, a simple equation the waste industry, individual scientists and environmental groups claimed was not possible in the long term. Environmental groups and several scientists claimed there were not enough spent solvents in Ireland to justify Hydrochlor's operation. Greenpeace said what the Limerick group had been saying for over a year, that Hydrochlor were in fact setting up the structure for a toxic waste incinerator, but the international environmental organisation were not the only observers in the drama. Byrne O Cleirigh completed its feasibility study on the incineration of hazardous waste in Ireland and the need for a commercial national incinerator. 'In order to protect the viability of (a national toxic waste incinerator), it will be necessary to discourage those competing facilities which are currently under investigation, or in planning, from going ahead.' Byrne O Cleirigh recognised that 'under existing legislation it may prove difficult, if not impossible' to tell companies like Hydrochlor to go away. Despite a recommendation from the Minister for the Environment that the toxic waste incinerator would not be built in a highly populated area, it was also clear that Limerick Corporation's problem involved finding a way of telling Hydrochlor to go away while avoiding a heavy compensation claim. Instead Hydrochlor informed Limerick Corporation that it was withdrawing its planning application. The site, they had decided, was unsuitable. And in February 1989 the Byrne O Cleirigh report recommended that planning for a national toxic waste incinerator should go ahead.

In September 1989 tenders were invited for the national toxic waste incinerator, and shortly thereafter a shortlist of five consortia was picked, among them the waste disposal companies Irish Environmental Services and Minchem – both exporters of Irish toxic waste. What did not emerge at this time was the hope in government that DuPont, in Derry, would let them off the hook by building a toxic incinerator at its factory at Maydown, which would take Ireland's toxic waste. It appeared to be the perfect solution. DuPont was an established chemical corporate and it needed a facility to get rid of its own toxic waste, so taking the toxic waste from the rest of the country was just the answer to the solution. But, as before, the communities struck back and, after an intense campaign that involved 70 groups culminating with an analysis that a national toxic waste incinerator was not economically feasible, DuPont went the way of all the others who had attempted to provide the state with a solution to the toxic waste problem; it gave up.

When DuPont abandoned its plans in December 1991 it left egg on the face of a government that had promised industry to have a high temperature incinerator in place to deal with the country's hazardous waste by 1992. Padraig Flynn had said Ireland had three options for the disposal of its toxic waste. 'The prevention of waste by using clean technologies and processes; recycling; and safe disposal of waste in the nearest and most suitable site relative to its point of production.' The latter option was Britain. In 1989 the British government said it had no problem taking toxic waste for treatment or incineration from other countries 'provided it is properly regulated at all stages'.

By 1993 this did not stop the Department of the Environment getting together with the engineering department of Trinity College Dublin to organise a conference on hazardous waste management with a single agenda: the establishment of a national toxic waste incinerator. In June 1993 Environment Minister Michael Smith announced that he would hold a seminar 'to promote discussion, and hopefully greater consensus' on incineration as an essential option for toxic waste disposal. At the time some environmentalists believed that the seminar would seek to legitimise industry's unqualified need for an incinerator. 'It will assist our consideration of waste disposal options to allow incineration to be included among them, as it now is in virtually all other EC states', said Smith, adding that the environmental opposition to incineration was an inordinately closed and limited one.

> Export of waste for disposal in other countries is a delicate issue – both politically and environmentally. It is now strictly controlled by the Basel Convention and the corresponding EC regulation on waste shipments. It follows that we must aspire as far as possible to self-sufficiency in waste management. This is a matter of political and environmental responsibility for the Irish government and people.

He was supported in this view by Liam McCumiskey, head of the new Environmental Protection Agency.

> We're not going to be able to export it. Are we going to close our eyes and pretend it doesn't exist? The pragmatic approach is to have a facility that can be operated efficiently and successfully and avoid illegal disposal.

To back their case, when the seminar was finally held in January 1994, the government wheeled out new estimates on hazardous waste returns which set industrialists and environmentalists at each other's throats, each arguing that inaccurate returns, confusion over definition and interpretation of data portrayed a false picture. The seminar was told that 82 per cent of the 66,500 tonnes of hazardous waste believed to be generated each year was disposed of in Ireland, of which 18 per cent was burned in five on-site hazardous waste incinerators. This left 18 per cent or approximately 12,000 tonnes, which the Department of the Environment claimed was exported. The waste disposal industry and the Irish Business and Employers Confederation argued that the total figure was higher, that as much as 20,000 tonnes was exported for incineration, while Waste Action, a new pressure group, demanded full disclosure of accurate data. Government figures showed that approximately 4,000 tonnes was incinerated in England and Finland. The Department of the Environment said it was still trying to complete its latest survey of the available data, and added that all but one local authority had returned the required information. Irish Business and Employers Confederation (IBEC) argued that a 'toxic waste disposal and processing facility in Ireland would protect existing jobs and increase the attraction of Ireland for new industries' adding that the estimated IR£50 million cost to build the incinerator should be sought from EC structural funds.

The formation of the EPA in 1993 and the introduction of the Waste Management Act, 1996 changed everything. For the first time in Irish history hazardous waste was to be classified and, it appeared, regulated. Unlike the bad old days of the 1970s and 1980s when the state had no idea how much waste was being generated, the EPA in conjunction with local authorities and the Department of the Environment was empowered to provide annual figures. When new EC regulations widened the definition of hazardous waste, this heightened industry's demand for a national toxic incinerator and the state's desire, using the regulations in the Waste Act and European funding, to provide one. The announcement of the EPA's first national waste inventory in 1996 showed that industry had generated 240,000 tonnes of hazardous waste in 1995. What were more alarming than the higher than expected figure were the EPA's figures on the recovery rate and treatment of this waste – which was lower than expected, despite government promises that recovery and recycling were now waste management priorities. These figures amounted to slightly over two-thirds, approximately 180,000 tonnes, leaving 60,000 tonnes that was either incinerated, exported or landfilled. The debate over figures had been resolved, but anti-toxic campaigners realised that for the first time a national toxic waste incinerator was economically viable, and the industry, supported by government policy, went to work to plan a giant incinerator while continuing to add on-site incinerators just in case.

Roche (formerly Syntex) in Clarecastle was the first to succeed, crushing without much fuss the 18-month community opposition in December 1996. Orla Ní Éilí of Ennis, the nearest town to Clarecastle, took Roche to the High Court but her case also rested on the evidence of experts whose testimonies were easily dismissed. Consequently the High Court decided the EPA's decision to grant a licence was 'rational'. Ní Éilí appealed to the Supreme Court and on 30 July 1999 the five judge court rejected that appeal, Justice Murphy stating that the conditions imposed by the EPA on the licence provided even more protection for the environment.

The campaign began with the formation of Care for Clare, a group representing fishing, farming and tourist interests. As the campaign became serious and the myriad groups realised that Syntex was, according to one campaigner, 'running rings around us' Clare Alliance Against Incineration was formed to take up the challenge. It started well. The groups thought they had an ally in Richard Fitzgerald, the environmental health officer with the Mid-Western Health Board, who started asking some awkward questions about existing dioxin levels in the area. In a letter to Clare County Council on 19 October 1995 about Syntex's application for planning permission for the incinerator he said: 'Is the applicant suggesting that such dioxins are "naturally" present in most soils or are they present as a result of toxic emissions from, supposedly, the chemical industry?' and: 'Can the applicants then comment on the possibility that such dioxins found were introduced to the lands by the use of the applicant's pharmaceutical plant?'

For some strange reason Syntex, which was bought by the Swiss chemical corporate Roche in 1995 when it was valued at $5.36 billion, never got round to answering Fitzgerald's questions despite the concern in and around Clarecastle about the health risks from dioxin. Instead the Mid-Western Health Board's Chief Medical officer, Dr Kevin Kelleher, said the Mid-Western Health Board were in the 'difficult position' of trying to assess the possible health risks from the proposed incinerator as against those from the pollution levels already in existence. Incineration, he said, 'was the most safe way of doing what is necessary on the site within the economic parameters allowed by the Act' adding that 'what is happening now does not meet the EPA requirements'. When asked about the ability of the health board to object on health grounds he said 'the legislation makes our position not dissimilar to a member of the public' yet, he added, there had been some meetings with the EPA resulting in a 'useful debate' on the subject.

Syntex claimed that new European and domestic legislation would eventually force it to abandon its practice of exporting its toxic waste to Britain (to Rechem near Pontypool, Lothian Chemical Company in Edinburgh, Chemical Manufacturing & Refining in east Sussex and occasionally to Cleanaway in Ellesmere Port) and occasionally to Finland. Syntex Ireland's managing director Bob Costello dismissed the 'outrageous claims' by those opposed to the incinerator.

> I remain absolutely convinced that our incinerator is essential to comply with environmental regulations and to allow the plant to expand in the future. I am also convinced that it will be safe and will not pose a threat to the health of people or animals in the locality.

This victory for Roche appeared to indicate that the industry had, after years of failure, finally found a way to defeat its opposition. Clare Alliance Against Incineration had campaigned to prevent the building of the incinerator by, in its own words, following 'every official means' of objection. It was a flawed strategy and its campaign failed because it did not learn from the successes and failures of previous anti-incinerator campaigns, but more crucially it failed to realise that the state was more determined than ever to include incineration in its waste management strategy. Kieran Keohane described the EPA's oral hearing, its first, on the granting of a licence to operate the incinerator 'an instance of systematically distorted communication'. The alliance of groups opposed to the incinerator could not understand why the EPA should be allowed to adjudicate on an appeal against its own decision. 'Some participants felt that the hearing was a cynical exercise in public deception,' said Keohane, 'a deliberate sham designed to give the appearance of a sincere discussion, deliberately intended not to re-examine, but merely to endorse a course of action already taken'. Keohane himself saw the hearing as 'white noise' but his added assertion that it was a 'sideshow' was closer to the truth.

Once again the state ignored evidence about the toxicity of the chemicals to be emitted from a toxic waste incinerator but, to the alarm of those who believed the war was being won, the protesters underestimated the state. In their report on Roche's application, following the oral hearing, the EPA said it did not believe that the new evidence on the toxicity of dioxins presented by the protesters justified their concerns. It was a remarkable statement and one that the state in collusion with industry would go out of its way to prove over the following years, initiating biased studies that would purport to show low levels of dioxin amidst Ireland's toxic hot spots.

By failing to notice that the industry was building incinerators that were able to reduce the amount of dioxin emitted, the protesters put their eggs in a basket that was made of old material. An EC directive, endorsed by the European Council in June 1993, required industry to apply new standards to their new incinerators in 1995 and to existing units by 1997. Many chemical companies in Europe immediately spent millions of euros installing new technology, including catalysts that they claimed eliminated 99 per cent of dioxins. BASF in Ludwigshafen in Germany spent €65 million on equipment upgrading its eight high-temperature incinerators. 'We now have a limit – a regulatory 0.1 nanograms per cubic metre and I say that is absolutely agreeable', Bayer's Gerhard Stolpa announced. 'In my personal opinion the risk of dangers from dioxins are heavily over estimated.'

While epidemiologists, oncologists and toxicologists were focusing on the impact from the range of chemicals being emitted from incinerators and other toxic combustion processes, Irish industry cleverly ignored the new evidence and concentrated on the older debates about dioxin. It is not known if the EPA was aware of the statement in 1993 by Linda Birnbaum, the USEPA director of environmental toxicology and co-ordinator of its reassessment of dioxin:

> If all you are worried about is dioxin, the levels of dioxin by itself are probably not that high. But when you look at the sum total of what is out there, that is where the body burdens may be high enough – so you might say we are having a response.

Birnbaum went on to add that 'the weight of the evidence is becoming overwhelming'. There was new evidence that toxic incineration produced the effects the Clare protesters claimed it did, but it appeared that they did not have access to it. Neither did they appear to understand that dioxin works in concert with other synthetic pollutants in different ways, and the Irish EPA was certainly not going to go out of its way to consider data that was not being presented to it. More frighteningly, by using experts who were not at the cutting edge of toxicological research, the protesters failed to address the issues zoologist Theo Colborn, among several scientists studying the impact of specific chemicals, had raised five years earlier in 1991. Dioxin was only one of the chemicals implicated by Colborn and her colleagues. Thus, by isolating the debate about it, the EPA were able to rule that dioxin, as they wanted to understand it using old data, was no longer a problem and therefore not an issue for Roche. It was a defining moment in the toxic war that was now turning in favour of the allied forces of industry and state.

What was more disturbing for communities who feared incinerators in their midst was the continued failure of the green lobby to apply some lateral thinking to their campaigning about the health effects of incinerator emissions. By concentrating on dioxin and ignoring the wider issues about incineration emissions the green lobby had applied a strategy that industry and state could handle. Awareness of the holistic health impacts of waste management has never been part of that strategy. Modern waste incinerators emit tiny particles containing hundreds of chemical compounds of which dioxin counts only as one. To concentrate the debate on dioxin was always going to simplify and not explain the reason communities fear incineration.

Particulate emissions from incinerators contribute to air pollution that has its source in the actions of animals, plants, geophysical activity and humankind. Animals exhale carbon dioxide, decaying vegetation produces methane, volcanic activity vents sulphur oxides, winds carry suspended particles from natural sources and humankind as a result of its technology pumps into the atmosphere sulphates, particulates, carbon monoxide, nitrogen oxides, oxidants (such as ozone), polycyclic aromatic hydrocarbons (such as dioxin), volatile organic compounds (such as benzene, formaldehyde and vinyl chloride) and various other chemicals, heavy metals and minerals. Combustion has been accepted as the major source of air pollution and if we were living in the nineteenth or twentieth centuries it would be easy to argue that there isn't much evidence about the health effects. Lester Lave and Eugene Seskin said as much in their 1977 book *Air Pollution and Human Health* when they stated that 'the scientific community has been slow to accept this evidence ... because of the methods used to gather it and the lack of studies using controls'. This is no longer true.

If you live in an urbanised area, near an industrial complex with or without an incinerator, a motorway or a combination of all three, the air that you breath daily will contain fine particles visible to the eye only as smoke, dust, soot or as a gas. They are not visible except as a general haze. They are far too small to be seen. They are not captured efficiently by modern pollution-control equipment, but we do know about them. It was the USEPA that started measuring particulate pollution, in 1987, describing it as PM10, particulate matter 10 micrometres or less in diameter. A micrometre is a millionth of a metre and a metre is about a yard. The dot above the letter i in a newspaper measures about 400 micrometres in diameter. PM10 is measured by weight, so 50 micrograms measured as a 24-hour running average means the total weight of particles with a diameter of 10 micrometres or less in each cubic metre of air (μg/m^3). One μg/m^3 is one millionth of a gram in every cubic metre of air. A gram is $^1/_{28}$th of an ounce and a microgram is a millionth of a gram. Therefore it is the size, shape and density of the particle that determines how long it remains suspended in the atmosphere and what happens to it if it is inhaled. 'Biological effects of a particle', state Douglas Dockery and Arden C. Pope, 'are determined by the physical and chemical nature of the particle itself (particularly its solubility), the physics of deposition and distribution in the respiratory tract, and the physiologic events that occur in response to the particle's presence.' According to Anthony Seaton:

> very small particles, below about 1 micrometre in diameter, may remain suspended for weeks, whereas those greater than 2.5 micrometres in diameter are removed by settling and by rain in a matter of hours. A cloud of the finest particles will thus drift for many miles and may cause pollution across national boundaries.

In a 24-hour period an adult breathes approximately 20 cubic metres or 20,000 litres of air. In a modern city, on many days, the air will contain 100 billion one-nanometre-diameter particles in each cubic metre of air, all of them invisible. By weight, these 100 billion particles will only amount to 0.00005 micrograms (one ten-thousandth of 1 per cent of the 50-microgram legal limit), yet they are responsible for much of the health damage created by particulate pollution. And size is the problem. Larger particles get caught in the nose and throat where they are removed by coughing, spitting or swallowing. Those particles that escape this natural filtering process get as far as the airways of the upper lung where they settle on the inner walls. The smallest particles however are carried into the air spaces known as the alveoli in the deep lung where gas exchange occurs between the air and blood stream, oxygen moving in and carbon dioxide moving out. Scientists estimate that between 50 per cent and 60 per cent of the smallest particles, below 0.1 micrometre in diameter, are deposited in the alveoli. If they are not soluble in water, they are retained in the deep lung for long periods (months or years). Because of their origin in combustion processes, most fine particles are coated with toxic materials – metals like lead and mercury, or toxic organics like polycyclic aromatic hydrocarbons (dioxin, for example) – so fine particles provide a uniquely efficient carrier, giving dangerous toxins direct entry into the blood stream. The toxicity of urban particles and urban particulate emissions depends in part on the type of metal compounds they contain, as well as their combustion-derived organic content.

To understand the biological mechanisms involved it is necessary to know how the lung functions, how it deals with pollutants and what happens when those pollutants penetrate the body's natural defences. The primary function of the lung is for gas exchange, to allow oxygen to move from the air into the bloodstream and carbon dioxide to move out. The lung also metabolises some compounds, filters toxic materials from the circulation and acts as a reservoir for blood, but it is the gas exchange at the blood–gas interface in the deep lung that is significant when dealing with fine particles. Gas is brought to one side of the blood–gas interface by airways and blood to the other side by blood vessels.

The lung is characterised by airways, which consist of branching tubes, and blood vessels, which encapsulate small air sacs called alveoli. There are about 300 million alveoli in the human lung. The alveolated region of the lung where the gas exchange occurs is known as the respiratory zone. This zone makes up most of the lung, consisting of airways and airspaces. Diffusion of gas molecules within the airways takes less than a second of the time we take to breathe in and breathe out. Inhaled particles or pollutants which are not trapped by the nose and throat, for subsequent excretion, are deposited in the alveoli where they are mostly engulfed by large wandering cells called macrophages. However this protective mechanism is not wholly reliable, and Seaton has suggested that the particles that reach the alveoli provoke inflammation, thus causing lung damage, and release natural chemicals into the bloodstream, causing coagulation of the blood. This, Seaton and fellow scientists hypothesise, can lead, in susceptible individuals, to acute respiratory illness and exacerbations of lung and heart-related diseases.

Reviews of the epidemiological evidence suggest that particulate pollution is causing or exacerbating a wide range of human health problems, including initiating and worsening asthma, especially in children; increasing hospital admissions for bronchitis, asthma, and other respiratory diseases; increasing emergency room visits for respiratory diseases; reducing lung function (though modestly) in healthy people as well as (more seriously) in those with chronic diseases; increasing upper respiratory symptoms (runny or stuffy nose; sinusitis; sore throat; wet cough; head colds; hay fever; and burning or red eyes); and increasing lower respiratory symptoms (wheezing; dry cough; phlegm; shortness of breath; and chest discomfort or pain); and heart disease. It appears also that there is no safe threshold, no level of particulate pollution below which deaths do not occur. In their review of epidemiological evidence of health effects of particulate air pollution, Pope, Dockery and Schwartz 'observed associations between particulate air pollution and various human health endpoints, including incidence and duration of respiratory symptoms, lung function, restricted activity, hospitalisation for respiratory disease and mortality'. They added:

> because of the public health relevance of these findings, there has been considerable interest about potential biological mechanisms, constituents of particle pollution, potential interactions with other pollutants and risk factors, sources of these air pollutants, and how these findings can be incorporated into public policy.

Air pollution is contributing directly or indirectly to a range of illnesses from respiratory disease beginning with asthma to heart, lung and brain disease depending on the vulnerability of the individual, to reproductive disorders and dysfunction. Of all the combustion processes in use in the modern world incineration is arguably the worst because the emissions and ash are deadly packages of toxic chemicals.

A debate about incineration in the Seanad in June 2000 revealed there was much confusion among politicians about the health effects. Their remarks showed remarkable ignorance, and at times the debate was theatrical rather than political. Galway Senator Fintan Coogan of Fine Gael prompted the debate with a motion to talk about the issues involved in waste reduction, recycling, composting, incineration and gasification, with particular reference to any possible consequences to public health. Coogan led the debate by arguing that communities were 'frightened' by incineration and that the facts needed to come out. 'I have two files with me', he said, taking an objective stance:

> one, a very thin one, is pro-incineration, containing claims that it is safe and that the dioxins produced are minimal. The other file is three times as thick and it contains evidence that incineration is dangerous. Included in that file is an Environmental Protection Agency report from the United States, which says that dioxins from incineration are carcinogenic, in other words, they cause cancer. I have no other proof of that and I do not know how this report was drawn up, but I assume the EPA in America is as qualified as the EPA here and that it did not lightly decide the dioxins are carcinogenic.

With this knowledge Coogan asked Noel Dempsey, Minister for the Environment and Local Government, why he believed incineration was safe. 'Will he assure me and everyone else – public representatives and those they represent – that its safety is guaranteed?' Coogan raised a crucial aspect of the debate, that he believed misinformation was rife, and that the government agenda on incineration included keeping the truth out of the public domain.

> This subject is worthy of a long debate. Senator Quill, other senators and myself have continually asked for a debate on this which we did not get, so we must compress the discussion into Private Members' time. We are not being informed of all the facts. I want to be convinced that the decision I make is based on all the facts.

Senator Jim Walsh of Fianna Fáil was happy to provide those facts – and a few his own government probably did not want to hear.

Walsh's speech was the most informed of any heard in the Senate or the Dáil on the environmental and social issues surrounding incineration. 'Emissions from incinerators threaten health and the quality of food. In the case of dioxins it is wrong to claim there are many other significant sources in Ireland', he said, referring to a government report that argued other sources for dioxin other than incineration and to the use of report as propaganda. The report acknowledged that data on dioxin sources was limited and that the calculation on the amount of dioxin in the Irish environment could only be based on estimates, significant points the government managed to overlook. Walsh clearly knew what he was talking about:

> Lists of other dioxin sources are used to mislead the Irish public since these measurements are from industrial and contaminated Europe. Burning straw in central Europe releases dioxins because incinerators have deposited dioxins on the lipid layer of grass. It would be wrong to justify introducing a major source of dioxins into this country on the basis of figures taken out of context. All sources of dioxin must be eliminated. If waste incineration is a source of dioxins, then it must be eliminated. This is why the EU Waste Management Directorate has stated that incineration is now being viewed in the same way as nuclear power – nobody wants it. Particulate matter from incineration is another problematic emission because it is so difficult to trap the dangerous parts. Smallest particles present the greatest threat, in particular those less than 2.5 microns. Pollution control devices in incinerators manage to catch only between 5 per cent and 30 per cent. These emissions cause heart attacks and strokes. It is not possible to eliminate all the risks from waste incineration simply because it is not possible to eliminate serious pollutants such as mercury, cadmium and other heavy metals, as well as the smallest and most dangerous particulate matter. Even the amounts of these that are removed must be disposed of in a landfill.

It was Labour's Joe Costello who made the most relevant point. 'This is unreal science', he argued. 'We do not know what incineration has in store for us.' And it was Fianna Fáil's Ann Ormonde who summed up the real problem:

I am sorry the debate was so curtailed. Senators Quill, Costello and I, with other Senators, have continually asked for a lengthy debate on this issue, which we failed to get. Unfortunately, we had to compress it into the few hours given to us tonight, as a result of which certain issues were not dealt with. Worst of all, we have come out with no further information or no greater knowledge which tells us what we should be doing. How can we go back to our local authorities and tell them we have made no progress? All we got was a one-sided response from the Government.

Throughout 2000 the government continued to argue that it had all the information it needed. Unfortunately that information was based on the infamous USEPA reassessment on dioxin, as if it was the only report that mattered. Of course this was exactly the line the state wanted to take. The Irish EPA would follow the lead taken by the USEPA because it had spent the 1990s procrastinating about dioxin and had insisted its report was still a draft and could not be cited because it had only put it into the public domain for peer review.

'The United States Environmental Protection Agency, USEPA, has, since 1991, been engaged in a comprehensive reassessment of dioxin science, which it hopes to complete this year', Noel Dempsey announced, taking a line that he hoped would quell the opposition to incineration who appeared far too ready to cite the USEPA assessment. He added:

Last June the USEPA published two chapters of its proposed report for the purpose of scientific peer review. In so doing, it cautioned that the material concerned should not be cited as the agency's final assessment of dioxin risks, and stated that the question of using the outcome of the reassessment for regulatory purposes does not arise until the review procedure is completed.

This has been the crux of the Irish state's position on dioxin through-out the 1990s, but Dempsey had a much more important point to make. He acknowledged the classification of dioxin as a human carcinogen by the International Agency for Research on Cancer, an agency of the World Health Organisation, and the position of the EU – that its emission limit of 0.1 nanograms was, as Bayer's Gerhard

Stolpa had argued on behalf of the chemical industry, to be the accepted standard. And Dempsey's point?

> In licensing incineration facilities in Ireland, the Environmental Protection Agency already applies a flue gas emission limit value for dioxins of 0.1 nanograms, that is, one ten thousand millionth of a gram, per cubic metre of gas emitted. This extremely stringent standard will shortly be adopted by the EU generally, under the proposed council directive on the incineration of waste. By comparison, dioxin emission standards issued by the USEPA last year, which will only apply to US hazardous waste incinerators from 2002, are between two and four times higher.

And to make sure that everyone was listening to the point he was really making he concluded: 'My department will monitor the outcome of the ongoing USEPA work.'

Dempsey, it could be argued, was simply doing the job his masters had mandated him to do: put the incineration line without compromise, and without reference to the thousands of studies in the public domain. The only studies Dempsey concerned himself with were those that had been sanctioned by the chemical industry who spent the 1990s making sure that the USEPA, in particular, did not make any rash conclusions about dioxin and other chemicals implicated in the toxic debate. Instead incineration became 'thermal treatment' as Dempsey sought to push his government's uncompromising policy on waste management. Dempsey said:

> The 1998 policy statement on waste management, *Changing Our Ways*, indicates that, where technically and economically feasible, and subject to appropriate attention to materials recycling, incineration with energy recovery or other advanced thermal processes are among the treatment options which should be considered in an integrated waste management strategy. That remains the position.

It was definitely the position in 2001 as the Dáil debated a government proposed bill to amend the Waste Management Act. The amendments were clearly designed to make the passage of incineration through the legislation as easy as possible, but one amendment in particular – designed to give county managers the power to implement waste management plans without consultation with elected councillors – epitomised the government's stance. Labour's Michael Bell was unequivocal about its impact on local democracy.

> The amendment of section 4 of the City and County Management (Amendment) Act, 1955, is an absolute disaster. County managers have sought its abolition over the past decade because it is the only power that elected members can invoke. The amendment of the section is the thin edge of the wedge as it has not been completely repealed. For example, Meath County Council was about to invoke section 4(4) in regard to the proposed incinerator but that will not be possible following the enactment of this legislation because the subsection is being deleted. The proposal to give county managers the exclusive power to make waste management plans is undemocratic. The Bill removes all power from elected councillors for the making of such plans. This extraordinary, dictatorial measure is designed to facilitate the Minister's agenda to construct five regional incinerators. As the recently published Labour Party strategy on waste management stated, this is the wrong approach. Investment in waste infrastructure should be concentrated on recycling, not incineration, and that is what the Minister's constituents are saying loudly and clearly to him.

Fine Gael's Paul Connaughton, a Galway Deputy, agreed with Bell's assessment.

> The Minister will go down in history as the man who set out to enhance local government and then disenfranchised the councillors. He has taken the players off the pitch and allowed the referee to finish the game. This will go down in history as one of the saddest occasions for local democracy in a long time. This legislation is draconian. It does not take any notice of the elected councillors, the local committees or the many different ways to dispose of waste which have been pioneered across the world, but it takes notice of the consultants who, at colossal expense to the Exchequer, draw up plans to dispose of waste through incineration and landfill sites which are placed in areas that families must leave.

The arguments were to no avail. By 54–43 the Bill was referred to the Select Committee on Environment and Local Government. One more obstacle had been removed. The way was paved for another attempt at the establishment of a national toxic waste incinerator, and inevitably the location chosen was Ringaskiddy in County Cork. The war had turned full circle back to the territory of the earliest toxic battles. In April 2001 Minchem, the hazardous waste disposal company set up in 1977 – becoming part of the Belgian Indaver group in November 1999 – and one of the state's contenders in 1989 to build a national toxic waste incinerator, phoned Braham Brennan of the Ringaskiddy and District Residents' Association. It didn't identify itself, other than to state it was a new industry wanting to locate in the area and could it meet the Ringaskiddy group in the Maryborough House Hotel to talk about its plans. 'Five of us arrived up to meet them and that was the first we knew who they were', Audrey Hogan, secretary of the group, recalled.

> Then they announced to the public who they were. They wanted to come to the community centre in Ringaskiddy and put their plans on show but we objected to this and sent them a letter to say that we had no interest in meeting with them, and that they would never be welcome.

Chastised by the community, Minchem/Indaver put its plans on display at the ferry terminal in Ringaskiddy on 1 May, and began a series of 'information' meetings in Carrigaline, Crosshaven and Cóbh to inform the communities that it planned to lodge an application with Cork County Council to build an incinerator that would handle 100,000 tonnes annually of hazardous waste. Indaver proposed to handle all the hazardous waste that was being exported for incineration. In 2001 that amounted to around 65,000 tonnes. The response from the communities was immediate. A silent protest was held at the ferry terminal and at each of the information meetings. 'We're willing to take this to the courts, and we'll even go to Europe if we have to', said Braham Brennan.

Groups were formed to motivate the communities against the proposal. On 5 September they came together to form an alliance. A month later when the Carrigaline group decided to use the name Cork Harbour for a Safe Environment the other groups rallied under the umbrella banner of CHASE. Linda Fitzpatrick, who had been the public relations officer for the Carrigaline group, and Sean Cronin, who was acting as its chair, inherited the same positions with CHASE. The following month the company lodged its application with Cork County Council. In response the objections began to pour into county hall. 'As a group,' Linda Fitzpatrick explained, 'CHASE lobbied local and national politicians, met party leaders, got party policies changed and clarified, held information meetings, brought in expert speakers, raised general awareness, and submitted detailed objections.'

One of the first responses of the groups to Indaver's initiative to involve the community was to accept an invitation to visit the corporate's operations in Belgium for two days at the end of February. Mary O'Leary, Alan Navratil and Carmel Cronin from CHASE; John Howard of the Ringaskiddy Residents' Association; Carmel Conroy of Cóbh; Howard Crowdy, a reporter with the *Southern Star*; Martin Mullane of Glanbia, Kilkenny, Councillor Tom Tuohy of Haulbowline and John Bray of GlaxoSmithKline were shown recycling parks, a 100,000 tonne municipal waste incinerator with energy recovery, a separation facility, two 45,000 tonne rotary kiln incinerators for liquid or solid industrial and hazardous waste, an 8,000 tonne static kiln specifically for highly chlorinated (30–40 per cent) liquid material and a municipal waste and ash recovery facility. Carmel Cronin, in a report to the communities back in Cork, noted that the community recycling park they had been shown would be similar to Indaver's proposed facility for Ringaskiddy. 'This consists of a huge tarmacadamed area similar to a big car park with skips and drop off stations for the various waste streams', she said.

Of more significance to the group were the comments of the incinerator plant manager who admitted that a decrease in waste affected its operation. He also told the group that the cost per tonne of recycling was considerably less than cost per tonne of incineration. They also learned that the recycling rates in the communities had risen from 21 per cent to 66 per cent, where they had remained constant since 1999, prompting the comment from Carmel Cronin: 'This begs the question, "could this be improved upon if the incinerator did not exist necessitating a constant feed at high fixed costs to the operator?"' On the second day the group were taken to see the hazardous waste facilities in Antwerp. 'Whilst we were there a large shipment of toxic waste came in from Luxembourg', reported Cronin.

We were told that 10 per cent of toxic waste is IMPORTED. If this is the case in the heartland of a heavily industrialised country, with a large petrochemical and polymer chemical industry to name a few, what guarantee is there that toxic waste will not be imported into Ringaskiddy?

After being told that routine checks are made on employees to ascertain any build-up of pollutants or heavy metals, the group asked if body fat was measured for the build up of lipophilic, fat-soluble organics. According to Cronin 'there was a vague but negative reply'.

With the 2002 General Election only months away the incinerator became a political issue. In Cork East and Cork South Central, the two constituencies closest to the proposed incinerator, every candidate, including Health Minister Michael Martin, declared, in their election literature, that he or she was against the proposal. Not one candidate, including those from Fianna Fáil, came out in favour of it. And every non-government candidate declared his or her party firmly against incineration. Fitzpatrick said:

> At the same time there was a level of apathy in communities such as Carrigaline. The old chestnut of the pharmachem industry raises its head again and again. People are not keen to voice objection to the incinerator if it could be seen as objection to the pharmachem industry, and thus their jobs.

This did not stop the communities from submitting 20,000 objections to the council as the debate about incineration and the need for a toxic waste incinerator in Ringaskiddy gathered momentum throughout 2002 and into the spring and summer months of 2003.

Despite this opposition it was clear when the politicians came around to discussing incineration again during the Protection of the Environment Bill in February 2003 the state had made up its mind and was doing everything it could to pave the way for incineration. Senator Paddy Burke, of Fine Gael, discussing the bill in the Seanad on 13 February realised this:

> The Minister spoke on national radio before he introduced the Bill to the House when he gave the impression that incineration was the way to go. He stated there were 16 or 17 incinerators in a country like Denmark which has a

population of much the same size. The Bill seems to be all about incineration. When Senator O'Rourke spoke, she said it all. She said landfill would not work and that she was not for incineration but what will we do? She said we were coming too late as a nation to recycling but it is never too late. Her comments lead me to believe the Bill is totally about incineration.

Two days later Fianna Fáil's Martin Cullen summed up the state's position on incineration:

> As politicians, we had better begin to understand about what we are talking when we refer to incineration. We are not talking about traditional incineration facilities associated in the public mind with mass burning. No such facilities will ever be built here. They would not be acceptable to the government or to any political party. The facilities in question have taken a huge leap in terms of technology and treatment, even in the past three to five years. Having addressed the waste problem so late, we have enormous difficulties in our waste management systems, Nevertheless, we are probably lucky because the technology we will introduce will be so advanced as to allow us to have managed facilities with very marginal emissions.

The following month, in response to a request for advice from Cork Council, the Health and Safety Authority agreed with Cullen. 'On the basis of the information the council has supplied to the authority and the information obtained directly from Indaver Ireland, the authority does not advise against the granting of planning permission in the context of major accident hazards', the HSA said in a report submitted to the council.

The HSA, CHASE said, had missed the point. 'We would consider accidents to include fugitive emissions, even though the HSA did not consider routine emissions. We would urge councillors to take the true risks into consideration if it comes before them', said Linda Fitzpatrick. On 24 March, Cork's planners said they had no objection to Indaver's application. They referred to a Health Research Board report, which claimed 'that modern incinerators, properly operated and controlled, met environmental standards set down by an EU directive'.

All that was left in the way of the council was its own County Development Plan, which excluded merchant incineration and landfill in industrialised areas. 'In order to grant planning permission,' Fitzpatrick explained, 'a material contravention of the existing County Development Plan is required as the proposed site is not currently zoned for industrial use.' County manager Maurice Moloney confirmed that the council would seek a material contravention of the County Development Plan. Fitzpatrick said they were 'optimistic' that the councillors would vote against the material contravention, but Indaver's managing director John Ahern said it planned to apply to the EPA for a licence in April and would appeal to An Bord Pleanála if the council vote went against them.

On 26 May 2003 Cork's councillors voted by 30 to 13 against it. CHASE rejoiced momentarily. 'Members of CHASE are pleased with the outcome of this vote', Mary O'Leary said. 'Cork County Councillors recognise the sentiment in Cork harbour, and the risks associated with this incinerator, and they have reflected the will of the people in their vote.' What worried CHASE was the planning board's decision to allow Indaver to go ahead with its municipal incinerator in County Meath, despite a recommendation from the appeal inspector to refuse it. What shocked it were the contents of Indaver's Integrated Pollution Control licence that showed the corporate wanted to burn 400 tonnes of asbestos waste a year. What spurred CHASE on was the knowledge that Cork communities had won before, and could win again. 'This proposal should not be allowed to proceed, and having defeated it at this first stage, it will provide motivation to Cork people to continue the fight for as long as necessary', O'Leary announced, aware that once again the communities plus the combined forces of state and industry would face each other in another mighty verbal battle on the top floor of the county hall.

6 Carndonagh: Anxiety Among the Women

> All the legislation introduced in the past 25 years has been designed to inhibit public input and not to protect the environment or public health.
>
> Derry Chambers (2003)

At 5.28 p.m. on 16 January 1992 an 8 pounds 9 ounce baby boy was born in Letterkenny Regional Hospital to Grainne and Jim McCarroll of the Malin Road, Carndonagh – the principal market town of the Inishowen peninsula in County Donegal with a population of approximately 1,800. The delivery had been perfect and baby Paul was fine.

A natural birth in natural circumstances and nothing out of the ordinary. For Grainne and Jim McCarroll it was more than that, it was the end of a three-year nightmare that had seen them lose two children in abnormal circumstances.

When Grainne McCarroll miscarried the first time, in November 1989, after an eight-week pregnancy, her husband Jim, the local vet, was convinced he knew what had caused the premature abortion. When another couple, who lived nearby, also lost a baby in similar circumstances a month later, all the active child-bearing women on the Malin Road became very worried.

Within a period of 14 months there were three miscarriages (including a second one to the McCarrolls), one premature birth (the child died later) and one child born with a disorder, to women living along the Malin Road. Between the summer of 1989 and the winter of 1991–2 the women lost six children out of nine pregnancies (two children were born with blood disorders, which later cleared up). Grainne McCarroll's baby boy was the first perfect child to be born along the Malin Road in nearly four years.

'I was very relieved that everything was all right', Grainne McCarroll said after the child was born. 'I found the pregnancy very stressful but he's a perfectly normal baby.' Grainne had been induced after a 38-week pregnancy.

The relief was not only felt in the McCarroll household but throughout Carndonagh, where the mystery of the unexplained abnormal births dominated the lives of the townspeople for four years. And the mystery remains.

It was Jim McCarroll who began to worry about the new owners of the local alcohol factory on the Malin Road in Carndonagh during the winter of 1986–87. Truloc, a Dublin listed company, had acquired the factory from the liquidator of Ceimicí Teoranta in 1986. McCarroll, who had learned that Truloc proposed to manufacture adhesives, immediately contacted the local authority and subsequently the chief fire officer in Donegal. Among the concerns expressed by residents along the Malin Road, McCarroll wanted to ensure 'that emissions emanating from these premises should not constitute a health risk to people or the environment' and all 'emissions be monitored and controlled by internationally accepted standards and tests'.

Following McCarroll's letter, a firm of local solicitors, working on behalf of a number of the Malin Road residents, wrote to Donegal County Council to enquire whether Truloc had applied for planning permission to operate an adhesives factory. It was the belief of the solicitors that Truloc had not made an application despite the fact that their operation would not be making industrial alcohol. This, stated the solicitors, was quite clearly a change of use of the factory.

The solicitors sent further letters to the council in April and May of 1987 before the county secretary replied to state that the regulations exempted some industries from planning permission. The council, he added, had launched an investigation to determine whether or not Truloc needed planning permission. It took the council some time to conduct its investigation and to inform the community and the Inishowen Environmental Group that Truloc did not need planning permission, because the change of use fell within specific classes of use under the local government planning regulations.

The Inishowen group, which had begun lobbying the council about Truloc during the summer of 1988, was told in February 1989 in answer to questions about Truloc's waste and waste disposal methods that an investigation was underway. It would, said the council, look at the 'possibility of air pollution'.

The complaints about the factory had begun in June 1987. Residents complained of breathing difficulties, headaches, streaming noses and eyes. They were convinced that emissions from the factory were the alleged cause of their ailments. Some people alleged that the smell from the factory had made them sick.

In 1988 the IDA in Dublin told Bev Doherty, chair of the Inishowen group, that it would be concerned if any individual or company were to damage the ecology of the area and affect the livelihood of people in the community. As autumn neared, Truloc, concerned about the rumours and allegations, invited the community to visit the plant, to, as Bev Doherty put it, 'allay local concern'. While the Inishowen group waited for the council to explain why it had failed to incorporate the 1982 EC (Toxic and Dangerous Waste) Directive into a county-wide waste management plan, Truloc explained to Bev Doherty that the company made two types of adhesives: cyanoacrylate adhesives (superglues) and anaerobic adhesives.

The process which made the superglue brought para-formaldehyde and cyano-acetate together in a chemical reaction. Several chemicals were blended to make the second adhesive. There was an odour from the process, Truloc's Donal Doherty told the Inishowen group, and he added that they were upgrading the internal structure of the factory. Their chemical waste, he said, was either recycled or sent to England for incineration.

Bev Doherty wrote to Earthwatch. Jeremy Wates, Earthwatch's Coordinator, advised the Inishowen group and the Malin Road residents 'to keep an accurate record of any anecdotal instances of health problems' and he indicated the kind of research they would need to do to find out more about local, national and EC environmental and health and safety law.

Meanwhile the county council was still reviewing Truloc's air emissions and its methods of waste disposal, and was preparing a comprehensive waste disposal plan (which would not come to light until January 1992 when it was revealed that Donegal County Council was among six north-west councils that had agreed to fund a study into municipal waste incineration). And following the long awaited initial meeting with the council in September 1989, the residents went away with several assurances that something would be done about Truloc. But it was not until 3 May 1990, three years after the first complaints and nearly four years since Jim McCarroll had first voiced his concerns on behalf of some of the Malin Road residents, that a serious meeting with Donegal Council's senior officers took place. Fourteen people travelled from Carndonagh to the council's offices in Lifford for an 11 a.m. showdown. During the two-hour meeting they discussed pollution, waste, emergencies and planning permission.

These were the stated issues because the purpose of the meeting was to establish that it was not the aim of the Carndonagh community activists and environmentalists:

> to close the Truloc factory, but rather to ensure that the plant is well run, that it poses no threat to the local community, through noise, emissions, toxic chemicals, toxic waste, accidents or emergencies that may occur because of the factory's location.

The Carndonagh residents who had campaigned about Truloc's operations had formed themselves into the Carndonagh Environmental Group. The meeting with the council allowed them to formally state their immediate concerns about ill health in the area and about localised pollution. Three residents said they would make a formal complaint about noise pollution from the factory but the main concern was about emissions. The residents asked if the council agreed that the emissions were serious.

'Yes', the council representatives said.

'How many different emissions does the council recognise?'

'Formaldehyde and a raw materials smell', came the answer. Donal Casey, Senior Environmental Officer, and Liam Kelly of the council stated that the factory was meant to have installed new equipment and that the smells were coming from the raw materials store which the company had been ordered to seal. The council would, however, operate the 1987 Air Pollution Act and attempt to take action against Truloc.

'Does the council acknowledge that these emissions have public health implications?'

'Yes', the council said.

On the subject of toxic waste stored at the factory the council admitted that it knew Truloc had transported toxic waste from its Dublin factory to Carndonagh. It was the council's intention, the residents heard, that Truloc would be ordered to move the waste. The residents also learned that some waste materials from Truloc had been dumped in a local tip, but the council insisted that none of this waste was toxic.

The council also admitted that many of the chemicals stored at the Truloc factory were toxic but that only the company or the Department of Labour could provide health and safety information on the specific chemicals.

The meeting had answered some of the residents' questions but they were not happy. In a letter to Liam Kelly on 21 May, Jim McCarroll said he could not understand why the council had not taken a prosecution against Truloc for repeated emissions in breach of the Air Pollution Act, despite assurances made at the September meeting that action would be taken by 31 December 1989 if Truloc did not comply with the legal notice served by the council under the Air Pollution Act. He also conveyed the Carndonagh group's alarm about toxic waste stored at Truloc, which the council had assured the residents would be moved.

The residents had been told at the September meeting that the barrels used to store the waste were in a poor condition, that the material was unsuitable for recycling and that the waste was a fire hazard. 'Hints were dropped at that meeting,' McCarroll told Kelly, 'and indeed at the meeting in May that the cost of moving this waste was prohibitive and that the waste must be incinerated in England.' Hopefully, McCarroll added, 'the personnel involved will spring into action and serve the notices' they had undertaken to make at the two meetings. Angrily McCarroll told Kelly that he found the council's 'procrastination inexplicable' and perhaps the council should consider 'relocating and compensating the residents of the Malin Road'.

McCarroll's anger can only be explained by the council's 'procrastination'. At the September meeting the council officials told Garda Philip Maree and schoolteacher Mike Doherty that 'everything would be okay by January [1990]'. Going into the May meeting the Carndonagh group had expectations. Jim McCarroll had prepared a comprehensive set of questions and the group was well briefed. He said:

> I think the council were surprised at the number of people who turned up.... We felt that the council officials were under pressure because they hadn't done anything. We thought this time something would happen. As the statutory authority they were going to take the issue seriously but they only took it as seriously as a council can. I anticipated we'd end up with the court case.

The Carndonagh group had decided it had to step up its campaign and lobby the Minister for the Environment, local politicians, the factory inspectorate and the Ombudsman. It also wanted another meeting with the council, within a month, and this time it wanted Doctor Mary Cooney, the North Western Health Board's Senior Medical Officer, to attend. But the cat had already been set among the pigeons when the Malin Road residents discovered that Truloc had attempted to move some of its toxic waste between the evening of Thursday 17 May 1990 and the morning of Friday 18 May.

Sometime after lunch on the Thursday, City Industrial Waste, a Derry based company, arrived in Carndonagh and began to move the waste which, according to the residents, was contained in 'deteriorating and rusting steel drums'. Eyewitnesses said the waste was leaking and there was a strong smell about the place.

Bev Doherty phoned her husband, Mike Doherty, to tell him what was happening. Doherty, who taught in a school in Derry, stopped at the customs post in Muff, on the border, to enquire about the transportation of the waste. The customs officers said they had no powers. When he got home Mike Doherty phoned Donegal and Derry councils. '[Donegal Council] said they couldn't contact the man with responsibility for this sort of complaint. Derry City Council, on the other hand, were most concerned and promised an immediate investigation by an inspector at the dump itself.'

Bev Doherty was led to believe that the waste was being taken to the Derry City Council dump on the outskirts of Derry, in Culmore, near the river Foyle, but the waste, apparently, was brought elsewhere. Subsequent investigation by the Doherty's revealed that the waste was destined for Portadown where it would be incinerated. But the council there denied any knowledge of the waste and said it had no facilities for incineration.

This incident sparked off a spate of angry letters from the Carndonagh group. Michael Doherty wrote a three-page letter to Junior Environment Minister Mary Harney and two one-page letters to Earthwatch and to Donegal County Council.

Doherty asked Earthwatch:

Would we be able to move against the council for its failure to:
- supervise a movement order when the factory first transferred waste to Carndonagh from Dublin (or more correctly, ensure that there was a movement order in the first instance)

- impose a movement order on Truloc since 1986
- prosecute after January 1990 for breaches of the Air Pollution Act (1987)
- take seriously the constant stream of complaints made against Truloc by residents about smells, noises, illnesses (streaming eyes, noses, breathlessness)?

To Liam Kelly of the council, Doherty asked:

- Did the factory follow all the required procedures for moving the toxic waste?
- Did Donegal County Council therefore authorise the movement?

The response by the Department of Environment in Dublin and the council was fairly immediate. In a letter to Harney's private secretary, Liam Kelly said the council had been in correspondence with Truloc since June 1989 about the alleged emissions. Kelly also clarified the council's position over the notice, served under the Air Pollution Act, in September 1989, which required the company 'to eliminate or reduce to a minimum emissions which might cause nuisance or be a hazard to public health in the vicinity'. Kelly added that as a requirement of the notice the company had employed consultants in Queen's University, Belfast 'to examine and report on the best methods to deal with emissions'. Truloc had, said Kelly, acted on the consultant's recommendations; subsequently the council had asked Truloc 'to employ either the same or other consultants to evaluate the effectiveness of the steps taken'.

Despite these assurances from the council and from the Department of the Environment, that it was up to the council to employ the Air Pollution Act, the residents of Malin Road were still suffering. Several residents wrote to Dr Mary Cooney of the North Western Health Board, imploring that someone investigate the health problems. Philip Maree wrote to an environmental consultant in Dublin but the cost (IR£250 a day) put the group off the idea of doing its own monitoring of Truloc's activities.

In a further letter to Harney's private secretary, Liam Kelly explained that samples had been taken at regular intervals by the council's chemist but the council's solicitor had advised caution because the onus was on Donegal County Council to prove that Truloc had breached the Air Pollution Act.

Infuriated by the council's inability to deal with the problem, Grainne McCarroll wrote to the North Western Health Board asking for reassurance that the emissions from Truloc had nothing to do with the abnormal pregnancies. Copies of her letter were sent to the council, to Environment Minister Mary Harney and to the Minister for Health, Dr Rory O'Hanlon.

The North Western Health Board replied and said it was not possible to prove or disprove that the emissions were the cause of the miscarriages. Dr Mary Cooney subsequently requested copies of the women's medical records and finally in January 1992 the NWHB revealed it had discovered nothing to indicate the cause of the miscarriages.

Truloc, meanwhile, continued to deny that the reports of ill health and the miscarriages had anything to do with its operations. Following another meeting with the county council on 30 January 1992 the Carndonagh group met to decide whether it should take a civil action. Then the council, deciding that it could take legal action, took a chance. During June and July at four sittings of the District Court in Donegal the case by the County Council against Truloc was heard. Truloc faced nine charges. Eight related to alleged emissions and one to the company's failure to use the best practicable means to limit and prevent emissions.

During the hearings the council's chemist Donal Casey alleged that samples taken from a vent in Truloc revealed the presence of cyanide and formaldehyde. The council recorded readings of formaldehyde of 5 parts per million (ppm) and cyanide of 30 ppm. Casey also alleged that when he first visited the factory in 1989 he found a 'very bad state of housekeeping'. He further alleged that recommendations made by Queen's University to curtail the emissions were either not followed or those that were followed were of a 'makeshift' fashion. During the court case several residents alleged they had experienced 'headaches, sore throats, dizziness, nausea, vomiting, burning sensations and fatigue'. Bridie Maree said she had experienced headaches and sore eyes before her miscarriage and that one of her children suffered from eczema.

At the fourth hearing, the judge found Truloc guilty on eight counts and fined it IR£2,400 (IR£300 for each charge). The company was also ordered to pay IR£2,000 court expenses and IR£2,000 witness expenses. Truloc's John Doherty, in a statement, said: 'The operations of Truloc Ltd, Carndonagh, do not present any threat to the residents of Carndonagh nor do they present any threat to the environment. Truloc has always and will continue to operate within the law.'

It is now virtually impossible to prove that industrial air pollution was the cause of the miscarriages in Carndonagh. No toxicity tests were undertaken after the foetuses were aborted.

7 Askeaton: In the Shadow of the Dragon

> In large communities it is called rumour but in small communities it is knowing. You cannot hide real events and call them by another name, because men are not fools and if you give them the evidence of their ears and eyes, and even with a minimum of intelligence, they can piece together all the facts.
>
> Walter Macken

North-west Limerick, a stone's throw from the Shannon estuary, is to the innocent traveller a place of quiet beauty and reserved solitude. Beef and dairy cattle are abundant on fields of luscious greenery. It's a scene common in the brochures of An Bord Fáilte. A glimpse of a time when the production of food was essential to the well-being of Irish communities, this seemingly rural setting is a false one, for beyond the fields on the western horizon the idyll is shattered by the smokestacks of industry and modern commerce, while the fields themselves give no indication of the industrial farming practices that now characterise modern agriculture.

The nearest stacks are those of Aughinish Alumina, where the refinement of alumina from bauxite results in the emission of 17,000 tonnes a year of sulphur dioxide. Beyond Aughinish further along the estuary lies Tarbert oil-fired power generating station and Moneypoint coal-fired station whose particulate emissions darken the sky. These industries spew thousands of tonnes of chemicals and heavy metals into the Clare and Limerick air, which eventually fall onto fields and farms as acid rain and are taken up by plants and animals.

Sometime during the late 1980s this deadly cocktail of pollutants, augmented by pollution streams from the European mainland and some say sand from the Sahara, began to change the lives of the local farmers, resulting in the deaths of approximately 400 animals on the farms of Liam Somers, Justin Ryan, Paddy Sheehy and Andy Sheehy; general ill health among animals on many farms including increased infertility and a decline in milk production; and the beginning of an awareness that the illnesses people were suffering from were somehow related to these toxic pollutants. 'Given the scale of emissions from industries in the Shannon estuary it would be surprising if there were no ill effects or manifestations of pollution in the region', scientist Rory Finegan lamented in the conclusion of his investigation into the vegetational and animal health problems on Somers's 59 acre farm near the ancient, monastery town of Askeaton in west Limerick.

Emissions from industry, the farmers believed, had 'impacted detrimentally' on particular farms in the Askeaton area in the early 1990s and they felt powerless – particularly Liam Somers in Ballysteen and Justin Ryan in Toomdeely who between them lost roughly 200 animals. Not only were they at the mercy of the state's obfuscations and industry's propaganda, they appeared unable to challenge the hierarchical systems which had disempowered them. In the midst of their despair and frustration they had become dependent on bureaucrats, scientists, politicians, journalists and environmentalists in the hope that these elites would somehow represent their plight to the wider community and that someone would actually do something positive when, inevitably they naively assumed, the cause of the problems were revealed.

This rested on a false belief that a solution acceptable to everyone implicated in this ecological soap opera would be discovered. Consequently, as the government procrastinated and bureaucrats deliberated, the farmers realised fairly quickly that their interests were secondary to local industry, Limerick County Council, the Electricity Supply Board (ESB – which operates the power stations) and the state. That the farmers' animals had been poisoned, their own health (and that of their neighbours) impaired and their livelihoods destroyed appeared to be of concern to all these pocket hierarchies. Yet, they feared, it would come to nothing. The state, at first it seemed, was reluctant to launch an investigation. 'The agency is not going to be a fire brigade for anyone', the EPA's Iain Maclean told the Cork Environmental Alliance when asked if it would investigate.

Still, Ireland's primary green groups all highlighted the animal health problems in west Limerick and took the farmers' case to higher authorities. The Green Party pledged its support to the farmers. Trevor Sargent toured from his Dublin constituency to see Somers. The Limerick and Cork print and electronic media dutifully reported the 'story' from most of the respective angles. Those who gain their news from the national (Dublin) media were told of events in west Limerick. Although generally quiet about pollution from the Shannon estuary several politicians, including the odd minister or two, expressed their concern. Many individuals supported the farmers' genuine claims. Yet despite this wider concern, from the state, industry, the media, the organised greens and individual activists, no one made an attempt to integrate the ecological, agricultural, social and political implications of the agricultural and industrial pollution in west Limerick into a holistic framework.

In 1995, following a public meeting that heard the communities of Askeaton and Rathkeale highlight their concerns about health problems, the Mid-Western Health Board initiated a serious of twelve studies – on births and congenital abnormalities, sex ratio, twinning rates, general practitioners' perceptions of health problems in their practices, a health status survey, an acute health effects/diary study, cancer incidence study, Askeaton mortality study, adolescent health study, child absenteeism study, a report on sampling of horticulture produce, and an investigation into media reports of suspected cases of chloracne (which is associated with acute dioxin poisoning).

The first was carried out by Dr Mary O'Mahony, Acting Director of Community Care at the board, who contacted six GPs in Askeaton and Ballysteen. She asked them to report skin rashes, eye/nose/throat irritation, respiratory problems, miscarriages and cancers. The GPs said there were no clusters of adverse health effects. Then, using data from 1994 and 1995, the first two years of the National Cancer Registry, researchers with the board also looked at the incidence of cancer in Askeaton and Rathkeale, using Ennistymon, Killadysert, Moyne/Littleton and Clarecastle (home of Syntex/Roche) as control areas, and comparing the data with the national average. When the research team came to report it claimed there was no evidence that cancer risk was greater among the 4,000 people living in Askeaton and Rathkeale compared with the control areas or the national average. Instead it found that the data indicated a lower level of cancer.

The Mid-Western Health Board compounded this research with a study based on a questionnaire sent out to 50 GPs, of which 34 participated from Askeaton, Rathkeale, Killadysert, Clarecastle, Ennistymon, and Moyne/Littleton, to determine the range of illnesses among the communities dating back to 1986. The GPs representing the Askeaton and Rathkeale communities reported they had concerns about the rates of miscarriages and general health. Realising there was a dearth of adequate and properly reported data on ill health in the area, the board conducted another study over 13 months involving 18 Askeaton farming families (76 individuals) who had experienced animal health problems. Its primary objective was to record the results of pregnancies. When it was completed the board stated there were no statistical differences between Askeaton and the control areas. Of the other illnesses the researchers noted that respiratory symptoms were the most common (19.5 per cent); followed by ear/nose/throat (16.4 per cent) skin (13 per cent), and fatigue (12.6 per cent).

Later that year the EPA finally took action and launched its investigation – in conjunction with Teagasc (the agricultural advisory board), the Veterinary Research Laboratory and the Mid-Western Health Board – which it announced would solve the mystery of the animal deaths and the ill health. All over the district, there was a genuine fear that nothing would be resolved. The conclusions of the investigation would rest solely on science and would not involve the social, political and economic subtexts. But it would only be the Irish state's science that counted. Independent studies would simply contribute to the scientific confusion in the minds of the public. And the science would not be judged by anyone. Simon White, one of the affected farmers and now the Irish Farmers' Association's representative in the area, was adamant about this when the farmers' fears were realised:

> The EPA and the Department of Agriculture, Teagasc, and the Department of Health are guilty of committing a great injustice to the affected farmers. They made a political judgement to exonerate industry, to blame the farmers and put it forward as a scientific judgement. This judgement was not based on good scientific method and is a case of hijacking science to prove a particular scenario, which was preferred by the most politically influential lobby. The question is: who wields the true power in Ireland today.

The EPA's agenda became apparent when its three interim reports were published in September 1995, April 1997 and August 1998. Unfortunately for the farmers the investigation was retrospective.

'It is clear', the authors of the second report state, 'that whatever adverse circumstances led to the cattle deaths and ill-health on Ryan's and Somers' farms in the late 1980s and early 1990s are now absent.'

The reason for the state's inability to address these issues holistically is both complex and simple. We live in a world that is dominated by the culture of consumerism; to survive we must enter the buyer–seller nexus. Social ecologist Murray Bookchin has described this to include every aspect of production, consumption, community life and family. 'Our agricultural epoch – a distinctively capitalist one – envisions food cultivation as a business enterprise to be operated strictly for the purpose of generating profit in a market economy.'

In west Limerick one method of profit making conflicted with a competitive and more lucrative method. Although the farmers around Askeaton practised industrial agriculture for the benefit of the national economy, they were unwittingly up against a global hierarchy – in the form of the chemical industry. The fact that food – milk in the case of the Limerick farmers – is a commodity, in much the same way that aluminium is, matters little here. Aluminium benefits the global economy, milk does not. If the milk should happen to become contaminated, the obvious course of action is to pretend there isn't a real problem, otherwise people would be wary of buying the product. Both the national and the global economies needed to be protected.

Hence an unmarked co-op milk lorry was seen at the farms of Somers and Ryan to collect the allegedly contaminated milk before both farmers were forced to accept deals from the state. The co-op – Golden Vale in this instance – paid the two farmers roughly ten pence less than the going rate for their milk which was taken off into the distance.

What became of it, you ask? That's a question Golden Vale would be best placed to answer. It claimed to have tested the milk and found nothing wrong with it, so why the unmarked lorries and the lower price to the farmers? Notwithstanding the spectre of pollution hanging over the land this was a fine solution, albeit a cursory one, for the farmers because the product must be maintained otherwise livelihoods and profits would be damaged. And while the farmers would become emotional in their cries about the aluminium factory, the state had to find a solution that would not drive the corporate out of the country while assuaging the fears of those who had been affected by the mystery illnesses.

According to Somers the arrival of the unmarked milk lorry quieted concern among the farmers. Meanwhile, behind closed doors, the cogs of government were maintained and the wheels of commerce rolled on. Industry went about the business of improving its image, not forgetting to stress the importance of its continued existence to the local economies. Yet the problems of pollution and ill health remained. No one in authority thought to genuinely consider the potential catalyst for the farmers' problems – arguably because they did not have to. The legislation governing integrated pollution licences would take care of that – when the time came. In western industrial society, diplomatic solutions are found for the problems of pollution: behind closed doors.

Farmers with generational knowledge of their land do not become bad farmers overnight, any more than people suddenly become ill without cause. 'My family have farmed here for 250 years and never had a problem until now', David Naughton said in 2002. 'Every farmer around here has bad problems', one farmer said in 1995, aware that until 1995 there hadn't been a genuine attempt to record exactly what the animal and human health problems were. The animal health problems identified on the farms of the affected farmers were seen by the majority of local farmers as the extreme end of the problem. The Askeaton, Ballysteen Animal Health Committee, when it was set up by the farmers in May 1994 to investigate 'the situation as far as possible', didn't have the funds to commission the kind of independent analysis which, augmented by the rich local knowledge of the people who live in west Limerick, would have conclusively revealed the extent of the pollution.

Significantly none of the regulatory authorities have been able to characterise all the local pollution, particularly atmospheric pollution, and as the wind patterns are variable this pollution has been widespread. A westerly carries most of the pollution over the farms of Somers and Ryan but their problems appeared to be unique. The reason for that would surely baffle any authority that did not wish to learn the truth. And there is no evidence from the investigation that the state has ever wanted to provide answers to the farmers, other than to prove that everything is okay now. Paul Toner of the EPA insisted in 1995 that until proven otherwise the existing pollution in the area was within safe levels, though he admitted that the overall problem could be quite complex.

Several scientists, notably Finegan, called in 1995 for more detailed information on the industrial processes to the west of the affected areas, namely Aughinish and the two power stations. Conversely Finegan was adamant that 'sick plants and sick animals' are a sufficient enough indication that 'environmental pollution is occurring'. There is, he said in 1995, 'a superimposition of pollutants' in the area. Yet Aughinish was able, in all innocence it seemed, to state it was not and never had been the source of the farmers' problems – its publicist Frank Dunlop rallying at the oral hearing into his company's integrated pollution licence (during the summer of 1997) that accusations against his company were unfounded. The hearing itself was seen as a charade, the Askeaton, Ballysteen Health Committee and the Sheehy family walking out, arguing that their withdrawal was a protest against the EPA because they did not expect a fair hearing. 'We do not see why we should have to defend ourselves like criminals against senior counsel because of our genuine concerns.'

But, as Finegan said, there is no comprehensive information on the effects on people, animals, wild and plant life from the pollution in west Limerick, irrespective of the sources. Aughinish knows it is not legally possible to claim that any one pollutant is responsible for any one illness, whether in animals or humans, and that is its defence. Instead of the onus being on Aughinish to prove it is not responsible, whether as the primary source or as part of an aggregation of sources, the farmers must prove that it is, and for the moment the law and science are not geared towards that eventuality. That however is not the point here. There is or was an animal health problem but no one appeared to know what to do. As research scientist Peter Montague put it in 1996, 'regulators and judges now insist that science has to "prove harm" before regulatory control can begin'. Those who study science know that science cannot categorically 'prove' anything. 'It often takes science decades – sometimes centuries – to reach a clear majority opinion and there will always be uncertainties, giving rise to nagging doubts which can only be laid to rest by further study.'

So when air pollution scientists Paul and Valerie Dowding highlighted the role of modern farming practice – which after all is encouraged by the state on behalf on industry – they simply isolated the issue, obscuring the overall or holistic viewpoint. Industrial agriculture (the use of pesticides, artificial fertilisers, genetic hormones, antibiotics and other chemicals) exacerbates the problems caused by intensive farming, thus depleting the soil of natural minerals. Many of the affected farmers practise industrial agriculture. Coupled with industrial atmospheric pollution, the land of the affected farmers isn't capable of maintaining animals that depend on the richness of the soil for their wellbeing. Thus already stressed animals have further burdens to contend with. Mineral deficiency was cited as a major cause of the farmers' animal problems. The Dowdings conducted their survey on behalf of Limerick County Council in 1993. Ten years later their conclusion was the refrain that the farmers were part of the problem, a point made by UCC sociologist Kieran Keohane. 'Irish agriculture can no longer be seen simply as in some sense the "victim" of pollution by industry, but, now as increasingly implicated in ecological problems. This is primarily because modern Irish agriculture has itself become an industrial process.'

The early 1990s coalition government of Fine Gael/Labour/ Democratic Left had urged the senior civil servants in the departments of Health, Environment and Agriculture to take seriously the farmers' problems and the perceived ill health in the area. Yet before the investigation began in earnest the government agencies involved were telling the media there was not a problem. The health board made it clear that it believed there were no human health problems associated with industrial pollution in west Limerick, contradicting the local knowledge that a high number of people suffered from a range of illnesses – but critics of the published studies have pointed out that their methodology was flawed, inadequate and therefore unlikely to find anything. Something is causing people to die of cancer and no one in authority appears to know what it is. The cluster of cancers in the area is, apparently, not unusual – a statement local people find hard to believe. The Consumers Association of Ireland agreed with them, in December 2001 condemning the IR£4.19 million investigation 'profoundly unsatisfactory' and 'inconclusive'. So when a 2002 survey of 800 people living south of Askeaton and east of Rathkeale, including Cappagh and Croagh, showed that 39 people had died from cancer among 64 cancers – three times the national average – people began to wonder about the ways scientists go about their business.

The EPA published weighty tomes, which look impressive but reveal nothing of substance. The investigation was set up to include a study of animal health on the affected farms (using a control group of animals from an unpolluted farm), an analysis of the animals' immune systems and a general study of all animal health in the area; sampling of soil, herbage, vegetation, animal feed, drinking water and milk; and atmospheric emissions. The samples were tested for minerals, heavy metals, organic and inorganic chemicals, including polyaromatic hydrocarbons, PCBs and dioxins. 'If it is industrial pollution we will attempt to prevent that pollution', said Paul Toner of the EPA in 1995. 'We are the regulatory authority and we will take action.'

As the investigation got under way the most affected farmers, Somers and Ryan, had to consider their plight. Both were asked to participate in the animal health study by Teagasc at their farms. Somers turned down three offers from the state to supplement his income as part of the study before finally agreeing to sell his herd of 93 cattle for a sum believed to be in the region of IR£80,000. Shortly afterwards, in January 1996, he said he believed that the investigators would say their analysis of his cattle and soil has revealed nothing. 'Telling us that they've found nothing is ridiculous after 96 animals dead', and so far Somers has been proved right. While the investigation was going on the government provided Somers with an income. 'We've enough to eat and it's keeping us off the dole', he sighed discontentedly a few months after the first interim report was published in September 1995:

> They are letting us have an income and we're letting them into the farm on goodwill. Otherwise I'd stand and fight a bit longer and get them to cough up for the dead animals. We've lost about IR£200,000 in dead animals, loss of milk quota and the benefits upgrading the farm would have brought over the past seven years. The EU want to bring up the standards in milk parlours, which brings farmers who meet those standards an extra three pence a gallon.

Interestingly, during the investigation, some farmers reported that the government had admitted that the problem had not been caused by the farmers. Which made them wonder. Following a meeting in September 1995 to discover how many farmers had animal health problems, it was learned that the government had told farmers they could have confidentiality if they wanted to join the investigation. Some 20 farmers took up this offer, but Justin Ryan sold his farm (adjacent to Weyth, a baby food factory) to the government for a package believed to be worth IR£367,000. Somers believed Ryan had no choice but he said he could not do the same. 'If I can't live on my farm, the fella next door can't live on it either. They have to sort it out. This is my family farm and I can't leave.' (The farm has been in the Somers family for over three generations.)

'I don't think we're ever going to get any answers with this investigation', Somers said in July 1997.

> The cattle are fair, but they can't say they are fine. Only about six out of the 28 are milking fair and they've no explanation for it. The ones that don't do well, they cull. Their milk yield is so low. They say they are doing 1,000 gallons a cow but they are just milking away until they get a yield.
>
> That's not viable farming. You don't feed cattle 365 days of the year and then milk them 365 days just to get a 1,000 gallon quota. They've been feeding them up to 19 pounds a day concentrate – an 18 per cent protein mix. I usually do 10 pounds a day of a 16 per cent protein. Normally I would feed them concentrate from February through to April but they've been feeding them concentrate throughout the winter, along with the silage from the farm, until June there. They want to feed them concentrate all the time. I would milk cattle for between 260 and 280 days and give them a two month dry period before calving. And get between 850 and 900 gallons per cow a year. It wouldn't be farming on a small farm to be doing what they are doing. They don't seem to mind about the cost. No ordinary farmer could afford to run a farm like that. I would spend between two and three thousand and a year on concentrate and they must be spending double that. They'd nil profit for 1996. The whole investigation is a terrible waste of money and nothing coming out of it.

The farmers have always believed they know who the catalyst is, why they are having problems; they know their land and they have eyes. They also have ears and believe that Somers and Ryan had no choice but to accept the government's financial packages to save their livelihoods. The Ryans choose a new life in Tipperary. 'Justin and I have had to leave our farm and our families in order to give our children a future because there is none left on the poisoned farm', Suzanne Ryan wrote in a letter to the Cork Environmental Alliance. 'We also know that the finger will never be pointed at the source of the problem.'

But Suzanne was wrong about that. In the winter of 1998 the finger was pointed and many people believe it was pointed in the right direction. The finger pointers were the Irish Equine Centre. Its independent study found aluminium at levels liable to cause death in animals and serious ill health in humans. This appeared to be the proof that was needed, but the EPA was adamant that 'there is no significant pollution in the area'. The farmers sighed and shook their heads. The EPA, raged Simon White, are 'more concerned with protecting industrial operations than they are in protecting the environment'. White's frustration at the EPA's insistence that there is 'no evidence of aluminium toxicity' in the area was an accurate reflection of the mood among the affected farmers and the local community. And it seemed there was nothing industry could not get away with, including the night of 11 March 2002. That night a power cut in the Aughinish Alumina factory resulted in a caustic blow-out. In the morning Somers noticed that all the shiny surfaces outside – his and his daughter's car, the bales of silage wrapped in black plastic – were covered in little pinkish white dots. The pink hue was reminiscent of the pink lining of the white sulphur dioxide-laden smoke plumes coming out of the twin smokestacks of the factory, and of the red mud dumped on the factory site that is the waste product of the refinement of alumina from bauxite. 'It was the first time I could pin it down to a day', Somers explained, believing that at last something would be done. 'I reported it. I called the EPA, asked if they had any other report. No, they hadn't. They came within an hour, took samples from my car, my daughter's car, herbage samples.' The incident made headlines and made the farmers feel better, especially as Aughinish Alumina admitted to the pollution, though a spokesman denied that it had caused any problem outside the plant.

Liam Somers goes around at times with the look of a pitiful figure. Other times he is frustrated. For most of the time he is patient. He has had to be. While everyone around him has gone quiet – 'people with problems won't come out in the open and admit they lost animals' – Somers himself has courted and played host to a succession of experts. Back in 1992 he was dealing with four to five organisations a day. 'I never refused an interview', he said ten years later. Sometimes he feels it has been a waste of his time and he wonders if it would have been better for him and his family if he had given up. 'I'm just lucky to be alive, to have the will to be able to fight', he said, declaring that in 13 years (1989–2002) the dairy farming population in the wider area around his farm has fallen from 70 to 12 (in Askeaton it has fallen from 29 down to 7).

'You can't farm normally in this area anymore, you'll always have losses', he said, his pride as a farmer hurt because 'farmers who have problems here are put down as bad farmers by the EPA'. So the majority say nothing. 'People around here, they wouldn't talk to you, they'd run, they'd be afraid they wouldn't be able to sell their produce.' He doesn't take it personally, but his family does. His grandchildren have had constant respiratory and immune system problems since they were born:

> For the first six months of their lives they were in and out of hospital. They get rashes, lots of rashes, and my wife is covered in them. I'm lucky, I'm the healthy one. Only thing with myself is the throat, suffer a lot from the constant cough.

It has been much worse for other farming families. 'The graveyard is full of miscarriages, still-borns, seven–eight months old', he laments. Somers is not a pitiful man though he has the right to be. He has the right to give up, as other farmers did, and he has the right to be frustrated. He has remained patient, hoping that 'somebody, somewhere, someday' will come, not influenced by government, who will take the decisive sample, make the conclusive test, identify the exact chemical that causes 'lumps from the size of a finger nail to the size of a football' to break out of his cows' hides, and trace the source of the pollutant.

But he may be waiting a long time. It is the belief of Simon White that a number one suspect does not exist, that the problem is synergistic:

> Pollutants are coming out, landing on farms, under certain conditions, and animals, ingesting the grass, become sensitised to it, then re-sensitised; it affects their central nervous system and makes them susceptible to secondary infection. But all the big boys wouldn't accept primary infection. And we can't put a name on a particular pollutant. I can't, nobody can.

Another belief may be closer to the truth; the respiratory illnesses are linked to the emissions from the power stations; the animal illnesses are linked to the emissions from industry and exacerbated by industrial farming methods (thus primary and secondary infections). All that leaves is an explanation for the cancers!

The Cork Environmental Alliance's warning, after the Hanrahan family's successful prosecution of Merck Sharp and Dohme for alleged chemical pollution in the 1970s and 1980s, that this kind of toxic tragedy should never be allowed to happen again has been ignored. 'From the very beginning this investigation was seen by many as little more than a "cover-up" designed simply as a damage limitation exercise to protect state industrial policy in the Shannon Estuary', the CEA's Derry Chambers said in October 1998. 'There can be no other logical reason for the incompetence displayed in the investigation procedure.' He put it another way:

> Most people are shocked when they hear about events on the Shannon Estuary, Yet there is no real mystery or Machiavellian cover-up of events there, for the simple truth that there was never any need. And therein lies the real tragedy for our society. In Ireland too few people cared or had the integrity to cry halt when animals began to be poisoned at Askeaton. As in the past, in Cork Harbour or Ballydine, we as a society willingly choose to accept the official version of what was happening. We choose to believe that industrial emissions were not the cause, that the farmers involved were lazy combo chasing bastards, that the state was determined to find the cause, that the best scientific principles were employed in the investigation, etc, etc. We choose to believe anything that would not upset our cosy view of ourselves as a good natured, caring and just society.

8 Against Money and Power

> The people who are affected ... become politicised. They form basic political groups and become involved in the political process. In so doing, they come face to face with the fact that rather than discussion and negotiation with the various parties involved, they are faced instead by money and power wielding forces.
>
> Kieran Keohane

This book has been about the community opposition to toxic capital and hazardous industry in Ireland, particularly the kind of industry that is now associated with globalisation. It is not a book about environmentalism or environmentalists. Neither is it a book about parliamentary politics or legislative policy. However it raises questions about the roles played by environmentalists, politicians and policy makers in these community struggles. This is an important distinction to make because communities by themselves are no match for industry and state. Single issue campaigns in the Ireland of the late twentieth century were like flaming meteorites falling to earth in wondrous martyrdom. The 1980s and early 1990s saw a plethora of groups emerge in Irish urban and rural life, operating either on the national stage or at community level. These groups spanned the social spectrum and focused on ecological, environmental, health and social issues yet, with few exceptions, they were all doomed to failure.

Despite more open government and a greater understanding among communities about the crucial issues, nothing changed in fin de siècle Ireland. The problem facing community (or local) groups remained the same in the 2000s as it had been in the 1970s, 1980s and 1990s – the paradoxical journey they must undertake to make their voices heard. Many are independently funded – aided primarily by public donation, subscription and membership – but for some (particularly the rural community groups) funds are sought from government via domestic and EU programmes, and that immediately plunges them into partnerships with the state, into a marriage that is forever turbulent. It has been generally accepted that as the state is the dominant partner confrontational or adversarial tactics are disallowed, which dilutes the role of the group. They become compliant partners. Community groups suffer most from this imbalance because they are almost entirely dependent on state funding or on donations from their members.

According to Galway sociologist Tony Varley 'community action in Ireland owes its marginal position to the stance politicians and the state have adopted towards it'. Despite the seemingly formidable collective force that these self-empowerment groups have become there is, argues Varley, 'no concerted will' by the state to involve them in mainstream Irish politics. Varley is not alone in his political analysis of rural and urban community groups and neither is he expressing an extreme view when he notes that 'many present-day politicians fear the disparate community movement, even the tendency based on inclusive/integrationist assumptions, as a potentially alternative non-party power base in Irish society'.

Yet this fear tells us more about the paranoia of Irish politicians because the disparity is paradigmatic itself, particularly in the rural areas, because these groups represent communities on their last legs. And like battle-weary combatants, bloodied, bruised and broken, many of these communities have no fight left. Self-empowerment alone is not enough to break the pattern. Paradoxically many observers believe that community action gives the larger community the impression that something is being done when in fact all it is doing is diluting the positive and negative attitudes to state policy.

Anthropologist Adrian Peace has described this community opposition to hazardous and undesirable development as 'local level developments' that are 'brief, volcanic eruptions'. They have, he wrote, 'exhibited extensive oratorical elaboration but little organisational structure'. The same argument can be applied to the green movement. Peace's analysis of the intercourse between communities and their green allies is based on his anthropological studies:

> Those involved have had no need for the scripts of 'movement intellectuals', since they are relatively at ease in constructing their own discourses. They have failed to develop major political programmes since this is rarely, if ever, a part of what they have proposed to do.

The reason for this is obvious. Opposition movements are generated, according to Peace, 'to defend ways of life, community identities, economic interests, people's rights, a sense of integrity and pride, and much else besides'. The issue is about the web of diverse issues. 'To reduce these concerns to mere elements of an Irish environmental movement would be to identify only the lowest common denominator.'

The environmental movement's inability to understand this aspect of opposition to globalisation has meant that any political analysis of the state's economic and industrial policies has been left, in Ireland, to parliamentary parties such as Sinn Féin and the Socialist Party – and their mandates have never allowed them to do more than make token gestures. It should be argued that a movement, such as that of the greens, that claims to oppose industrialisation because of its impact on both the biodiversity of the planet and the health of its species, would be capable of mounting a successful strategy against polluting industry coupled with alternatives to the economic and social policies of the state. The history of opposition to hazardous and undesirable development in Ireland reveals that individuals have proposed such strategies but the greens, as an authoritarian and hierarchical movement, have failed to adopt them. This has been evident amidst the various community campaigns. Peace again:

> The extent to which local groups are able to mount effective forms of opposition is determined by their ability to interpret, assess, and process the variegated bodies of knowledge available to them in complex cultures. This involves contesting the political discourses of development, growth, and progress – which are, above all, the weapons of the powerful – which also engages the broader population on their own discursive terms. The language of the powerful has to be contested, while at the same time the language of the powerless must be confirmed. This entails an infinitely more difficult task than that faced by corporations and institutions commanding economic and political power, for theirs is only to insist that in late industrial society, the authority of technical rationality remains unsurpassed and, quoting Foucault, that truth 'is centered on the form of scientific discourse and the institutions which produce it'.

As this book has shown, communities, with few exceptions, have done it all on their own, in their own ways. Where the green movement has got involved the opposition has become diluted. In many instances, instead of lending advice and support, as the anti-Carnsore anarchists once did, the green movement has attempted to control the discourse of protest. No better example of this came during the campaign to prevent DuPont building a toxic waste incinerator at its Maydown factory in Derry. Despite the presence of almost 70 autonomous groups, Greenpeace tried everything in its power to wrestle control of the campaign and to lead it so that it could claim the glory in victory and donations from its admirers for its adventurous stance. It never occurred to Greenpeace that the groups needed the NGO's experience on incineration so that they could fight the battle on their own terms. In the end the Donegal and Derry local groups won because they defeated DuPont with an economic argument; the science Greenpeace wanted to use was not needed.

The DuPont and Sandoz campaigns epitomised the green movement's one-dimensional approach to the issue of environmental protection and that of the health of the communities. Rarely during the campaigns did the green movement see the whole picture or even the brush strokes at the edges of the canvas. All they could see was the need to engage in a direct, vainglorious conflict with the state and industry. There was no lateral thinking to their approach. Against Sandoz, where the green movement was in the vanguard of the opposition, the corporate won. Against DuPont, where the autonomous groups were in control, the corporate lost.

The failure of the green movement to recognise social, economic, political and emotional factors in its campaigning, repeatedly, has allowed detractors to discredit its arguments, particular because few environmentalists take radical perspectives or can argue credibly about how the country should be run. Local autonomous democracy is not an integral aspect of their campaigning. Greens in Ireland tend to be bourgeois in their orientation and careerist in their outlook, with little understanding of life in a low-income family or on a council estate or what it is like to work in or live near a chemical factory. Community groups without the direction of the greens always fared better than their allies because they were, at least up to the late 1980s, dogged and persistent, and because their non-violent (and sometimes violent) actions challenged government and industry in a manner that reflected the seriousness of their concerns. Because they have never had a global agenda, like the larger green NGOs such as Greenpeace, and start off largely apolitical, community groups can oppose proposals for hazardous development with an increased mandate from within their own communities.

Throughout the 1970s and 1980s the state and industry frequently underestimated the strength and tenacity of the communities opposed to its proposals, content instead to attempt to discredit the likes of Greenpeace and latterly Cork Environmental Alliance because these groups sought a vanguardist position in the power relations between the state and the environment, failing to understand that the issues were not solely about the environment – that they were also about human rights and social conditions.

Asked how effective the green movement are as political lobbyists Fine Gael's Jim Mitchell once answered: 'Not as effective as SPUC, thank God' – SPUC being the Society for the Protection of the Unborn Child.

If the qualification was meant to imply that the green movement could have an enormous social, economic and political impact on Irish society if it added a social dimension to its ecological stance, there are many who would agree with him. If, in fact, he meant that it is just as well that the green movement are not as effective as SPUC there are many in industry and government who would agree and express a sigh of relief. A green movement that is eco-social or a mixture of green (ecologist and environmentalist), red (socialist) and black (anarchist) based on grassroots autonomous assembly would be a powerful force against globalisation. The reason for the greens' ineffectiveness has much to do with their tentative beginnings and present nebulous existence in Irish life.

In Ireland the emergence of the green movement had more to do with the state's economic policies of the late 1950s and less to do with the issues that were framing ecological and environmental concerns in places like North America and continental Europe. At first the movement was radical and effective. Anti-toxic and anti-mining groups evolved out of the anti-nuclear movement of the mid-1970s who joined with local communities, concerned largely with the proposed Carnsore nuclear power station, asbestos waste in Cork, uranium mining in Donegal and the toxic legacy of mining all over the country. Gradually other environmental groups with varying – mostly single issue – agendas began to form, some with local and radical bases, others with national concerns. Sociologist Hilary Tovey argues that two distinctive environmental movements evolved during this period, an 'official' urban-based movement that relied on expert knowledge to resolve environmental problems, and a 'populist' rural movement that became more socially realistic and less politically naive.

An Taisce would argue that it preceded this 1970s explosion of radical green groups by several decades. Founded in 1948 with a mandate from its members to encourage care of the environment, An Taisce initially concerned itself with the Irish landscape, architecture and settlements, thus getting a reputation as a heritage group dealing with soft environmental issues. Along with the Irish Wildbird Conservancy and the Irish Wildlife Federation, An Taisce was seen to be part of an elitist conservationist movement. The fact that it was also tied to the establishment by the 1963 Local Government Act so that it would have a small input into the planning process meant that its orientation was academic rather than radical. That changed with the introduction of the extraction and toxic industries into Ireland. In the early 1970s the extremely vocal Cork branch of An Taisce led the fight against toxic industry, and got into a fight with Pfizer. An Taisce's move into hard environmental politics was not without criticism, from other green groups and from government and industry – simply because it appeared to take an establishment line one minute and a radical one the next. Several anti-toxic groups were amazed when the An Taisce chair Philip Mullally called for a national toxic dump in 1980. Yet An Taisce's call during the same year for a comprehensive register of waste disposal activities, which would record all movements of toxic waste, was the first attempt in Ireland to introduce a toxic release inventory.

While the 1970s green campaigns were primarily about nuclear issues (Windscale/Sellafield, Carnsore, radioactive waste dumping) a general concern about environmental degradation prompted some people to drop out of society. Rural parts of Ireland became green havens for foreigners and Irish alike. And these defined the green movement in Ireland more than the small radical groups that were fighting globalisation and the industrialisation of Ireland. It is now a generalisation to say that the majority of the active greens in the Ireland of the 1970s were from Britain, continental Europe and North America – specifically because this was the public image that persisted into the 1990s. These people, it was claimed, were only interested in their own agendas and wanted Ireland to be a 'green haven' for their benefit. Of course it wasn't as simple as this. The indigenous Irish did care about their environment and their health but it was not until the 1980s that they realised what they had let themselves in for, that the radicals did know what they were talking about and that the state, which they believed was providing jobs for them, was also providing hazard they did not want in their communities. So from the beginning there existed a dilemma and only those who could afford to were able to opt out of the rat race and wage-slavery.

In 1971 Matt Murphy left his job in Cork and moved with his family to Sherkin Island, where he started an environmental newsletter *Sherkin Comment* (which is distributed to politicians, civil servants, school principals and company executives), launched the Sherkin Island Marine Centre and initiated regular environmental conferences on the island.

Common Ground, a magazine which was started in 1977 as the *North-West Newsletter* by a group of people living alternative lifestyles, became a green flagship selling 10,000 copies. The original editorial group were all 'blow-ins' from abroad and then gradually it became an all-Irish affair. '*Common Ground* has always been run by a free floating editorial group, with people coming and going at will', said Charley Langrish.

> It is a fairly anarchic set up which works well most of the time. The magazine relies unashamedly on pieces written and sent in by readers. Nobody is paid a dime, which is probably why the magazine has kept its head above water for so long. It began as a fairly practical publication, a platform for the exchange of personal experiences concerning the writers' various endeavours towards living their lives as far as possible divorced from the capitalist system.

By the end of the 1970s alternative living and environmentalism were sexy terms, and more and more groups began to form. Those who believed it was possible to work within the capitalist system and still raise the green agenda began to move, as academic Sue Baker put it, 'towards lifestyle issues, alternative energy sources and what may be called "green politics"'.

Then, in a flush of activity, the green movement began to grow out of all proportion to its 1970s origins. Many of the individuals involved in green politics became involved in Comhaontas Glas (Green Alliance), which had evolved out of the Ecology Party, formed in 1981. Throughout the 1980s the Green Alliance attempted to elevate green issues onto the political agenda, and when some of its members decided that hardcore politics were not their forte the Alliance split and the Green Party was subsequently formed in 1988. Within a year the Green Party had in Roger Garland its first parliamentarian when he took a seat in the Dáil to represent those who had voted for him in the Dublin South constituency.

An Taisce lost its mantle as the only body stating the environmental issue. Out of HOPE (Help Organise Peaceful Energy) a west Cork group formed in 1980 to oppose radioactive dumping, Earthwatch was formed in 1986 and subsequently became a member of Friends of the Earth International.

And various individuals personified specific environmental causes. The preservation of broad-leafed trees became the obsession of Australian Jan Alexander and she formed Crann (tree in Irish) in 1986. German Karin Dubsky fought to increase awareness of the state of Ireland's coastline. Her Dublin Bay Environmental Group launched its coastline survey in September 1987 and followed it up two years later with another survey, Coastline Europe. In May 1987, former Sea Shepherd activist John Bowler was appointed Greenpeace Ireland's national coordinator. In November 1990 Deonoibrithe Caomhantais (Conservation Volunteers Ireland) was established by 16 voluntary NGOs, including An Oige, An Taisce, ECO, Irish Peatland Conservation Council and others, and became a member of the International Conservation Action Network. In April 1991, following a conference in Trinity College, Dublin titled 'Women and the Environment: What can we do?' an Irish Women's Environmental Network was founded to empower women to act on the environment.

Yet despite all this activity Ireland's ecology and its environment was getting worse by the minute; the air became polluted, the lakes, rivers and streams became poisoned and the land became denuded and stripped of its fertility. All the while the health of the people deteriorated as the country began to exhibit the same kinds of illnesses that characterise the world's industrial populations. This left many communities and some individuals, who wondered what was happening to their country, questioning the roles of the greens who proclaimed to care – because it appeared that was all they did.

Of the green NGOs, An Taisce has certainly had the most impact, particularly in raising public awareness, yet Philip Mullally was not sure if the organisation had made a lasting impact. 'I think the issue really is that we have not yet linked into the real needs of the country and its people', he said in 1986 – a comment that was still true in 2003.

When asked in the early 1990s about their impact on Irish society, Earthwatch and Greenpeace sounded arrogant. 'Substantial and positive', said Earthwatch, but both NGOs admitted that it was almost impossible to quantify this impact. 'The issue of waste management/incineration/clean production is now a serious debate but how do you gauge exactly how much of this is due to Greenpeace', said Greenpeace administrator Margaret Ward in 1993.

Jeremy Wates, Earthwatch's coordinator, was more cynical about it around the same time:

> Not that many years ago, Irish politicians were not embarrassed to stand over bad environmental policies. The environment was simply not an issue. Then they began to be embarrassed but they did not do anything to improve the policies. The only thing they did was learn to talk green.

While Greenpeace was fairly effective on single-issue campaigns, like its anti-toxic and anti-nuke stances, the political parties generally believed that Greenpeace and Earthwatch were not effective lobbyists, a point Jeremy Wates agreed with:

> In general, I think the environmental movement in Ireland is not particularly sophisticated in its lobbying efforts, but I would also level some criticism at parliamentarians and other decision makers who have failed to adequately use the valuable information resources of the environmental movement.

While the green movement as a whole is not seen as an effective lobbying force, individual campaigners, like the former Dublin Zoo Keeper Brendan Price for example, have managed to bend the ears of several politicians and gain some respect for their environmental arguments. Leo Hallissey in Letterfrack with his sea weeks and his bog weeks has raised awareness without making political capital out of it.

When Jim Mitchell stated that the green movement was 'very active and articulate with lots of sensible ideas' he was repeating a

general belief, but the Progressive Democrats echoed another sentiment, that the public perception of the green movement is that it is
'well meaning but idealistic'.

There has been a strong argument that the green movement in
Ireland will not evolve if it continues to progress using established
economic, legal, political and scientific modes of activity. But the
argument in support of small, local and autonomous eco-social
groups working outside the system, which first surfaced during the
anti-nuclear campaigns in the mid-1970s, only began to find favour
in the mid-to-late 1990s when the anarchist movement woke up to
the reality of globalisation in Ireland and the impact it was having
on Irish society, getting involved in the Grassroots Gathering
collective (and the Grassroots Network Against War), which sought
to bring diverse groups and individuals together to fight the
globalisation of Ireland.

Back at the end of the 1980s the signs were there that
autonomous solidarity groups were the answer, individuals and
groups with varying agendas coming together to fight common,
local and national causes. While some groups remained small, local
and autonomous, others formed into regional alliances, like the
Cork Environmental Alliance, the Derry/Donegal Alliance and
Cork Harbour Alliance for a Safe Environment, which, according
to some critics, diluted their power. Yet it did give them a combined
regional strength that they used to their advantage. But it also gave
them the same headaches as national and global NGOs, lack of
funds, inadequate resources and few professional full-time workers.

The ideal that concentrated power lies with a mass eco-social
movement developing outside traditional parliamentary politics,
which was also first expressed during the anti-nuclear campaigns,
was beginning to gain ground in the early years of the 2000s as the
issues of globalisation began to galvanise a new generation. In the
early 1990s such an ideal was indeed revolutionary, and the inability of groups to see what should be done led to failure – a good
example being the anti-toxic campaigns described in this book,
which brought back some of the same activists involved in the anti-
nuclear campaign. In her study of the Irish ecology movement Sue
Baker argued in 1990 that the anti-toxic movement remained
'nebulous' and because of this was unable to develop:

> to successfully launch campaigns of opposition to indus-
> trial development strategies for their area. Lacking a

national organisational dimension, longer-term and planned goals, being reactive rather than primarily pro-active in nature, they are in a weak position in terms of their ability to influence the direction of a national indus-trial development policy so rooted in the ideology of all the main political parties since the 1950s.

One major criticism that the green movement, particularly the national NGOs, had difficulty with was the conflict between social issues and environmental goals. When Greenpeace said on many occasions that it did not accept that jobs and a clean environment are incompatible its critics argued that it did not look at social realities. Sinn Féin's environment spokeswoman, Anne Speed, said her party:

> would like to see the campaigning green movement in Ireland pay particular attention to the impact of their demands on those living in poverty and unemployment. This does not mean diluting their environmental demands. It means taking other issues on board.

And this has been its problem since toxic industry came to Ireland. The state and, in particular, the IDA can say, by bringing these corporates into the country, they have created thousands of jobs and boosted the economy. Throughout the 1980s and 1990s greens were frequently asked to elaborate on the social and economic poli-cies they would bring in to replace industrialisation. Sadly few were able to offer little more than gestures and empty promises. No more was this more evident than during the Merrell Dow campaign when many environmentalists promised to create clean industries that would offer badly needed jobs in the area. Instead the job creation was left to the initiatives of the communities while the greens got on with improving their own lives, living in green bubbles immune from the harsh social realities of life in modern Ireland, searching out job opportunities in government, industry and academia.

Community groups, as the Merrell Dow campaigners showed, need wider support if they are to win toxic battles but, as socio-logist Kieran Keohane proved, the process politicises and people start to look closer at the society they live in. So they turn to green NGOs and green politicians, believing that these people are their allies, and gradually they find that the green agenda is not so different from the agendas pursued by the establishment.

If we need evidence of this you only have to look at the Hanrahans' battle with Merck, then at the east Cork opposition to Merrell Dow, the campaign against Sandoz and finally the Askeaton tragedy. Hanrahan took Merck Sharp and Dohme on with only the support of his family, some friends and a very small number of people who believed in him; the organised greens were nowhere to be seen. Again in the extremely well organised and ultimately successful campaign against Merrell Dow the greens were unable to offer more than token gestures. Against Sandoz they got involved, giving the communities the impression that they knew what they were doing, and bit-by-bit they compromised with the state and with industry, and Sandoz got to build its factory. But the greens' greatest failure has been their inability to interpret and do something about the tragedy of Askeaton.

Despite the relative successes around the country since hazardous and toxic industry came to Ireland in the late 1960s, Irish people now live in a society that is dominated by hazard, corporate capital and the rules of globalisation, while the green movement's history is one long and glorious failure. It had the chance to make the country into a food and craft producing haven with a clean environment and healthy people; instead Ireland got the chance to catch up with the rest of the industrialised world and its elites got to bask in avaricious glory, leaving many communities marooned on toxic islands amid an ocean of corporates.

Though isolated these communities began to exhibit different characteristics and employ demographically astute strategies during the early years of the 2000s. Cork Harbour Alliance for a Safe Environment, in the campaign against Indaver, based its strategy on social politics, leaving the environmental science to the greens without compromising the issue. 'One of our main aims in the campaign was to make it political, and that, to my mind was one of the most telling things about the amendment Bill raised in the Dáil by the Greens', Linda Fitzpatrick, public relations for the Cork alliance opposed to Indaver's plans, said.

> We were surprised at the extent of participation from opposition parties. When we started, Fine Gael still had incineration as part of their waste policy. We were fortunate to have their Environment spokesperson in our constituency to lobby directly, and it was she who got their policy changed. That is how we now have their support 'en masse' officially.

It would be presumptuous to say that Cork is the final battle-ground, that Ireland's image as a pure, green land has been corrupted by globalisation and the industrialisation of every means of production, and that all that remains is for people to escape to somewhere else. The problem, as Linda Fitzpatrick has articulated it, is that there is nowhere in Ireland that has not been changed by globalisation, and by the policies of the Irish state and successive governments. The debate about these policies and their impact on Irish society has been crushed – and the history of how it all came about has been marginalised, with very little criticism in the public domain on the roles played by the state and semi-state bodies.

On 19 June 1997 the Askeaton/Ballysteen Animal Health Committee and the Sheehy family delivered a stinging retort to the methodology of discourse employed by the EPA at its oral hearing into Roche's application to the agency for a licence to operate a high-temperature hazardous waste incinerator on its Clarecastle site. 'They cannot act impartially as both judge and jury of their own licence determination', the group and the Sheehys, in a written submission, said. 'We do not see why we should have to defend ourselves like criminals against Senior Counsel because of our genuine concerns.'

In his critique of the EPA Kieran Keohane wrote that 'the institution of the EPA Public Hearing is best understood as an instance of systematically distorted communication'. The rules and procedures, which are determined by the EPA, he said, are for a discourse that 'favours bureaucrats and company directors' against ordinary people 'to whom such language and practices are unfamiliar and intimidating' leaving them at a distinct disadvantage. And despite objections, this 'discourse remains overwhelmingly that of bureaucrats and scientists'. Keohane added:

> Some participants felt that the hearing was a cynical exercise in public deception, a deliberate sham designed to give the appearance of a sincere discussion, deliberately intended not to re-examine, but merely to endorse a course of action already undertaken.

This last analysis could also describe the history of the state's reaction to successive generations of opposition to the industrialisation of Ireland, for which all departments of the state have come in for strong criticism – simply because they have always been seen to be on the side of industry, and never of the people. The IDA, justifiably, has come in for the most criticism, followed closely by the IIRS, the local authorities and An Bord Pleanála. The roles played by the Department of the Environment and the Taoiseach's Department have also been criticised.

Set up in 1950 the IDA survived its unpopular early years, according to Joseph Lee 'to become later a virtually independent republic in the formulation of industrial policy'. Barry and Jackson flesh out this skeleton:

> The system of grants and incentives to multinational companies is fully managed by the Industrial Development Authority which describes itself as a 'one stop shop'. This means that multinational companies planning to set up in Ireland can carry out their negotiations with a single organisation. This autonomy, which is jealously guarded by the IDA, has meant that the process of a new multinational establishing a subsidiary in the country is not complicated by overlapping agencies, parallel power structures or bureaucratic inertia. The IDA spends about 11 per cent of the government's capital budget each year and until [the early 1990s] tended to operate without critical review or assessment.

The IDA was allowed this autonomy because in the 1970s, noted Lee, 'government effectively abdicated to the IDA responsibility for industrial policy'. As long as the job approval announcements kept coming, the politicians were happy. They were also prepared to ignore any criticism of the IDA. Initially the IDA was accused of attempting to induce local communities into accepting toxic developments, of preventing the implementation or deferring the implementation of proper environmental safeguards and of attracting dirty industry to Ireland. Keohane reported one community's perception of the IDA:

> Of all the parties involved other than Penn itself, the IDA was regarded as the worst offender. People considered it to be hand in hand with Penn, and that it was the voice behind the scenes which directed the county council and An Bord Pleanála.

One major charge has been that the IDA attracted dirty industry by presenting Ireland as a pollution haven. It is a charge that the IDA continually found itself forced to deny, especially during the 1980s. The issue first arose in 1974 when the IDA was attempting to attract the US corporate DuPont to Ringaskiddy. At the time DuPont was considering Ireland, Scotland and France as possible locations for a titanium dioxide factory. A highly critical article in the *New Scientist* in July 1974 warned: 'Are polluting developments of this type to be directed wherever conservationists are worst organised?' The following week DuPont denied that the major reason it was considering locating its factory in Cork was the opposition from environmentalists in Llanelli, Wales.

Accusations that corporates have chosen Ireland to site their most environmentally hazardous factories have been consistently made since. Perhaps the most paranoid presentation of this analysis was made by a publication of the Cork Noxious Industry Action Group:

> A recent article in the *New York Times* reported that the owners of noxious industry have genetically screened the workers of the world. They have looked at the genetic history and the chromosome make-up of workers in different parts of the world. They have determined that Ireland is one of the three countries where the workers are most suited to work in noxious industry, in Ireland the effects of the toxic substances wouldn't readily show up and there is a high incidence of Down's Syndrome (mongolism) in Ireland and an increase in die rate might not be easily detected.

Less paranoid versions of the hazard export charge have been supported by outside observers. In 1989 scientist Rosalie Bertell told RTE's *Today Tonight* programme:

> In more industrialised countries, there have been many disasters. The more polluting industries are looking for places to locate. You can usually tell such a company when the raw material is imported, it's processed in a country and then the product is exported. That's your key. It's cheaper to have the plant where the raw material is, or where the finished product is going. So there's some reason why the intermediary process is done in another country, and usually that is the polluting part of the process, and that is where you have the toxic waste.

In 1984 the American magazine *Multinational Monitor* argued that US corporates were using Ireland as a pollution and tax haven. Petra Kelly of the German Greens was more blunt when she spoke to a Women's Political Association meeting in Dublin in the early 1980s: 'Ireland has become the dumping ground for factories other EEC countries wouldn't accept.' Irish academics have also argued such a position. Keohane and Harris are two examples. Harris also writes of 'firms that have been attracted to Ireland in some measure precisely because of incompetent local implementation of health and environmental legislation'. Despite IDA denials, Leonard has shown that in the early 1970s the IDA paid little if any attention to the environmental impacts of industrialisation. Speaking of the period immediately after the reorganisation of the IDA in 1969 John Gannon said: 'There wasn't much planning, we just assumed we would have to take what industry we could get, and that dear Ireland would have to take some trade-offs.'

Although IDA made no explicit effort to attract industries that were causing severe environmental problems in other countries, the agency generally assumed that some of the industries migrating to Ireland would be ones that faced an inhospitable climate at home owing to concern about pollution. To ensure the cooperation of the local governments actually responsible for approving specific industrial proposals, IDA officials held a series of closed-door meetings to advise local officials that, for the sake of the economy and jobs, some of the dirtier industrial facilities from the advanced industrial nations might have to be sited on terms that offered less stringent pollution controls than in Europe or the United States.

Whether Ireland was a specific target for hazard export or not, the IDA's strategic decisions on the direction industrial development policy should take were bound to result in problems relating to pollution. Leonard describes what he sees as three phases in IDA industrial policy. In the early 1960s the emphasis was on labour-intensive industry: textiles, clothing, footwear, food processing, paper and printing. As competition from peripheral countries with even lower labour costs made this an increasingly vulnerable policy, the IDA therefore changed tack towards more technologically advanced industry.

The petrochemical and metal processing industries were a natural target for the IDA's planners. The IDA's plans included lead and zinc smelters, oil refineries and large-scale organic chemical projects, particularly in the Cork harbour area. Leonard cites two

Pfizer factories from this period – the Pfizer factory in Cork and the Quigley Magnesite factory in Dungarvan, County Waterford – which received considerably greater pollution rights than they would have received in metropolitan countries at the time. If the IDA was unsuccessful in these plans, it was not for want of trying: at various times refineries from BASF, smelters from Japanese companies and others, the DuPont titanium dioxide factory and other projects were announced but eventually failed to appear, mainly due to the economic and overcapacity crises of industry following the oil embargo of 1973. In fact the only really major heavy industry of this type attracted by the IDA was the Aughinish Alumina factory on the Shannon estuary, and there was a price to pay for that deal.

While it may not have got DuPont, the IDA found it was having increasing success in attracting US healthcare corporates. In its third phase, the IDA concentrated on the healthcare industry, particularly the pharmaceuticals sector, and then on electronics. Recognising the crisis in basic chemicals, the IDA set its sights on the seemingly recession-proof pharmaceutical industry. Of course this industry has its own pollution problems, but the IDA disingenuously argued that it was safe and that it was the heavy chemicals industry that was hazardous. Thus the IDA propaganda emphasised that pharmaceuticals was a clean bright industry, but here again the hazard export argument reappeared. While the IDA claimed it chose the pharmaceutical industry because it was environmentally clean, the IDA has succeeded in attracting the most hazardous sector of this industry. According to Keohane, 25 per cent of all the waste produced by the pharmaceutical industry is classified as hazardous. The active ingredients sector produces 75 per cent of this. The hazardous waste produced by the active ingredients sector tends to be the most hazardous, the most difficult and consequently the most expensive to treat and dispose of. Practically all the plants of the corporate pharmaceutical industry that have been established in Ireland have been active ingredients plants.

In 1980, for instance, Noel Murphy, Gaeleo managing director in Ireland, explained that the reason his company had chosen Little Island, County Cork, as its site was because 'we wanted a place with a similar infrastructure to the home country without so many government restrictions'. No doubt he felt comfortable making such a remark to an industry magazine with a small circulation in Ireland. No such comfort was available to the marketing manager for the Danish company Nordisk Gentofte who explained to the *Financial Times* in 1989 that the reason the company chose Ireland was the ease in obtaining permission to set up compared with the trouble it would have over environmental regulation at home. In general then, the industry has seen Ireland as 'a good country to do business in' and has offered praise for 'the sympathetic business-minded attitudes by central government and local authorities'.

Another example was the story of W&E Products, renamed the Soap Company of Ireland, which is presented as a textbook case of hazard export. The company produced a hazardous product, mercury soap, which had been banned by the EC and whose main developing market was in Africa where it was used as a skin whitener. The British government was also moving in on the company, at least partly because of problems of overexposure of W&E's workers to mercury in their English factory. Nevertheless in time honoured Irish fashion, planning permission was received before anyone realised what was going on. It was a Dublin MEP, Mary Banotti, who blew the whistle on W&E, but the debate focused on the hazard of the product rather than the hazards to workers. Ironically perhaps there was no community opposition to this factory. Opposition came mainly from the development lobby, as well as from the Consumers Association of Ireland and Earth-watch. The local Chamber of Commerce in Arklow came out in support of the factory, expressing the requisite confidence in the IDA and the IIRS, while Mary Banotti was criticised for being 'more concerned about a sensational headline than about Irish economic development'.

The IIRS was brought in to do a survey on the hazards of mercury soap and then refused to publish it. Access to it was restricted to the IIRS building in Ballymun. Coincidentally, the authors of the report discovered that the product was a health risk even if used properly. The IIRS denied that it originally intended making the report public and then changed its mind.

A quote *The Phoenix* attributed to John Hayden of the IIRS, that the IDA would finance gas ovens, summed up one widely held view of the IDA at the time. Here the IDA's position was that it did not operate on the basis of morality. This seemed incredible to an Earth-watch interviewer of the IDA's Padraic White who explained, 'I don't want the IDA to be in the position of being moral guardians of people in other countries.' The interviewer responded, 'We're not asking you to be moral guardians, just make a moral decision sometimes.'

A further illuminating example of the IDA's moral choices was shown over its handling of the Raybestos Manhattan dispute. Here an extremely revealing insight into the IDA is provided by Leonard, who reports criticism of Raybestos Manhattan by Irish officials. According to Matt Lynch of the IIRS in March 1980 'it is safe to say that if we had had the information we have today about asbestos or acrylonitrile, neither Raybestos nor Asahi [the Japanese chemical factory based in Ballina, County Mayo] would have been permitted to come to Ireland except under very restrictive circumstances'.

This is Leonard's version:

> But IDA also faced a big problem about what to do when the storm broke over Raybestos. Earlier IDA had made certain promises to Raybestos, including the commitment to find a new dumpsite when the original site in Ovens was vetoed. The success of an organisation like IDA depends more than anything else on its reputation among international businesses for keeping its promises and helping to ease the siting and eventual operating process for foreign companies. In the Raybestos case, IDA felt obliged to stand by the company publicly, because it was concerned that any failure to support Raybestos would tarnish its reputation with other foreign companies.

It is worth recalling Ted Deane's statement, before he headed back to the United States, that without the support of the IDA the company would have foundered in Ireland. The IDA's political masters also supported this position in which nothing was too important to sacrifice to industrial development.

After the Sandoz affair, criticism of the IDA began to wane, but that may have more to do with the simple fact that Sandoz was the last of the raw chemical giants to locate in Ireland. Between 1990 and 1998, according to the IDA's figures, 65 'major pharmaceutical investments were initiated in Ireland totalling $3 billion'. Sounds impressive except that 47 of these were expansions of existing factories and the rest were 'finished product' companies – the cleaner end of the industry. 'Research and development' became the IDA's buzz phrase of the 1990s as the agency managed to persuade the corporates that Ireland was now a secure base for the industry. After all, it boasted, 'nine of the world's top 10 pharmaceutical companies and ten of the world's top 15 medical products companies'. More significantly by 2003 Ireland was home to '200 overseas pharmaceutical, chemicals and healthcare companies'. Total investment was estimated in 2003 at $7 billion.

The Institute for Industrial Research and Standards (IIRS/Eolas) was another body that took the brunt of community criticism. Its failure to protect the health of the public and the environment was based on a mis-apprehension of the IIRS's role. It was set up as a state-sponsored body responsible to the Minister for Industry and Commerce. Its role was to facilitate industrial development through the fostering of technological research and through standardisation. It never had any statutory responsibility for protecting the environment, unlike the EPA, a point made in an IIRS document from 1977:

> It is important to emphasise that IIRS does not have any statutory function in setting emission standards or environmental standards.... In the absence of clearly defined statutory or local requirements regarding the environment, IIRS fulfils its responsibility by advising government and local (including planning) authorities on acceptable norms for industrial practice in relation to effluents, emissions, noise and vibration, solid and hazardous waste.

The IIRS wasn't an official standard-setting body in these areas; instead it acted as an unofficial standard-setting body. What were involved were 'acceptable norms for industrial practice' rather than 'best available technology' or similar regulatory demands.

Another problematic position the IIRS found itself in was that it was commissioned by the IDA to report on the environmental implications of projects being grant-aided by the IDA. Thus any industry a community would oppose already held the IIRS seal of approval. Unfortunately, due to the state's addiction to secrecy, these reports were not made public. The IIRS's credibility was undermined because it was seen as the scientific servant of the IDA.

A similar problem of credibility arose from the fact that much of the IIRS's work involved contract and service work for corporates. and this dependence on the private sector increased as the state cut its subventions and eventually merged the IIRS and the National Board for Science and Technology (NBST) to form Eolas. The IIRS's opinion on any subject was seen to be captive to whoever was paying for it. Yvonne Scannell summed up this public perception of the IIRS:

> The role of the IIRS in the field of pollution control is, however, suspect. It derives a substantial proportion of its income from private industry, and there appears to be potential, if not an actual, conflict of interests in this body which advises both controlling bodies and those who are likely to cause pollution.

Thus the IIRS found itself in the same quandary as other state bodies. It was required to promote and serve industrial development, and give expert advice to those supposed to regulate industrial development. Working to obtain some balance, it was inevitable it would come under heavy attack from the communities who wondered how it could serve two masters. A more cynical view of the IIRS is reported by Ives: 'The IIRS is another state organisation involved with toxic industry. Its function ... is to provide a scientific and technical veneer to state projects designed to diffuse anger and fear.'

It is undeniable that the IIRS was consistently used as a means of reassuring communities that companies locating in their midst were environment-friendly, having judged the safety and environmental impacts of the companies for the IDA and having found them reassuringly acceptable. The continual use of the IIRS in this manner led to eventual public disbelief in these reassurances from the IIRS. One constant criticism of the IIRS's work on the environmental impact of factories was that it was too committed to industrial development to approach its task always in a scientific manner: Keohane described how the IIRS approached its environmental impact statement for Penn Chemicals:

> The report concluded that the development would not be in any way detrimental to the local environment. The authors appeared to go out of their way to prove this. Less than one year prior to the EIS being conducted, the management at Penn established a bird sanctuary adjacent to the plant. The IIRS scientists referred to the existence of the sanctuary in the proximity of the plant as evidence that Penn was causing no environmental damage. If there were any ill effects they would not come to light for a number of years. No baseline

study of the birds had been conducted nor was there any examination whatsoever carried out at the time of the EIS, yet the IIRS saw fit to use this totally unscientific casual observation as evidence of the environmental safety of the plant.

Similar attacks were made on other EISs produced by the IIRS and Eolas. During the Merrell Dow oral hearing Eolas was criticised for producing an EIS that suffered from 'a poor reporting of method' and 'use of inappropriate methods, lack of data for various requirements and confusion over the accuracy of calculations presented in the EIS'.

Given that this toxic development was a cooperative project by the Irish state and foreign capital, the state was concerned not to put too many obstacles in the way of this development. One reason why the IIRS got so much criticism was the failure of the state to set up any adequate regulatory bodies to monitor and control this industry. In a stroke of bureaucratic genius the responsibility for monitoring the highly sophisticated and technologically advanced industry the IDA was attracting was handed over to the local authorities. Aside from being notorious polluters themselves, the local authorities were also co-promoters of state development policy and in competition with other local authorities to attract these industries to their local areas – South Tipperary and Merck being the classic example. In most cases, the local authorities were simply not equipped, a point made by Keohane: '[They] lacked the experience, the expertise and the resources to use effectively the legislation, and penalties for transgressions were negligible.' Leonard made the same point: 'There appears to be overwhelming evidence that pollution-control regulations are not enforced in a consistent and concerted manner. This fact is openly acknowledged by government officials and multinational corporate executives.' In his December 1984 published study for the Conservation Foundation in the United States based on his research in Ireland, Spain, Mexico and Romania, Leonard writes:

> [Ireland is not] adequately equipped to evaluate proposals or to make reasonable assessments about the long term implications of accepting the industry. For example there is still an absence of awareness about problems that may develop when small amounts of chemicals build up in

receiving waters or human bodies over the long term or
when workers and the public are exposed to hazardous
substances that do not smell or burn.

That it was lack of enforcement rather than lack of legislation to
enforce that was the problem was also the opinion of environmental law lecturer Yvonne Scannell:

> Some people here say the problem is that there is not an
> adequate body of environmental law in Ireland. But that is
> not true. There are 55 or so laws that affect what private
> industry can do to the environment. They are just not
> enforced. You can take it for granted that every single law
> is not being adequately enforced.

Enforcement, however, was not as easy as it sounded, as Donegal
County Council discovered when it tried to punish Truloc in Carndonagh for infringements of the legislation.

The Cork Environmental Alliance's criticisms of the EPA
suggest that little has changed since the early 1990s when the state
overhauled its system of regulation, placing the EPA in the role of
regulator. It was the CEA's opinion that the EPA was not established
to protect the environment.

> Rather, the true objective of the Agency has been to nullify the
> environmental conflicts between communities and the incom-
> ing multinational corporates. The Agency has been aided by
> the State industrial promotion agencies, such as the IDA and
> Local Authorities, in their effort to achieve this aim.

The CEA concluded in an analysis of the EPA that its 'underlying
environmental philosophy' was one of 'pollution control rather than
pollution prevention'. The Cork group demonstrated this with a
review of the prosecutions taken by the EPA in 1997. Their analysis
showed that:

> There were seven prosecutions taken in all during that year.
> These yielded an average fine of IR£418 each. The
> approach of the EPA is to always prosecute in the District
> court where only summary or minor prosecutions are
> meant to be tried. Typically this is the court where traffic

offences and shoplifting cases are tried. The EPA would need to contact the DPP before the case could proceed to a court higher than the District court. This happens routinely with other state bodies. We have all become familiar with the phrase 'a file has been sent to the DPP'. Well in the case of the EPA a file has never been sent to the DPP. It would be one thing for the DPP to decide that a case should not be tried because of some evidential deficiency. However, for the EPA to have never allowed the DPP to make this kind of decision is nothing short of scandalous.

The CEA argued that the EPA was 'seriously underfunded and, as a consequence, cannot carry out the limited role as an environmental protection agency ascribed to it under the EPA act' – the same act that obliged the EPA to 'have regard to government policies'. This, the CEA argued, undermined the EPA's independence.

And so it was proved when the EPA faced its first challenge following the allegations by Askeaton farmers against Aughinish Alumina in June 1997. The corporate had operated in Limerick since 1974 under a planning permit issued by the local council, which had never carried out any emission monitoring at the factory. When the EPA attempted to impose an integrated pollution licence on the corporate it discovered a sweetheart deal agreed with the IDA. Not only did Aughinish Alumina object to 40 conditions in the licence, it argued that a reduction in its sulphur dioxide emissions from 50 tonnes a day to 14 tonnes a day, would be in breach of the agreement it had made with the IDA because of the extra costs involved. The EPA's draft licence suggested that SO_2 emissions could be reduced by using a fuel oil with a lower sulphur content. The corporate swiftly produced the relevant paragraph from the 1974 deal: 'the Government will not impose discriminatory taxes, rates and charges on the property of the Irish company, the products and materials used by it, or on its operations'. And when the CEA asked for the full document, so that it could it could be introduced into evidence for the oral hearing against the licence, the corporate, then the IDA and finally the state told them to get lost. The company, the CEA protested, 'were allowed to rely on a document at the oral hearing that we were denied access to'.

What was at stake here was the corporate's wellbeing, both to its image and its profits. The allegations of pollution from its factory were, said Frank Dunlop, its public relations expert, 'totally completely unfounded with no basis in fact or science'. The conditions imposed by the EPA would, said Cynthia Carroll, the corporate's managing director, cost IR£9.5 million and possibly force Alcan, its parent company, to close down the Limerick operation and put people out of work. Aughinish Alumina, the oral hearing heard, employed 450 full-time people and 200 contractors making up annual wages of IR£14.4 million and contributions of IR£40 million to the local economy and IR£55 million to the national economy. Financial Controller Michael Collins said that Aughinish's projected profits for 1997 would only be IR£11 million, which he said was only 3.7 per cent of their capital investment.

The problem communities were now faced was with a set of new legislation that actually gave the impression that something was being done about pollution when in reality the state had come up with a clever strategy to lessen the opposition. Planning was left to the local authorities, pollution control and prevention were given to the EPA. Many critics saw the pitfalls immediately. Since the introduction of the EPA Act in 1992 and the Local Government (Planning and Development Act) in 1993, communities opposing new developments had to make objections to the local authority on the planning permission and then again to the EPA on the licensing permission. Instead of one process, objections to the local authority and then to An Bord Pleanála, communities were now up against money and power, the two ingredients in this mix they were short of. They had to plan a strategy to oppose planning permission by challenging the local authority with objections and then go through the costly planning appeals oral procedure. Once that had been done they had to do it again with the EPA. So it was no surprise that objections to the chemical and pharmaceutical industry have fallen away since the mid-1990s, and that Roche got to build its incinerator.

As there have been problems with regulation, so there have also been problems with monitoring. Between the 1960s and the mid-1990s the industry was effectively allowed to monitor itself, with a few exceptions – for example, when the state undertook the task. In both cases the public were refused access to the data. When the data was revealed it was found to be flawed, as I found out when I conducted research for Greenpeace on the pollution of Cork harbour in November 1988:

> Whilst companies are obliged to conduct analyses for
> specific pollutants in their waste, in general, they are only

required to analyse regularly for 5-day biological oxygen demand (BOD), chemical oxygen demand (COD) and pH. This provides wholly inadequate characterisation of the waste entering Cork harbour. In addition, toxicity tests by Eolas appear extremely limited in scope, providing only acute toxicity information. There is no indication of possible long-term sub-lethal effects, or the effects of combined effluents such as those released by the IDA pipeline. Monitoring data presently held by local government is not available to the general public and it is our considered opinion that it should be.

The major criticism the monitors faced was their relationship with the industries they were monitoring, plus their lack of expertise. The National Board of Science and Technology (NBST) reported on the deplorably weak state of toxicology in Ireland: 'The state apparatus in terms of legislation and of manpower dealing with monitoring and control of food and environmental quality is underdeveloped.' Furthermore, in the opinion of the NBST, government standards for a healthy environment were also underdeveloped, and based on 'relatively weak legislation' and poor staffing at official levels.

The original Cork County Council chief environmental officer who drew up Penn's planning permission in 1973 was a civil engineer who knew 'nothing or very little about toxic waste'. While the chief environmental officer made a valiant effort, it cannot be said that the situation was satisfactory. In 1975 Penn was granted planning permission for the production of a wider range of products, including cimetidine, but no new conditions relating to air pollution were added to the planning permission, despite the fact that the cimetidine process resulted in the emission of methyl mercaptan, one of the recognised sources of odour problems in the area. Keohane noted:

> This reveals that the Chief Environmental Officer who drew up the conditions (a) was not aware that Methyl Mercaptan was a by-product of the new process or (b) knew nothing of the properties of this substance. Either way it reveals a serious deficiency of expertise.

Local officials were expected to regulate an industry that was much more highly sophisticated technically, as well as being much richer in resources and influence. Similarly the officials' ability to act was circumscribed by their political masters, who were prepared to put pressure on local authorities not to crack down on corporates. This was evident during the Hanrahans' mighty battle with Merck, but it was also prevalent throughout the country. Cork County Council officials told Keohane they had been advised by the state not to prosecute corporate transgressors. This was still evident in the 1990s. After years of obfuscation and secrecy, the state encouraged the IDA, the corporates and their agents, local authorities and its own bureaucracy to communicate, cooperate and make their documentation available to the public. One aspect of this was the freedom of access to information introduced in 1993. This made compliance monitoring figures available to anyone who asked for them. The CEA did, and from the data it compiled a study of effluent emissions between January and June 1993 from twelve corporates operating in Cork harbour. Despite 1,740 documented breaches of water pollution licence conditions the CEA learned that 'no action was taken by the licensing authority'. Cork County Council refuted the allegations that the power of the corporates dictated whether they sought prosecutions.

The corporates, of course, had their own set of strategies operating. As Keohane argued, if the IDA targeted the pharmaceutical industry, the corporate pharmaceutical industry also targeted Ireland. The IDA generally let the corporates set up where they wished, while providing stronger incentives in certain designated areas, primarily in the west. While a good proportion of the chemical and pharmaceutical industry clustered around Cork harbour, the rest chose isolated greenfield sites throughout the country. While planning and setting up their operations, the corporates were able to use the hunger of the local authorities for economic development to play one local authority off another to obtain the best possible deal locally. (Planning conditions are of course decided locally.) One result of this was that certain local authority officials were unable to do their job adequately. An example of this was provided by Captain Brian McMahon, speaking at an IIRS seminar in Cork in 1977:

If the local Chief Fire Officer raises any objection they can – and do – threaten to move the plant to another local authority area. They would come to one local authority and say 'OK, we'll set up our factory here provided we do not have to do this, that or the other'. And if the local authority did not agree they would go to some other local authority and make the same deal with them. That local authority might agree. Therefore when there's a possibility of a large industry setting up in a certain area the local Chief Fire Officer's comments are in most cases, if not all, either smothered or entirely ignored, because the local authority was faced with establishing a factory and providing jobs. And the local authority in many cases chose to close its eyes to the safety aspects of the proposal it was handling.

Some corporates pushed their luck very strongly. In the case of Eli Lilly's application to set up a factory at Dunderrow, Kinsale, County Cork, the original planning application failed to include any details of the specific products the company intended to produce. When the local authority asked for further information, the company responded by providing a list of classifications into which the products would fall. Thus if the local authority had allowed permission on the basis of the planning application, Eli Lilly could have produced pretty much what it wished at the site. This proposal was so outrageous that An Taisce was forced to move into action, with the eventual result that Eli Lilly and Cork County Council signed an agreement that the company would specify what it would produce and, if it wished to produce some other product subsequently, it would also need to apply for planning permission specifically for that product.

The corporates did their best to obstruct the regulatory process, usually by withholding information or making access to factories available only at the corporate's convenience. Fishery Board inspectors suffered more than most. When North Western Fisheries Board had the job of sampling the effluent from Asahi's factories, its Pollution Officer Siobhan Shiel had to make an appointment the day before she wished to call. 'Having to make an appointment defeats the whole purpose of monitoring. If I thought it was any use I would go to take samples more often', she said. Asahi responded to complaints over this by refusing to change the system for 'security reasons'. It wasn't just the corporate that refused to cooperate. The local authority refused the North Western Fisheries Board access to the detailed results of the monitoring of Asahi by the Western Health Board.

Asked why the council had refused to give the Fisheries Board the results of the chemical analysis of the Asahi effluent, Michael O'Malley (Mayo County Manager) said the data had to be confidential because it could be of value to Asahi's competitors. 'I'm not going to have everybody coming in and monitoring me', he responded to further questions.

Similar problems were described by James Rogers, Manager of the Southern Regional Fisheries Board, at the Bord Pleanála hearing on Merrell Dow:

> In my present position, for the last six years, I have had very great experience, unfortunately, of my pollution control staff being impeded, ostensibly for safety reasons, at factory entrance gates and in many instances they are impeded ... for so long that their subsequent inspection of the effluent handling area is virtually a waste of time.

Throughout the 1970s, 1980s and 1990s this was a characteristic of the corporates' operations in Ireland, leading to the understandable paranoia among communities that the corporations have something to hide. Speaking in the Cork Circuit Court in July 1979 in relation to the Nohoval toxic waste dump plan, Cork County Council's Chief Environmental Officer, Matthew Whelan, said the council had been denied certain information on where certain toxic wastes were then being dumped in County Cork:

> We have a problem getting enough information to help us evaluate a proposal or identify the source of a problem that develops downstream because the companies claim that they cannot divulge trade secrets. Sometimes we have to assemble a whole team of experts and go through a number of tests just to find out basic things that the companies could tell us in a minute.

Corporates consistently refused to provide information on their environmental impact, almost invariably citing the 'confidential trade secrets' excuse. This excuse has also been consistency backed by state authorities. An early example was provided by the refusal of the IDA and the IIRS to release details of toxic waste arisings in Ireland in 1980, as it contained confidential information that the corporates had agreed to give only if it was concealed from the public. Nothing changed much throughout the 1980s and 1990s except the image the corporates wanted to show of themselves, as people who were prepared to share information. Of course, what companies are offering here is public relations, not information. The original Sandoz information campaign was a prime example of the lack of substantial information being provided by companies to local communities. The 'Popemobile', as it was christened by local activists, which made its way around Cork harbour to inform the lucky locals how wonderful a company Sandoz was, failed to provide any detailed information on Sandoz's proposals for its intended Ringaskiddy factory. So when Indaver sought to use these same tactics, it got a rude shock. From the moment it tried to engage the communities it was told to go away – repeatedly. When its staff tried to attend a public meeting in Ringaskiddy, two years after its first attempt to provide information to the community, they were told they would never be welcome. Audrey Hogan, Secretary of the Ringaskiddy and District Residents' Association, said: 'John Aherne and his assistant Laura Burke showed at that meeting and they were not allowed to put on a PowerPoint presentation, it was purely a question and answer session.'

Before the Internet became prevalent in Irish households, support for the communities fighting toxic capital came from assorted academics, anarchists, environmentalists, republicans and socialists. The trade union movement, which could have been expected to consider what would be a hazardous industry to its members, instead allied itself to the industry. In the case of Raybestos Manhattan, Irish Trade and General Workers Union members picketed and struck in support of the asbestos firm. On a more national level, certain unions – notably the ITGWU – were accused of arranging 'sweetheart deals' with the corporates before the factories being organised had even opened. Even that sector of the left that had doubts about the state's industrialisation policies was critical of aspects of their implementation rather than questioning the ideology of development itself. Thus the social opposition to toxic development in Ireland did not come from the area traditionally expected to combat capital, the left and the unions, but from areas and groups that would not normally, due to their rural location, be in an antagonistic relationship with capital. The greenfield orientation of the corporates ensured that most conflicts would be rural. Few of the stories in this book involve opposition by workers to toxic capital; only in the case of Raybestos Manhattan is such opposition seen.

Instead the opposition movements were spontaneous, local and rural. In most cases groups grew up in response to a specific local threat and dissolved when the threat was defeated or when the community was defeated. Women played a central part in these movements. These groups were highly mercurial and they were not unique to Ireland.

According to Leonard and Morrell:

> What is significant about grassroots environmental politics, however, is its appearance in virtually all geographic areas of the developing world. It takes place among groups with little or no expressed interest in formal politics, living under a wide variety of governments. For many farmers, fishermen and urban poor, protest of this sort is the only means available to articulate interests, claims and demands for political action. As often as not, the decision to stand up and speak out is a spontaneous action motivated by immediate self-interest.

Leonard and Morrell also put their finger on one of the most frustrating aspects of these movements for the political establishment: they are spontaneous and difficult to control and they can 'suddenly impinge upon the political system in unpredictable and uncontrollable ways'. This has certainly been a characteristic of Irish opposition to toxic industry, which, as Leonard notes, has led to concern over what Daniel O'Connell, Assistant Principal at the Department of the Environment in 1980, described as an 'overuse of democracy'.

The Irish state has been strongly concerned about limiting this overuse of democracy wherever possible. This is inevitable given that this industrialisation is a joint project between the Irish state and corporate capital. The consequences of this for individuals, groups and communities opposing toxic developments locally was that at every stage they faced an unresponsive if not outrightly hostile state bureaucracy imbued with a culture of secrecy and a grim aversion to public accountability. The major agencies they found themselves opposing were semi-autonomous arms of the state such as the IDA and the IIRS/Eolas in the early years and latterly the EPA. The dominant state and indeed public ideology at the time was pro development, pro industry, pro science and technology and pro foreign direct investment.

Baker, in her survey of the ecological movement in Ireland, describes one major line of cleavage within the movement. On one side were the groups with traditional organisational structures, chairpersons, secretaries and so on. These groups wished to use the legal and administrative processes that were provided by the state. On the other side were autonomous political and community-based groups. These were local groups without formal membership or structures and using direct democracy. These groups did not wish to restrict their activities to the processes provided by the state to channel such dissent but were prepared to use direct action. Of course this distinction cannot be made rigidly, as Baker points out, and it's better to see the groups as forming part of a continuum from participation in planning and court appeals on the one hand, to direct action to block drilling, construction or dumping on the other hand. What place on the continuum groups will occupy depends to a large extent on the local situation and the dynamics of the struggle itself. The most successful struggles have involved a combination of both legal/administrative and political/direct action tactics.

Opposition within the communities varied. It's important to emphasise that groups opposing toxic developments were often strongly in conflict with other influential sectors of the community, especially in the early stages. In some cases, anti-toxic activists were dismissed as mercenary, individualistic, litigation-orientated or simply not right in the head. In the case involving Schering Plough, the local opponents were threatened with the calling of a total boycott against them. Dissent in one case led to other residents armed with shotguns arriving at night to visit the local dissenters.

Strong attempts were made to marginalize these groups. Some were made by trade union groups that denounced any opposition to industrial development as being rooted solely in the property interests of those opposing the developments. Other groups were dismissed as being 'blow-ins' to the local area and unrepresentative of local opinion. In 1978, for example, the chairperson of Kinsale Urban District Council attacked objectors to the proposed Eli Lilly factory as 'little more than guests in the country': how dare these 'guests of the nation' criticise the state's policy of inviting corporates in? In this case traditional anti-imperialist sentiment was used by a section of the bourgeoisie to support the introduction of foreign capital. Opponents were also smeared as associating with terrorists: the *Cork Examiner* reported no less a group than the Red Brigades had participated in a national anti-toxic conference in Cork in 1982. Linda Fitzpatrick, was told she should remember what side her bread was buttered on. As a former employee of the

Cork Chamber of Commerce she understood exactly what the comment meant.

The opposition was also politically marginalized and disenfranchised. As a consequence of government support for foreign direct investment, it did what it could to prevent groups or communities from interfering in the creation of this brave new island. As struggles developed in response to toxic developments, public fora and opportunities for the expression and channelling of dissension rapidly evaporated, with the result that the state itself forced groups to take actions that were illegitimate, as they were outside the politically approved process of decision making. Thus, after a group in County Clare succeeded in preventing Beecham's from setting up a pharmaceutical factory in 1978 through use of the planning and legal process, the state moved to change the planning laws to eliminate such use by community groups. It would be the first of many such moves by the state. Each time a community group found a way of manipulating the system the corporate's political lobby ensured that the state closed the loopholes with ever more increasing sophistication.

Such actions only emphasised the lack of participation by local people in state plans for their area. and this question of local democracy was one that constantly recurred. Communities that had no desire to move outside the normal political channels found themselves having to do so if they wished to block the threat to their area. In their struggles communities have used whatever means necessary to block toxic developments. While in the cases of Nohoval and Beecham, legal challenges were sufficient, they proved unsatisfactory methods in the case of Raybestos, and the community then took up direct action as the only option left open to it. Other struggles, such as those waged by the Donegal Uranium Campaign, the Limerick Environmental Health Protection Group, the Womanagh group and Cork Harbour Alliance for a Safe Environment, have showed excellent use of local clientelist politics. However, when it became obvious that other tactics needed to be employed, these campaigns also used direct action methods. The Limerick group organised picketing of the county council meetings while the bedrock of the Donegal campaign was the direct action by local farmers, which prevented the prospecting companies from exploring the area.

Similarly, the development of this opposition must be seen historically. Thus when individual people first, and then community organisations, began to question the dubious benefits of industrialisation, they found themselves facing a united front of state agencies, corporates, trade unions, and, in the beginning at least, local elites and quite often the general public locally. The only change that has come over the decades that this book deals with is that the community groups are now in a position where they still face the same united front with one major exception: in recent times, community opposition has moved from a minority, marginal position to one where the majority of a community opposes toxic development. The mobilisation of east Cork and west Waterford against Merrell Dow showed a strong, united yet diverse community opposition, which was a majority in the area. One element in the growth of the movements and in their increasing strength is their ability to mobilise other local interests that are threatened. The Merck Sharp and Dohme case was to provide a forerunner for this issue, raised previously only in the case of Nohoval, which, notes Baker, 'forced policy makers to confront two conflicting interests: those of agriculture and industry. This was a conflict of interest that is especially important in a newly industrialised country where agriculture is still an important component of GNP.'

In the Merrell Dow controversy, the interests mobilised were not only local agriculture, but also fishing, mariculture and tourist interests. In the Merrell Dow case there were to be problems over this issue, when attempts were made to mobilise support from other Cork communities for the anti-Merrell Dow struggle. Thus opposition to Merrell Dow broke down between those whose position was not in Killeagh – people who wouldn't be overwhelmingly worried if the factory was sited in Ringaskiddy – and those who felt no place in Ireland was an appropriate site for such a factory. The first position was held more by those in the immediate reach of the factory, while supporters from Youghal and Waterford would have inclined more to the latter position, though this is necessarily a very crude dichotomy. Some support for the second position nationwide was shown by an MRBI/*Irish Times* opinion poll, which found that a majority (51 per cent) of Irish people did not think the IDA should attempt to attract chemical or pharmaceutical companies to Ireland.

Leonard and Morrell observed that:

Most examples of this sort of environmental protest have occurred 1) when environmental problems arise because of a lack of vital public services; or 2) when pollution from

one sector of the economy impinges on the economic livelihood of a particular group or class – e.g. when industrial
pollution from a factory kills fish or destroys crops.

This is partly borne out by the Irish experiences: thus in Bantry
opposition to the proposal to reopen Whiddy Island was strongest
in those involved in the shellfish industry, who saw their economic
and employment interests threatened.

But this is only a partial explanation. While some people
become active purely to defend their economic interests, others
become involved because of a more basic interest: that of their
safety and health, and ultimately their survival. The interests that
have fed opposition to the pollution of Cork harbour cannot be
explained purely on economic grounds: concerns over public health
are paramount here.

It would be nice, but unreal, to present a general increase in
sophistication in community struggles since the 1960s. But social
movements, particularly local, spontaneous and reactive, do not
always learn from the lessons learned in earlier struggles. Similarly,
by its reactive nature, the anti-toxic movement was limited in its
options and strength. Attempts to begin building an anti-toxic
movement on the model of the successful anti-nuclear movement
failed. Nevertheless, as community groups learned from experiences
in other parts of Ireland, particularly from the experience of the
Hanrahan family, opposition strengthened and deepened to total
opposition to toxic developments rather than reformist demands
for monitoring and legislation. Sadly it was always being betrayed.

It would also be polite to say that the new eco-social and
social movements that began to emerge in Ireland at the turn of
the millennium are different from the models employed by previous generations because they understand globalisation and the
needs of Irish communities, who themselves are demanding local
control of economic and productive activity in a manner that is
considered basic to most models of 'ecological' society. The
evidence is still contrary. A more generous view of these social
movements, which recognises both the limits of these movements
and their possibilities, is provided by Manuel Castells:

> So, faced with an overpowered labour movement, an
> omnipresent one-way communication system indifferent to
> cultural identities, an all-powerful centralised state loosely

governed by unreliable political parties, a structural economic crisis, cultural uncertainty ... people go home. Most withdraw individually, but the crucial, active minority, anxious to retaliate, organise themselves on their local turf.

Thus [these] movements do address the real issues of our time, although neither on the scale nor terms that are adequate to the task. And yet they do not have any choice since they are the last reaction to the domination and renewed exploitation that submerges our world. But they are more than a last, symbolic stand and desperate cry: they are symptoms of our contradictions, and therefore potentially capable of superseding these contradictions. They are the organisational forms, the live schools, where the new social movements of our emerging society are taking place, growing up, learning to breathe, out of reach of the state apparatuses, and outside the closed doors of repressed family life.

In this context, what has been remarkable about Ireland's late industrialisation has been the absolute failure of the opposition against it. Communities, as we have seen, were always in the thick of battle, sometimes winning, mostly losing, yet the failure of the anarchists, ecologists, environmentalists, journalists, republicans, politicians, socialists and others with anti-industrial and social ideologies (as groups and individuals) who sought to support their struggles is harder to understand. The history of industrialisation in Ireland has been about lies, obfuscation and secrecy from the state and industry, and about ignorance and stupidity from those with political agendas, but perhaps that is the reason that the industries of hazard (and that includes the electronic and software plus the extraction and agro- and biochemical industries that have been beyond the scope of this particular book) have been able to dictate their own agenda from the first day the state welcomed them to Ireland. Selfish avarice, desire, greed and ignorance have allowed those with hidden agendas (particularly academics, who have got involved with community groups – especially in County Cork, and environmentalists) to pretend they cared when all they really cared about were their own careers. Why, during the history of the early industrialisation of Ireland, did only the few ask the relevant questions, in the Dáil, in the media, in public halls, in meetings? Some communities tried very hard to stimulate debates about the failure of the state and of industry to provide answers to simple questions.

These questions, as naive as they sound in the atypical European democracy that is modern Ireland, still need to be asked:

- Who gave the IDA a mandate, or more pertinently what piece of legislation allowed it to negotiate secret 'sweetheart' deals with the corporates?
- Where is the evidence of a mandate from members of trade unions so their leadership could negotiate 'sweetheart' deals with the corporates?
- Why has the state continually refused to release documentation from its liaisons and meetings with the chemical and pharmaceutical industries? (The answer to this one is known: it's to protect corporate secrets.) Is this a constitutional question?
- What is the role between the industry confederations, IBEC for example, and the state? Again does this infringe constitutional rights?
- Has there been a hidden hand authoring the draft changes to environmental and planning legislation, and if there is who is it attached to?
- Why has the state in all its forms refused to accept peer-reviewed epidemiological, oncological and toxicological science on the impacts of pollution on both the environment and human health? Why does the state continue to argue bad science?
- What is the extent of community and political donations from the chemical and pharmaceutical industries?

We know the answers to some of these questions, and even if we were to be told the answers to all of them it would not matter. The battles have been fought, the war over the industrialisation of Ireland has been lost, and Irish people now have new choices to make. According to the OECD Ireland remains the most globalised country in the developed world. However economists agree that the boom of the mid-to-late 1990s is over, as the spectre of relocating factories haunts dependent communities. Since 2000 foreign investment in Ireland has fallen by 50 per cent while Romania, Russia, Bulgaria, Ukraine, Turkey, Hungary, Czech Republic and Estonia are attracting manufacturers because of their low labour costs and increasing number of English speakers. Ireland, the first country to decolonise in the twentieth century and the first to recognise the value of English as a lingua franca, now faces an uncertain future. Throughout the 1990s Irish workers bought into the cult of consumer spending; personal debt levels are the highest in Europe. The state now faces a tough challenge; how to redress the deficit in public finances while developing a strategy to consolidate the inflated standards of living of the newly affluent Irish. They will have to do so without the cushion of EU structural funds, which run out in 2006. They will have to address the decline of rural Ireland as small farmers sign on the dole and their children flee to the professions in the cities. In addition Irish society is becoming more multi-ethnic, creating new social and political challenges.

Meanwhile the Celtic Tiger economy is starting to diminish just at the time when people are flocking to the country. Many are returning home, coming back with their hopes and dreams intact, from a homogenising Europe that no longer needs cheap Irish labour. Others are coming from Britain, desperate to escape a disintegrating society, and some are even coming from America – believing in the romanticism of their forebears' homeland. It would be very easy to shatter their dreams with a negative view of modern Ireland, because the Ireland they have returned to has been changed dramatically by global politics.

Any one of these people by taking the time would see there is still opposition in Ireland to state and global policies, by people who are trying to change Irish society simply by changing their own lives in a pacifist manner by setting examples through their actions. These are people who by their own nature are not cynical or selfish or fascist, but are altruistic and caring and sharing. They are the dispossessed but they are not weak. Tom Collins sees the nature of the society that is emerging amongst the dispossessed on the fringes of Irish society as:

> one which has a renewed interest in traditional Irish society, but has rejected its caricature; it equates personal growth with social commitment; it espouses spirituality but discards religiosity; it is committed to democracy but distrusts politicians; it has fundamental commitment to work but is likely to be unemployed; it is locally committed but globally oriented; it is coming from the outside in rather from the inside out.

So this book can be no more than a lament for the Ireland that we have lost and a tribute to those who fought to change it into a country where money and power are not the defining articles of existence.

Sources

Introduction

For a historical analysis of the development of the green movement in Ireland see Tovey, H. (1993) Environmentalism in Ireland: two versions of development and modernity. *International Sociology* 8(4): 413–30, December.

Chapter 1 The Politics of Pollution

Peter Hammill's lyrics are from *Mirrors, Dreams and Miracles*, 1982, Sofa Sound, PO Box 2, Westbury, Wiltshire, England; Chemical World © Peter Hammill. Readers interested in the industrialisation of Ireland should consult Bew and Patterson (1982), Telesis (1982), Crotty (1986), Kennedy (1989), O'Malley (1989) and Mac Sharry and White (2000). Statistics on US direct investment in Ireland come from the US Department of Commerce. Readers unfamiliar with this department should read, *A Guide to BEA Statistics on U.S. Multinational Companies* (Survey of Current Business, March 1995), available from Bureau of Economic Analysis by calling + 1 202 606 9827 or www.bea.gov/bea/ai/0395iid/maintext.htm or BEA Order Desk, BE-53, Bureau of Economic Analysis, US Department of Commerce, Washington, DC 20230. Chemical industry statistics come from the Central Statistics Office, Ardee Road, Dublin 6; tel: + 353 1 498 4000; email: information@cso.ie; web: www.cso.ie and the Federation of Irish Chemical Industries (now the Irish Pharmaceutical and Chemical Manufacturers Federation) Confederation House, 84–86 Lower Baggot Street, Dublin 2; Tel: + 353 1 605 1584; email: matt.moran@ibec.ie. Sinn Féin's *The Quality of Life in the New Ireland, Sinn Féin Policy Document*, May 1973 is available from Sinn Féin, 44 Parnell Square, Dublin 1; tel: +353 1 8726100; web: www.sinnfein.org/

An overview of the chemical industry, from the ecological and economic perspective, in Ireland appeared as Allen, R. and Jones, T. (1990) *Poisoned Island*, Magill, May. IDA's reports and press releases are available at its HQ, Wilton Place, Dublin 2; tel: + 353 1 603 4000; email: idaireland@.ida.ie; web: www.idaireland.com. OECD yearly and occasional reports on Ireland are available from the Organisation for Economic Cooperation and Development, 2 rue André Pascal, F-75775 Paris Cedex 16, France; tel.: + 33 1 4524 8200; web: www.oecd.org/. The figures on profit repatriation are from the CSO's *Balance of International Payments*. Statistics on the number of chemical companies come from the IDA, CSO and FICI; export figures CSO; environmental control from a survey conducted by the author, also published in the *Sunday Tribune*. The Stop Legal Pollution documents are available in the ENFO library; 7 St. Andrew Street, Dublin 2; tel: + 353 1 888 2001 or 1890 200 191; email: info@enfo.ie; web: www.enfo.ie. Peter Montague is quoted in *Rachel's Environment & Health Weekly*, Environmental Research Foundation, P.O. Box 5036, Annapolis, MD 21403; email: erf@rachel.org; web: http://www.rachel.org. The NIOSH and German studies are: Fingerhut, M. A. *et al.* (1991) *Mortality Among U.S. Workers Employed in the Production of Chemicals Contaminated with 2,3,7,8-Tetrachlorodibenzo-p-dioxin (TCDD)*. Industry wide Studies Branch, Division of Surveillance, Hazard Evaluation and Field Studies, NIOSH, Cincinnati, Ohio 45226 (from the National Technical Information Service, NTIS PB 91-125971, 5285 Port Royal Rd., Springfield, VA 22161, (800) 525-NTIS); and Manz *et al.* (1991). Cancer mortality among workers in a chemical plant contaminated with dioxin, *Lancet* 338: 959–64. Linda Birnbaum was quoted in *Science News*, 11 January 1992; and see Birnbaum, L. (1993) *Re-evaluation of Dioxin*: a presentation to the 102nd Meeting of the Great Lakes Water Quality Board, Chicago, Illinois, 15 July 1993; Birnbaum, L. (1994) Endocrine effects of prenatal exposure to PCBs dioxins, and other xenobiotics: implications for policy and future research, *Environmental Health Perspectives* 102(8): 676–9; Birnbaum, L. (1993) The USEPA's scientific assessment of the risks of exposure to dioxin, *Organohalogens* 14: 1–4.

The scientific data on endocrine disruptors is now extensive. Readers should start with: Wyrobek, A. *et al.* (1983) An evaluation of human sperm as indicators of chemically induced alterations of spermatogenic function, *Mutation Res* 115: 73–148; Carlsen, E. *et al.* (1992) Evidence for decreasing quality of semen during the past 50 years, *British Medical Journal* 305: 609–13; Sharpe, R. and Skakkebaek, N. (1993) Are oestrogens involved in falling sperm counts and disorders of the male reproductive tract? *Lancet* 341: 1392–5, 29 May; Sharpe, R. (1993) Declining sperm counts in men – is there an endocrine cause? *Journal of Endocrinology* 136: 357–360; Swan, S. *et al.* (1997) Have sperm densities declined? A reanalysis of global trend data, *Environ Health Per* 105: 1228–32; Sharpe, R. *et al.*, Gestational and lactational exposure of rats to xenoestrogens results in reduced testicular size and sperm production, *Environ Health Per* 103(12): 1136–43, 1995. (In Europe sperm production is falling 1 per cent a year, in the United States 1.5 per cent a year.) Harris, J. R. *et al.* (1992) Breast cancer. *New England Journal of Medicine* 327(5): 319–28; El-Bayoumy, K. (1992) Environmental carcinogens that may be involved in human breast cancer etiology. *Chem Res Tox* 5(5): 585–90; Danish Environmental Protection Agency, *Male Reproductive Health and Environmental Chemicals with Estrogenic Effects*, April 1995, Miljo-Kopenhawn, Denmark; Giwercman, A. and Skakkebaek, N. The human testis – an organ at risk? *International Journal of Andrology* 15: 373–5; Peterson, R., Moore, R., Mably, T., Bjerke, D. and Goy, R., Male reproductive system ontogeny; effects of perinatal exposure to 2,3,7,8-TCDD in Colborn and Clement (1992); Eaton, S. B. *et al.* (1994) Women's reproductive cancers in evolutionary context, *Q Rev Bio* 69(3): 353–67; Whitten, P. L. Chemical revolution to sexual revolution: historical changes in human reproductive development, in Colborn and Clement; Rier, S. E. *et al.* (1993) Endometriosis in rhesus monkeys following chronic exposure to TCDD, *Fund App Tox* 21: 433–41. (Chemicals known to disrupt the endocrine system include 2,4-D, 2,4,5-T, alachlor, amitrole, atrazine, metribuzin, nitrofen, trifluralin, benomyl, hexachlorobenzene, mancozeb, maneb, metiram-complex, tributyl tin, zinab, ziram, beta-HCH, carbaryl, chlordane, dicofol, diedrin, DDT and metabolites, endosulfan, heptachlor and heptachlor epoxide, lindane (gamma-HCH), methomyl, methoxychlor, mirex, oxychlordane, parathion, synthetic pyrethriods, toxaphene, transmonachlor, aldicarb, DBCP, cadmium, dioxin (TCDD), lead, mercury, PBBs, PCBs, pentachlorophenol (PCP), penta- to nonylphenols, phthalates, styrenes.) The Cork Environmental Alliance's report *Emperor's New Clothes: Protection or Pollution* is available in ENFO; see also www.iol.ie/~cea/

Chapter 2 Ballydine: Tears in the Valley

The quote by Jean-Jacques Rousseau is taken from his 1755 essay on the *Origin and Foundation of the Inequality of Mankind*, of which there are many translations. One of the best is in the 1913 Everyman's Library edition of *The Social Contract and the Discourses*. The research for this chapter is from interviews conducted by the author with the Hanrahan family, local people, councillors, Merck, and others who were either involved professionally (scientists, vets, local officials) or interested observers (journalists, academics, film makers) plus documentation made available to the author. These interviews took place on occasions between 1983 and 1991. Readers interested in the chronological story should consult the local newspaper, the *Clonmel Nationalist* (1976 to 1991), *The Irish Times* and *Irish Independent* (particularly 1982 to 1985), *Magill* (June 1983, pp.26–38, July 1984, pp. 19–21 and August 1988 pp. 36–39), *Irish America* (May 1988). *Magill* is archived from October 1977 in the National Library – call number Ir 05 M21. Gaeleo Managing Director Noel Murphy was quoted in *Eire's Chemical Industry* by Sandra Heathcote (Chemistry and Industry, 15 November 1980); he also said: 'We wanted a place with similar infrastructure to the home country without so many government restrictions.' Readers wishing to read the IIRS report should consult ENFO or contact the Eolas library and if that fails make a Freedom of Information request. Merck's questionable payments were reported in *Making Their Merck on Ireland*, MSD Study Group, available in ENFO. The (Irish) Supreme Court judgement of Justice Henchy, 5 July 1988, on *Mary Hanrahan, John Hanrahan and Selina Hanrahan v Merck Sharp & Dohme (Ireland) Limited 1982 No 2138P and 1985 No 316* is available in the Four Courts library. See also www.ucc.ie/law/irlii/cases/316_85.htm

Chapter 3 Killeagh: Power and Effluent

Rory Finegan's writings are available at Trinity College library. His reports for the Womanagh group were *Environmental Effects of a Proposed Pharmaceutical Factory at Killeagh, County Cork*, (July 1988) and *Adverse Environmental Effects of a Proposed Pharmaceutical Manufacturing Industry at Killeagh, County Cork*, December 1988. The Resource and Environmental Unit report, *The Proposed Merrell Dow Pharmaceutical Plant at Killeagh – A Critique of its Environmental Impact Assessment (including additional technical information)*, August 1988 is available from the library at UCC. The account of the Bord Pleanála oral hearing at Cork County Hall between 6 and 16 December 1988 is derived from notes and recordings taken by the author and from documentation supplied to the Bord Pleanála inspectors by many of the parties who contributed to the hearing. Everything noted was verified by the verbatim reporting of Doyle Court Reporters, Dublin, notably their transcript of proceedings, which were commissioned by Merrell Dow. For Yvonne Scannell's work on green laws see Scannell Y. Environmental impact statements: the legal framework and implications, *Irish Journal of Environmental Science* 1(1): 14–17; *The Lawyer's Role in Environmental Assessment*, given at Trinity College, Dublin seminar on Environmental Issues (Present and Future), 5 May 1989; and Scannell, Y. and Stevenson, C. Environmental impact assessment: new European obligations, *Irish Journal of Environmental Science* 4(1). For Wall see *Overview of the Irish Chemical and Pharmaceutical Sector* and *Industrial Relations in the Chemical Sector*; (both papers given by Wall at a seminar in Cork, 6 April 1989), available from the Irish Congress of Trade Unions, 31/32 Parnell Square, Dublin 1; tel: +353 1 8897777; email: see website; web: www.ictu.ie *Developing for Growth: A Framework Development Plan for Irish Tourism*, Bord Fáilte, April 1989 is available from Bord Fáilte, Baggot Street Bridge, Baggot St, Dublin 2; tel: + 353 1 602 4000; web: http://www.ireland.travel.ie/

Chapter 4 Cork: Poison Harbour

The Greenpeace report by this author, *Sea Dumping Operations and Pollution in Cork Harbour: A Preliminary Report*, November 1988, is available in ENFO. For sources on hazard export and the case against asbestos see Castleman, B. I. (1979) The export of hazardous factories to developing nations, *International Journal of Health Services* 9(4): 572–3; Holmes, K. (1982) The export of hazardous products and industries: a bibliography, *International Journal of Health Services* 12(3): 517–21; Mac Sheoin, T. (1985) The export of hazardous products and industries: a bibliography, *International Journal of Health Services* 15(1): 145–55 and 17(2): 343–64; and Castleman, B. and Vera, M. (1980) Impending proliferation of asbestos, *International Journal of Health Services* 10(3): 390. For the asbestos industry's conduct in America see Brodeur (1985) and Castleman, B. I., *Asbestos: Medical and Legal Aspects*, Clifton, N. J. (1984) *Business and Legal*.

The interviews with the activists with the Ovens Women's Action Group and the Cork Noxious Industry Action Group were given on the condition that their names would not be published. The working conditions of the asbestos workers were reported in Dalby, S. The nuclear syndrome: victory for the anti-nuclear power movement in Ireland, *Dawn Train 3*, winter 1984/1985. Kieran Keohane's *Ecologist* piece, Toxic trade-off: the price Ireland pays for industrial development, is vol. 19(4), 1989. SCRIP (1985) *Ireland – An Investment Opportunity for the Pharmaceutical Industry*, Richmond, Surrey: PJB Publications (expensive and not in the public domain). Sue Baker was writing in Dependent Industrialization and Political Protest: Raybestos Manhattan in Ireland, *Government and Opposition*, 22 (3), summer 1987.

The meeting with Sandoz in the IDA's Cork office is based on the transcript of a tape of the press conference made by the author and from notes taken and documents supplied by Sandoz. The Penn workers in dispute with management put all their grievances on paper, mostly in letters to management, their union and to the media. This account is based on that documentation and on casual conversations with several workers who asked not to be identified. When one aspect of the dispute reached the media, Penn suspended the union shop steward, demanding that he reveal who leaked the information to the media. The worker sought legal advice and told Penn it was a union matter, that the media had learned about it through sources in the union. Penn later reinstated the worker. On the issue of locus standi see de Blacam, Mark, SC, in *Judicial Review* (2001), Butterworths, Dublin. Tara Jones's criticism of the Cork alliance appeared in *An Phoblacht/Republican News* on 10 January 1991.

Chapter 5 Toxic Ireland

To follow the Nohoval court case see the *(Cork) Examiner*, 12 July 1979; 17 and 24 June 1980 and 27 January 1983. The *(Cork) Examiner* is the best source for the Gradogue disaster: 12–14, 17–20 June 1980 and 31 July 1980. An Taisce statements on the disposal of toxic waste from this period are available in ENFO. Keating's report is in UCC library. There was to be continued disagreement between the local opposition and Dublin County Council officials over exactly what was dumped at Dunsink. See, for example, the letter to *The Irish Times* (20 January 1982) from the Co-ordinating Committee Against the Toxic Dump, West Finglas Tenants' Association, and the response (30 January 1982) from D. O'Sullivan, Principal Officer, Dublin County Council. Lynch spoke at the second economic conference of the Irish chemical industry, 21–22 March 1983, discussing 'environmental and planning legislation in Ireland'. Sources consulted for the Hydrochlor story include Hydrochlor's planning proposal (the revised proposal, February 1989); Byrne O Cleirigh's feasibility study on the incineration of hazardous waste in Ireland; statements by the Limerick group; press releases and comments by Hydrochlor and their public relations company; interviews with David Thompson of the Limerick group; and with sources in the waste disposal industry, specifically Minchem (now Indaver). See also *The Phoenix* (19 May 1989). See Allen (1992) for a fuller account of the DuPont campaign.

Reports from the seminar at Trinity College are available in TCD library and possibly from the Department of the Environment. The disposal of toxic waste in England, Scotland and Wales is the focus of Allen (1992) and includes the history of the community opposition to Cleanaway, Rechem and others. See also www.bluegreenearth.com. For Keohane's analysis of the oral hearings see Keohane, K. (1998) Reflexive modernisation and systematically distorted communications: an analysis of an environmental protection agency hearing, *Irish Socheolaiochta na hÉireann* 8: 71–92. Readers wanting to learn more about particulate pollution should start with Lave and Seskin (1977) and move onto the work of Douglas Dockery, Arden C. Pope and Joel Schwartz, starting with Dockery, D. W., Schwartz, J. and Spengler, J. D. (1992) Air pollution and daily mortality: associations with particulates and acid aerosols, *Environmental Research* 59: 362–73; Dockery, Pope *et al.* (1994) An association between air pollution and mortality in six U.S. cities, *New England Journal of Medicine* 329: 1753–9; Dockery and Pope (1994) Acute respiratory effects of particulate air pollution, *Annual Review of Public Health* 15: 107–32; Schwartz, J., Dockery and Neas (1996) Is daily mortality associated specifically with fine particles? *Journal of the Air Waste Management Association* 46: 2–14; Schwartz (1994) Nonparametric smoothing in the analysis of air pollution and respiratory disease, *Canadian Journal of Statistics* 22: 471–87; Dockery and Pope (1994) Acute respiratory effects of particulate air pollution. *Annual Review of Public Health* 15: 107–32; and then Pope (1991) Respiratory hospital admissions associated with PM 10 pollution in Utah, Salt Lake and Cache Valleys, *Arch. Environ. Health* 46: 90–7; Pope and Dockery (1992) Acute health effects of PM 10 pollution on symptomatic and asymptomatic children, *American Review of Respiratory Disease* 145: 1123–8; Pope, C. A. and Schwartz, J. (1992) Daily mortality and PM 10 pollution in Utah Valley, *Arch. Environ. Health* 47: 211–17; Pope and Thun (1995) Particulate air pollution as a predictor of mortality in a prospective study of U.S. adults, *American Journal of Respiratory Critical Care Medicine* 151: 669–74; Schwartz, J., Slater, D. *et al.* (1993) Particulate air pollution and hospital emergency room visits for asthma in Seattle. *American Review of Respiratory Disease* 147: 826–31; Schwartz and Dockery (1992) Increased mortality in Philadelphia associated with daily air pollution concentrations, *American Review of Respiratory Disease* 145: 600–4; Schwartz, and Dockery (1992) Particulate air pollution and daily mortality in Steubenville, Ohio, *American Journal of Epidemiology* 135: 12–23; Shprentz, D. (1996) *Breath-Taking: Premature Mortality Due to Particulate Air Pollution in 239 American Cities.* May. USA: National Resources Defense Council (NRDC); Ackermann-Liebrich *et al.* (1997) Lung function and long term exposure to air pollutants in Switzerland, *American Journal of Respiratory Critical Care Medicine* 155: 122–9; Pope *et al.* (1995) Health effects of particulate air pollution: time for reassessment, *Environmental Health Perspectives* 103(5): 472–80; Pope *et al.* (1995) Particulate air pollution as a predictor of mortality in a prospective study of US adults, *American Journal of Respiratory Critical Care Medicine* 151: 669–74; Pope *et al.* (1991) Respiratory health and PM 10 pollution, *American Review of Respiratory Disease* 144: 668–74; Mott, L. *et al.* (1997) *Our Children at Risk: The 5 Worst Environmental Threats to their Health*, Nov, USA: NRDC; Bates, D. (1995) The effects of air pollution on children, *Environmental Health Perspectives* 103, Supp. 6: 49–54. See also Seaton, A., MacNee, W., Donaldson, K. and Godden, D. (1995) Particulate air-pollution and acute health-effects, *Lancet* 345: 176–8; Prescott, G.J. *et al.* (2000) Investigation of factors which might indicate susceptibility to particulate air pollution, *Occup. Environ. Med* 57(1): 53–7, 1 Jan; Seaton *et al.* (1999) Particulate air pollution and the blood, *Thorax* 54(11): 1027–32, 1 Nov; and Montague at www.ejnet.org/rachel/rehw 440.htm.

Chapter 6 Carndonagh: Anxiety Among the Women

See also Allen, R. (1992) Why are our babies dying? *Independent*, 10 May 1992, London.

Chapter 7 Askeaton: In the Shadow of the Dragon

With the exception of the reports by Finegan, the Cork Environmental Alliance (in its magazine *Green Times* – available in UCC), EPA, and Alloway this chapter is based on interviews with the affected farmers and observations made throughout the 1990s and early 2000s by the author, and by Anne Ruimy on behalf of the author, including Ruimy, R. (2002) An ordinary day in Askeaton, *Bluegreenearth* 2(33), 12 May. See also www.rockyroadmagazine.com. Readers interested in the chronological story should consult the *Limerick Leader, Clare Champion, (Cork) Examiner, Sunday Business Post* from 1991. Alloway, B. (2002) *The Final Reports of the Investigations of Animal Health Problems at Askeaton: A Review*, Nov. from Irish Farmers' Association, Irish Farm Centre, Bluebell, Dublin 12; tel: + 353 1 450 0266; web: www.ifa.ie. Finegan's reports on Askeaton are: Finegan, R. (1994) *Preliminary Report Concerning Vegetation and Animal Health Problems at Issane, Ballysteen, County Limerick, September 1994*; Finegan, R. (1994) *Notes on the Toxicity of Fluoride and Aluminum in Relation to Environmental Contamination at Issane, County Limerick, October 1994*; Finegan, R. (1995) *A Program for Investigation of Environmental Contamination at Issane, County Limerick, January 1995*; Finegan, R. (2001) *Opinion Concerning an EPA (Ireland) Report on Investigations of Animal Health Problems at Askeaton, County Limerick,*

November 2001. EPA (2000) *Investigations of Animal Health Problems at Askeaton, County Limerick,* six volumes, 6 January 2000, from EPA Dublin Regional Inspectorate, St Martin's House, Waterloo Road, Dublin 4; tel: + 353 1 667 4474; email: info@epa.ie. Also EPA HQ, Ardcavan, Wexford; tel: + 353 53 47120; web: www.epa.ie. And see Summary, Background and Findings at: http://www.epa.ie/ press%20releases/askeaton%20summary%20report.pdf and *Interim Report to September 1995; Second Interim Report to December 1996;* and *Third Interim Report to December 1997.*

Chapter 8 Against Money and Power

See also Varley, T., and Cearbhaill, D. O. (1996) An Irish community development movement's experience of crisis conditions: Muintir na Tíre's struggle for survival, *Journal of the Community Development Society* 27(1). See the first edition of this book, *Guests of the Nation,* for a history of opposition to mining.

The IDA's early history can be found in Lee (1990). The 'one stop shop' analysis by Barry and Jackson is discussed in Elson and Pearson (1989). The Cork Noxious Industry Action Group's 1980 report, *Oppose Toxic Waste Dumps!* is available in ENFO.

The *Multinational Monitor* feature is Harty, S. (1984) The multinationals' squeeze on Ireland, June. The incompetent local implementation of health and environmental legislation by Harris is discussed in Elson and Pearson (1989). The IDA's closed-door meetings to advise local officials are revealed in Leonard (1988).

Ireland as 'a good country to do business in' is reported in *Chemistry and Industry,* 15 November 1980. White was quoted in the magazine of *Earthwatch,* Summer 1989. The Institute for Industrial Research and Standards's report, *The Role of the IIRS in the Environmental Field,* was approved by the board of IIRS on 26 July 1977, available from the Eolas library or possibility in ENFO. Keohane's quote on the lack of experience in local authorities is from his *Ecologist* piece, Toxic trade-off: the price Ireland pays for industrial development. The Cork Environmental Alliance's analysis of the regulatory process is in its report *Emperor's New Clothes: Protection or Pollution?* Just after the start of the EPA hearing, on 3 June 1997, the Cork Environmental Alliance released the following press release:

> Cork Environmental Alliance has today lodged an official complaint with the Office of the Ombudsman following the Failure of the Minister for Enterprise and Employment, Richard Bruton TD, to comply with the Irish Regulations governing the

EU Directive on Freedom of Access to Information on the Environment.

The complaint relates to a document, alleged to be a secret agreement between the IDA and the Co Limerick based industry, Aughinish Alumina Ltd, which the company claims guaranteed that 'the Government will not impose discriminatory taxes, rates and charges on the property of the Irish company, the products and materials used by it, or on its operations.'

Aughinish Alumina Ltd maintain that a condition of the Environmental Protection Agency's recently issued Pollution Control licence, which requires a reduction in sulphur dioxide emissions from 50 tonnes/day to 14 tonnes/day, would be in breach of this agreement.

The CEA had sought full disclosure of the agreement in preparation for the forthcoming Oral Hearing of appeals against the Pollution Control licence which takes place on 19 June in Limerick. Having failed to secure copies of the agreement from both Aughinish and the IDA the Alliance made a formal request under the FOI Directive to Minister Bruton on 21 April. Despite repeated requests the Minister has failed to comply with the regulations which mandate him to respond within a one-month time frame from the date of the initial request.

'With just two weeks before the scheduled opening of the Oral Hearing, it now seems unlikely that the Ombudsman can investigate our complaint and adjudicate on the matter in time for the Alliance to properly prepare its case for the Hearing', said Derry Chambers of the CEA. 'It is probable that we will have to seek a postponement of the Hearing until such time as the matter is sorted out. Judging by the fact that Aughinish Alumina Ltd have objected to forty conditions of this licence one could be forgiven for assuming that any delay in implementing this licence would be welcomed by the company. Any such delays can be laid firmly at the Minister's door', he concluded.

At the end of the hearing, 20 June 1997, the CEA issued this statement:

Cork Environmental Alliance strongly urges the Inspector to recommend to the EPA board to approve the proposed IPC licence with the amendments already made in our submission, for the following reasons.
1.   The IDA letter which is unsupported and only partially revealed, in and of itself does not preclude the Agency from its function of environmental control. We draw your atten-

tion to the points relating to this in our submission made by Derry Chambers.

2. Aughinish Alumina Ltd. have not been able to present satisfactory evidence that the licence conditions are not BATNEEC. We have seen however that the company is in a profit-making situation and estimate profits of $16.3 million in 1997. Alcan, its parent company showed a profit of $410 million in 1996 and a first quarter profit (unaudited) of $143 million in 1997. We feel therefore that it is not unreasonable to request improved environmental performance in emissions to air of sulphur, nitrous oxides and particulates.

3. Aughinish Alumina Ltd have not presented satisfactory evidence that the improvements will not result in improved environmental performance. The fact is that no conclusions have been arrived at by the Agency regarding the animal health problems in Askeaton and until such time that some conclusions are made, we urge the Inspector to err on the side of caution and fully endorse the precautionary principle by supporting the conditions relating to air emissions in the draft licence.

4. Aughinish Alumina Ltd themselves have compared their plant to others within the EU that do not have to bear additional energy costs. We ask the Agency not to buck the trend put in place by Ireland's signatory to the Oslo convention. European legislation has steadily reduced the level of sulphur emissions which are allowed from a wide range of sources. The European Commission has accepted its own environmental directorates proposal for a directive to limit the sulphur content of fuel oil. The EU also intends to ratify the 1994 Sulphur Protocol. In March the Commission decided as part of the strategy, to propose adoption of a directive concerning the sulphur content of certain fuel oils. According to a draft of this, there would be a general limit of 1 per cent sulphur in heavy fuel oils, taking effect in 2000. Some member states of the European Community have already taken steps in advance of these directives. In Sweden for example, coal, peat and oil are now all taxed for sulphur. Oil however only being taxed when the sulphur content exceeds .1 per cent by weight. The measures which we request of Aughinish Alumina Ltd are not unprecedented within the European Union. Many plant owners throughout the EU have made efforts to bring their emissions below those prescribed in EU legislation.

For example a German oil fired plant at Ingolstadt, Bayern-werk has sulphur emissions of 10mg/mj of fuel. This plant is only one of a number within the EU which not only meets the existing directive but have even brought their emissions down to levels below those now proposed by the commission to accord with Best Available Technology.

It is a basic principle of EU law that Member States should conduct themselves within European Treaty provisions. Article 130t of the Maastrict Treaty specifically allows Member States to maintain or introduce more stringent protective measures so as to protect the environment.

5. We are surprised at the resistance by Aughinish Alumina Ltd to the requirement for insurance. It seems self-evident that if their processes are so environmentally benign then insurance should not be a problem.

6. Closure fund: Aughinish Alumina Ltd, the licensee and therefore the person legally responsible under the terms of the licence has in fact no assets. We therefore feel strongly that the closure fund must be retained, as under the terms of the draft licence. However, we urge that a separate account be established in which the necessary funds are kept separate from the funds of the licensee or other companies within the Alcan group, perhaps in a joint account with the EPA. Under the terms of the original planning permission granted to Alcan by Limerick County Council, section 6:

   a) the taking down and removal of all plant, equipment and installations in the event of the plant having, in the opinion of the planning authority, permanently ceased to function as an Alumina extraction plant.

   b) the reinstatement of the site to agricultural or such other use as maybe agreed by the planning authority. In the event of disagreement the form and the amount of such bond shall be as determined by the Minister for Local Government.

As the company has already agreed to the condition and in fact it remains in force until the licence is determined, we cannot understand why the company objects to the term being retained.

The report on Cork harbour is Allen, R. (1988) *Water Pollution and Sea Dump Operations in Cork Harbour: A Preliminary Report*, Nov, Dublin: Greenpeace Ireland, available in ENFO. The Cork civil engineer who knew 'nothing or very little about toxic waste' is referred to in Keohane (1987). Spontaneous community resistance is discussed in Leonard H. J.

and Morrell, D. (1981) Emergence of environmental concern in developing countries: a political perspective, *Stanford Journal of International Law* 17(2), Summer. The 'overuse of democracy' quote is from Leonard (1988). The Red Brigades comment is referred to in Jones, T. (1986) Hazards for export: double standards? *Radical Science* 20: 35. The ideal of an ecological society is discussed in Bookchin and earlier in Kropotkin. The quote from Tom Collins comes from *Power, Participation and Exclusion*, a report published in 1992 by the Justice Office of Conference of Religious of Ireland (CORI), Tabor House, Milltown Park, Dublin 6; tel: + 269 7799; web: www.cori.ie

Print media

The Irish Independent www.unison.ie/irish_independent/
The Irish Press (no longer published)
The Irish Times www.ireland.com/
Cork (now *Irish*) *Examiner* www.examiner.ie and archives.tcm.ie/
Sunday Business Post www.sbpost.ie and archives.tcm.ie/
Sunday Independent www.unison.ie/sunday_independent
Sunday Press (no longer published)
Sunday Tribune www.tribune.ie/
Irish News www.irishnews.com/
An Phoblacht/Republican News www.irlnet.com/aprn/
Clare Champion www.clarechampion.ie/
Clonmel Nationalist www.nationalist.ie/
Limerick Leader www.limerick-leader.ie/
Southern Star www.unison.ie/southern_star/
Irish Law Times
     www.smlawpub.co.uk/products/cat/mydetails.cfm?title=4454&
     detail=4454
Magill (no longer published)
Irish America www.irishabroad.com/irishworld/irishamericamag/

Newspapers and magazines are available from:

National Library of Ireland Newspaper Library
     www.nli.ie/co_newsp.htm
British Library Newspaper Library
     www.bl.uk/collections/newspapers.html
Dáil and Seanad debates and speeches are available at:
Parliamentary Debates www.oireachtas-debates.gov.ie/

Further reading

Allen, R. and Jones, T. (1990) *Guests of the Nation: People of Ireland versus the Multinationals*, London: Earthscan.

Allen, R. (1992) *Waste Not, Want Not*, London: Earthscan.

Ashford, N. A. and Millar, C. S. (1991, 1998) *Chemical Exposures: Low Levels, High Stakes*, London: Van Nostrand Reinhold.

Baker, S. (1990) The evolution of the Irish ecology movement, in W. Rudig (ed.), *Green Politics One*, Edinburgh: EUP.

Barry, U. (1986) *Lifting the Lid*, Dublin: Attic Press.

Barry, U. and Jackson, P. (1989) Women's employment and multinationals in the Republic of Ireland: the creation of a new female labour force, in D. Elson and R. Pearson (eds), *Women's Employment and Multinationals in Europe*, London: Macmillan.

Bew, P. and Patterson, H. (1982) *Sean Lemass and the Making of Modem Ireland 1945–66*, Dublin: Gill and Macmillan.

Bookchin, M. (1971) *Post-Scarcity Anarchism*, Toronto: Black Rose Books.

Bookchin, M. (1971, 1991) *The Ecology of Freedom*, Toronto: Black Rose Books.

Bookchin, M. (1980) *Toward an Ecological Society*, Toronto: Black Rose Books.

Bower, J. L. (1986) *When Markets Quake: The Management Challenge of Restructuring Industry*, Boston: Harvard Business School Press.

Brodeur, P. (1985) *Outrageous Misconduct: The Asbestos Industry on Trial*, New York: Pantheon.

Castells, M. (1982) *The City and the Grassroots: A Cross-Cultural Theory of Urban Social Movements*, E. Arnold.

Colborn, T. and Clement, C. (eds) (1992) *Chemically-Induced Alterations in Sexual and Functional Development: The Wildlife/Human Connection*, Princeton Sci.

Colborn, T., Myers, D. and Dumanoski, J. P. (1996) *Our Stolen Future*, London: Little, Brown.

Crotty, R. (1986) *Ireland in Crisis: A Study in Capitalist Colonial Underdevelopment*, Dingle: Brandon.

Davies, D. (2002) *When Smoke Ran Like Water: Tales of Environmental Deception and the Battle Against Pollution*, New York: Basic Books.

Epstein, S. (1978) *The Politics of Cancer*, San Francisco: Sierra Club.

Harris, L. (1989) Women's response to multinationals in Co. Mayo, in D. Elson and R. Pearson (eds), *Women's Employment and Multinationals in Europe*, London: Macmillan.

Hawken, P. (1993) *The Ecology of Commerce*, London: Weidenfeld and Nicolson.

Ives, J. (1985) Hazard export in the developing Irish Republic, in J. Ives (ed.), *Export of Hazard: Transnational Corporations and Environmental Control Issues*, London: Routledge and Kegan Paul.

Jones, T. (1988) *Corporate Killing: Bhopals Will Happen*, London: Free Association Books.

Kennedy, L. (1989) *The Modern Industrialization of Ireland 1940–1988*, Dublin: Economic and Social History Society of Ireland.

Kropotkin, P. (1898, 1912) *Fields, Factories and Workshops*, Toronto: Black Rose (among others).

Kropotkin, P. (1902) *Mutual Aid: A Factor of Evolution*, Toronto: Black Rose (among others).

Kropotkin, P. *Evolution and Environment* (originally published as *Modern Science and Anarchism* (1901) with a collection of essays written between 1910 and 1915), Toronto: Black Rose (among others).

Lave, L. and Seskin, E. (1977) *Air Pollution and Human Health*, Baltimore: Johns Hopkins University Press.

Lee, J. (1990) *Ireland 1912–1985*, Cambridge: CUP.

Leonard, H. J. (1984) *Pollution and Multinational Corporations in Rapidly Industrialising Nations*, Washington, DC: Conservation Foundation.

Leonard, H. J. (1988) *Pollution and the Struggle for the World Product*, Cambridge: CUP.

Lyons, F. S. L. (1973) *Ireland Since the Famine*, London: Collins/ Fontana.

Macken, W. (1968, 1999) *Brown Lord of the Mountain*, Dingle: Brandon/Mount Eagle.

Mac Sharry, R. and White, P. (2000) *The Making of the Celtic Tiger*, Cork and Dublin: Mercier.

O'Callaghan, J. (1992) *The Red Book*, Dublin: Poolbeg.

O'Faolain, S. (1947, 1969) *The Irish*, London: Pelican.

O'Malley, E. (1989) *Industry and Economic Development: The Challenge for the Latecomer*, Dublin: Gill and Macmillan.

Peace, A. (1997) *A Time of Reckoning: The Politics of Discourse in Rural Ireland*, Newfoundland: ISER.

Peace, A. (2001) *A World of Fine Difference*, Dublin: UCD Press.

Rousseau, J-J. (1913, 1993) *The Social Contract and the Discourses*, New York: Knopf (among others).

Scannell, Y. (1983) *The Law and Practice Relating to Pollution Control in the Republic of Ireland*, London: Graham and Trotman.

Scannell, Y. (1995) *Environmental and Planning Law in Ireland*, Dublin: Round Hall Press.

Stewart, J. (1985) Aspects of the financial behaviour of multinational companies in Ireland, in J. Fitzpatrick and J. H. Kelly (eds), *Perspectives on Irish Industry*, Dublin: Irish Management Institute.

Telesis Consultancy Group. (1982) *A Review of Industrial Policy*, Dublin: National Economic and Social Council.

Index